SHELLEY AND THE APPREHENSION OF LIFE

Percy Bysshe Shelley, in the essay 'On Life' (1819), stated 'We live on, and in living we lose the apprehension of life.' Ross Wilson uses this statement as a starting point to explore Shelley's fundamental beliefs about life and the significance of poetry. Drawing on a wide range of Shelley's own writing, and on philosophical thinking from Plato to the present, this book offers a timely intervention in the debate about what Romantic poets understood by 'life'. For Shelley, it demonstrates poetry is emphatically 'living melody', which stands in resolute contrast to a world in which life does not live. Wilson argues that Shelley's concern with the opposition between 'living' and 'the apprehension of life' is fundamental to his work and lies at the heart of Romantic-era thought.

ROSS WILSON is Lecturer in Literature at the School of Literature, Drama, and Creative Writing, University of East Anglia.

CAMBRIDGE STUDIES IN ROMANTICISM

This series aims to foster the best new work in one of the most challenging fields within English literary studies. From the early 1780s to the early 1830s a formidable array of talented men and women took to literary composition, not just in poetry, which some of them famously transformed, but in many modes of writing. The expansion of publishing created new opportunities for writers, and the political stakes of what they wrote were raised again by what Wordsworth called those 'great national events' that were 'almost daily taking place': the French Revolution, the Napoleonic and American wars, urbanisation, industrialisation, religious revival, an expanded empire abroad and the reform movement at home. This was an enormous ambition, even when it pretended otherwise. The relations between science, philosophy, religion and literature were reworked in texts such as *Frankenstein* and *Biographia Literaria*; gender relations in *A Vindication of the Rights of Woman* and *Don Juan*; journalism by Cobbett and Hazlitt; poetic form, content and style by the Lake School and the Cockney School. Outside Shakespeare studies, probably no body of writing has produced such a wealth of comment or done so much to shape the responses of modern criticism. This indeed is the period that saw the emergence of those notions of 'literature' and of literary history, especially national literary history, on which modern scholarship in English has been founded.

The categories produced by Romanticism have also been challenged by recent historicist arguments. The task of the series is to engage both with a challenging corpus of Romantic writings and with the changing field of criticism they have helped to shape. As with other literary series published by Cambridge, this one will represent the work of both younger and more established scholars, on either side of the Atlantic and elsewhere.

For a complete list of titles published see end of book.

SHELLEY AND THE APPRENHENSION OF LIFE

ROSS WILSON

CAMBRIDGE
UNIVERSITY PRESS

CAMBRIDGE
UNIVERSITY PRESS

University Printing House, Cambridge CB2 8BS, United Kingdom

Published in the United States of America by Cambridge University Press, New York

Cambridge University Press is part of the University of Cambridge.

It furthers the University's mission by disseminating knowledge in the pursuit of education, learning and research at the highest international levels of excellence.

www.cambridge.org
Information on this title: www.cambridge.org/9781107041226

First published 2013

Printed in the United Kingdom by CPI Group Ltd, Croydon, CRO 4YY

A catalogue record for this publication is available from the British Library

Library of Congress Cataloguing in Publication data
Wilson, Ross, 1979–
Shelley and the apprehension of life / Ross Wilson.
pages cm. – (Cambridge studies in romanticism)
Includes bibliographical references and index.
ISBN 978-1-107-04122-6 (hardback)
1. Shelley, Percy Bysshe, 1792–1822–Criticism and interpretation.
2. Life in literature. I. Title.
PR5438.W55 2013
821′.7–dc23
2013004685

ISBN 978-1-107-04122-6 Hardback

Contents

Acknowledgements

I have benefited in writing this book from the inspiration, assistance and encouragement of many individuals, including Rowan Boyson, Adelene Buckland, Kate Campbell, Cathy Caruth, Robert Clark, David Ferris, Tony Gash, Denise Gigante, Tom Greaves, Paul Hamilton, Mary Jacobus, Ewan Jones, Laura Kilbride, Jeremy Noel-Tod, David Nowell-Smith, Fred Parker, Reeve Parker, Ian Patterson, Rachel Potter, Henry Power, Rupert Read, Alexander Regier, Michael Rossington, Rebecca Stott, Stefan Uhlig, Nick Walker, John Wilkinson, my father Mike Wilson and Peter Womack. I am grateful to Linda Bree, Anna Bond, Liz Hudson, and Rob Wilkinson, to two anonymous reviewers for Cambridge University Press and to James Chandler, whose advice on the manuscript was invaluable. I am indebted to the following institutions, without whose support work on this book would have been impossible: the Leverhulme Trust; the Sir Isaac Newton Trust; the Faculty of English, University of Cambridge; Emmanuel College, Cambridge; and the School of Literature, Drama, and Creative Writing, University of East Anglia.

An earlier version of Chapter 5 appeared as 'Shelley's Sounds of Air' in *Thinking Verse*, Issue 1 (www.thinkingverse.com/issue01.html), and some sections of Chapters 3, 4 and 5 draw on 'Poetry as Reanimation in Shelley', in Ross Wilson, ed., *The Meaning of 'Life' in Romantic Poetry and Poetics* (2009). Likewise, much of this book has its genesis in papers presented to various conferences, colloquia and seminars; suffice to say that I am grateful to the organisers and audiences of numerous such events over the past five years.

I should like to mention four individuals in particular for special acknowledgement. Lyndsey Stonebridge's support has been of the highest value, as has the friendship and intellectual companionship of Tom Rutledge. Adequate acknowledgement of my debt to Simon Jarvis scarcely seems possible; without the inspiration of his work and thought, and his practical advice and encouragement, this book would barely have been conceived. Finally, I should like to acknowledge the tireless support of my wife, Lesley Wylie. This book is for her, once again, and for our daughter, Flora.

Abbreviations

BSM I	*'Peter Bell the Third' and 'The Triumph of Life'*, ed. Donald H. Reiman (New York: Garland, 1986).
BSM V	*The Witch of Atlas Notebook: A Facsimile of Bodleian MS. Shelley Adds. e. 6*, ed. Carlene A. Adamson (New York: Garland, 1997).
BSM XVII	*Drafts for 'Laon and Cythna', Cantos V–XII: Bodleian MS. Shelley Adds. e. 10*, ed. Steven E. Jones (New York: Garland, 1994).
BSM XVIII	*The Homeric Hymns and 'Prometheus' Drafts Notebook: Bodleian MS. Shelley Adds. e. 12*, ed. Nancy Moore Goslee (New York: Garland, 1996).
BSM XIX	*The Faust Draft Notebook: A Facsimile of Bodleian MS. Shelley Adds. e. 18*, ed. Nora Crook and Timothy Webb (New York: Garland, 1997).
Hutchinson	*Shelley: Poetical Works*, ed. Thomas Hutchinson, 2nd edn, corr. by G. M. Matthews (Oxford University Press, 1971).
Letters	*The Letters of Percy Bysshe Shelley*, ed. Frederick L. Jones, 2 vols. (Oxford: Clarendon, 1964).
Poems I	*The Poems of Shelley*, vol. I: 1804–1817, ed. Geoffrey Matthews and Kelvin Everest (London: Longman, 1989).
Poems II	*The Poems of Shelley*, vol. II: 1817–1819, ed. Kelvin Everest and Geoffrey Matthews (Harlow: Longman, 2000).
Poems III	*The Poems of Shelley*, vol. III: 1819–1820, ed. Jack Donovan et al. (Harlow: Longman, 2011).
Prose	*The Prose Works of Percy Bysshe Shelley*, ed. E. B. Murray (Oxford: Clarendon Press, 1993).

SPP	*Shelley's Poetry and Prose: Authoritative Texts, Criticism*, 2nd edn, ed. Donald H. Reiman and Neil Fraistat (New York: Norton, 2002).
Works	*The Complete Works of Percy Bysshe Shelley*, ed. Roger Ingpen and Walter E. Peck, 10 vols. (London: Benn, 1926–30).

In citing from the *BSM* volumes above, I give first the Bodleian pagination followed by that of the Garland reprint.

Introduction

In a fragmentary essay of 1819, Shelley poses a question that had concerned him since the beginning of his career and would continue to preoccupy him until its end:

> What is life? Thoughts and feelings arise, with or without our will and we employ words to express them. We are born, and our birth is unremembered and our infancy remembered but in fragments. We live on, and in living we lose the apprehension of life. How vain is it to think that words can penetrate the mystery of our being. Rightly used they may make evident our ignorance to ourselves, and this is much. For what are we? Whence do we come, and whither do we go? Is birth the commencement, is death the conclusion of our being? What is birth and death? (*SPP*, p. 506)

In its movement from the initial posing of the question, to attempts to begin to address it, to recognition of the futility of such attempts and, at last, to renewed and proliferated questioning, the passage above hopes at best to 'make evident our ignorance to ourselves'. The three sentences following the opening question each seem to offer different ways of approaching it, but each, in fact, ends up distancing us further and further from being able to say what life is. First, Shelley offers what might be a way of characterising life – 'thoughts and feelings arise, with or without our will' – as a starting point. But even though thoughts and feelings are said to arise either voluntarily or involuntarily, the fact that they 'arise', as if by some miasmic process, surreptitiously downplays their potential willed aspect and, moreover, hardly dispels the obscurity of their genesis. Evincing thoughts and feelings as characteristic of life would only seem, then, to deepen the mystery surrounding the initial enquiry. Shelley renews his attempt to establish some purchase on the question by turning back to what we might think of as the origin of life, namely, birth. Again, however, and even before Shelley asks whether birth is indeed the 'commencement' of our being, this turn to a putative origin enables little progress to be made, since this origin has in fact sunk into oblivion, and, what is more, the period following birth is likewise unreliable as a source of information concerning the nature of life because of the friable, discrepant character of any recollection of it. Finally, the last of these three sentences is a remarkably concentrated consolidation of the sense that the course of life itself is inimical to the attempt to grasp what life might be. It is because we 'live on' that we are progressively (or regressively) distanced from the knowledge of life. 'What is life?' We cannot know because we live.

'We live on, and in living we lose the apprehension of life.' This book is an extended reading of this statement. It is an 'extended reading' in the sense that it takes Shelley's concern with the opposition between 'living' and 'the apprehension of life' to be central to his work, from early poems like 'The Wandering Jew' and *Queen Mab* to the late and incomplete masterpiece 'The Triumph of Life', and from seemingly ephemeral fragmentary scrawls to *Prometheus Unbound*. In particular, I argue that Shelley does not merely acquiesce in the obliteration of 'the apprehension of life' by 'living'; on the contrary, his work is at once a profoundly informed, incisive critique of what might be called *mere* life and an attempt to bring the resources of poetic imagination to bear on the restoration of what he calls 'the apprehension of life'.

We can already see from the statement that 'in living we lose the apprehension of life' that 'living' and 'life' are, in Shelley's thinking, internally riven terms. That life is, so to speak, chequered is an insight hardly unique to Shelley, of course. Here is Keats's *Endymion*, for instance:

> But this is human life: the war, the deeds,
> The disappointment, the anxiety,
> Imagination's struggles, far and nigh,
> All human; bearing in themselves this good,
> That they are still the air, the subtle food,
> To make us feel existence, and to show
> How quiet death is.[1]

Whereas for Keats, however, the negative aspects of human life nonetheless bear 'in themselves' the capacity to make us feel alive, it is those aspects of life that, for Shelley, in fact deaden us. Life is not so much characterised for him by events, actions and emotions that are at once clearly negative but at the same time enlivening; life is instead at war with itself. Laura Quinney captures this well when she remarks that Shelley's 'vocabulary is composed of words hovering around deeply antithetical uses'.[2] Quinney's remark is notable too, however, because it suggests that 'life' is not the only one of Shelley's recurrent terms that is ambivalent: in fact, his whole vocabulary is constituted of just such terms. For instance, 'Power' in 'Mont Blanc' is, similarly to 'life', cast as potentiating and enervating, creative and destructive. Yet, even where the inaccessibility of power is considered in 'Mont Blanc', power itself does not weaken but ultimately abides aloof from the fray of mortal activity: it 'dwells apart in its tranquillity', whereas, faced with the consequences of power, there is by contrast no safe habitation for human beings: 'the race / Of man flies far in dread, his work and dwelling / Vanish like smoke' ('Mont Blanc' [Text B], *Poems* I, pp. 547, 548; ll. 97, 118–20). To be sure, like those of power, the effects of life upon human beings can certainly be ruinous, but in holding destructive sway over living beings, life is at the very same time destructive of itself. Life's frequent indifference to the living is not, for Shelley, a token of its serene majesty but rather of its own self-annihilation as well.

Life's relation with itself is thus central to Shelley's understanding of it. In an essay that in part addresses Shelley's 'The Triumph of Life', Jacques Derrida claims with particular regard to 'living on' that '[l]iving on is not the opposite of living, just as it is not identical with living. The relationship', he goes on to say, 'is different, different from being identical, from the difference of distinctions – undecided, or, in a very rigorous sense, "vague".'[3] This identity and non-identity of 'living on' with living, astutely teased out in Derrida's reflections on the implications of what it means to live *on*, is one of the key focuses of this book. Indeed, it is instructive that the surviving manuscript of the essay in which Shelley makes the statement that is at the heart of this book is catalogued in the Pierpont Morgan Library under the title 'Life and the World: Autograph Manuscript of an Essay Written on the Leaves of a Note-Book'.[4] The opening sentence of the essay, from which the Pierpont Morgan catalogue entry takes its title, might suggest that Shelley's view of what is involved in the question 'What is life?' is already very diffusive, even culpably (rather than rigorously, as Derrida suggests) vague. 'Life, and the world, or whatever we call that which we are and feel, is an astonishing thing' (*SPP*, p. 505). At best, it seems, Shelley has fallen victim to the astonishment to which he testifies, failing altogether to circumscribe the question of what life is and incapable even of defining its terms: he collapses right at the start into musing on 'whatever we call that which we are and feel'. John Middleton Murry, glossing Baudelaire's words, 'the deep significance of life reveals itself in its entirety', remarked, for example, that 'Life, in this phrase, means the universe of the writer's experience.'[5] 'Life', that is to say, is similar in usage to 'everything'. Likewise, in his study of those instances of 'life' used to mean, as he disarmingly put it, 'what I like', C. S. Lewis commented, generously enough, that 'the use of *life* to mean whatever the speaker values is serviceable language [...] *Life*, thus employed, is as useful a word as *good* or *nice*. The only danger is lest we should think it somehow more precise or scientific than they.'[6] In Shelley's case, it would seem that the imprecise and unscientific nature of the meaning of 'life' is due, in fact, to his deployment of it both for something he values – it is 'an astonishing thing' – and also for something the value of which is seriously open to question: it is life itself that causes the loss of its own apprehension.

One crucial attempt to rescue Shelley's understanding of life from the quandary into which it would seem to have mired itself has been the effort to recover his knowledge of what was indeed the scientific and increasingly precise account of life being developed around the beginning of the nineteenth century. Long ago, A. N. Whitehead argued for the importance of recognising the 'absorption of [Shelley's] mind in scientific ideas'.[7] Whitehead's emphasis on Shelley's knowledge of science was, of course, polemical and aimed at the disregard for his intellectual integrity displayed by his detractors and defenders alike. 'It is unfortunate', Whitehead wrote, 'that Shelley's literary critics have, in this respect, so little of Shelley in their mentality.' (By which he meant that their assessments of him were based on a dilatory treatment of the scientific aspects of his work.) 'They tend to treat as a casual oddity of Shelley's nature what was, in fact, part of the main structure of his mind, permeating his poetry through and through.'[8]

Of course, Romantic studies generally, and commentary on Shelley in particular, has developed in a number of different directions since Whitehead and his immediate followers. But it is worth emphasising that, as in Whitehead's work, the recently renewed focus on what has been called (in what is hoped to be a provocative move) 'Romantic science' has quite explicitly conceptualised and stressed its place in, and revision of, Romantic criticism.[9] Two aspects of this conceptualisation need to be drawn out with regard, in particular, to the Romantic understanding of 'life'. First, a number of important Romantic studies have aimed to recover the idea of organicism from post-structuralist strictures on it. In particular, it has been powerfully argued that the critique expounded and thence inspired by Paul de Man rests upon an oversimplified version of organic form that neglects or under-elaborates the complexities of the conceptualisation of the organic in a range of Romantic authorships.[10] Second, recent work on Shelley in particular has aimed to demonstrate his engagement with the controversy carried on between John Abernethy and

William Lawrence concerning the nature of vitality and thus has aimed more deeply to historicise Shelley's materialism. Sharon Ruston's *Shelley and Vitality* is paramount here, and she is especially interested in the political consequences of the 'vitality debate' in, for example, the implicit conservatism of Abernethy's reliance on an immaterial spirit as the basis for vitality versus the radicalism of Lawrence's more thoroughly physiological approach.[11]

The explicit emphasis on Shelley's knowledge of the emerging life sciences, found in Ruston's work, and the consequence of it for our understanding of his supposed materialism is supplemented by consideration of the significance of scientific thinking for Shelley's poetic practice, taking, for example, the assimilation of alien material by organisms – extensive consideration of which was central to theories of vitality – as a metaphor for the poetic process. Denise Gigante, in her account of Romanticism's 'epigenesist poetics', has advanced this interchange between science and poetry still further. Crucially, she views Romanticism's rejection of neoclassical standards as congruent with the realisation, intensified during the eighteenth century, that living beings accord not with a pre-established form but are instead characterised by their dynamic production of life from moment to moment.[12] Life and poetry alike are thus not conformable to a set of pre-given criteria but, instead, come to be and pass away constantly. Gigante offers a reading of Shelley's 'The Witch of Atlas' in which she takes his 'vitalist "Witch"' to be an enactment of his epigenesist sense that '[w]hat was distinctive about poetic or metaphoric language […] was its capacity to sprout new relations, and from these, organic forms.'[13] In particular, '[v]italist poetry aims not to narrate but aesthetically to enact natura naturans', and, furthermore, the vital power taken to be embodied in the figure of the witch herself, an understanding of Shelley's engagement with science shows us, 'may be less a metaphysical abstraction than something he believed really to exist'.[14]

The strength of accounts such as Ruston's and, especially, Gigante's rests in their recognition of the interrelation of science, poetics and aesthetics, a recognition perhaps missing or, at least, insufficiently emphasised in earlier discussions of Shelley's knowledge of scientific theory.[15] I do still, nevertheless, have questions about the kind of account advanced by Ruston, which have to do, on the one hand, with the degree to which science is allowed (extensive apologias to the contrary notwithstanding) to dictate to poetry and, on the other, with a potential neglect of sources other than science for thinking about what 'life' means.[16] Moreover, my emphasis throughout this book is not on recovering a more nuanced version of organicism as it might emerge from Shelley's work but rather on articulating what I want tentatively to call the *post-organic animism* that I see his poetry as evincing. The focus, then, of this articulation is neither on the place in Shelley's thinking of scientific theory nor even so much on the role of form (however 'open') but rather on the animistic investment of his verse in the sounds of particular words and letters. Poetry and 'life' are, in Shelley's work, mutually disclosing, and, thus, life is, in this book, neither an exclusively conceptual nor more broadly thematic concern but is rather a dynamic of poetic representation and performance itself.

In order to develop the reading of the interrelation between poetry and life sketched here, it will be necessary first of all to return in more detail to some of the ways in which my focus differs from other recent considerations of 'life' in Romantic studies. Therefore, Chapter 1 examines Shelley's conception of different theories of life as well as the ways in which that conception has been accounted for in approaches to his work in the twentieth century and more recently. And the minutiae of Shelley's verse composition, though they are pivotal throughout this book, are explicitly addressed in Chapters 4 and 5. At this point, however, I want to return to the apparently vague concept of life deployed in Shelley's 'On Life' – a vagueness, of course, that demonstration of his debt to science is meant to diffuse. The seeming vagueness of a locution such as 'life, or the world, or whatever we call that which we are and feel' is due not, I would like to suggest, to a deplorably lax handling of terms but rather, on the contrary, to the fact that life is fundamental and prior to our perception of the world and is indeed all 'which we are and feel'. This is what Shelley means when, slightly later in 'On Life', he gives what can only provisionally be called a *definition* of life when he says 'Life – that which includes all' (*SPP*, p. 506). This is not a mere evasion of definition but a recognition that life is the inevitable basis of our perception of all things.

The consequences of the realisation that life 'includes all' are central to Chapter 5, where I examine the thought experiment in 'On Life' in which Shelley imagines an artist who 'merely conceived in his mind' of the cosmos and everything in it, 'these things', counterfactually, 'not before existing' (*SPP*, p. 505). But it is worthwhile here to attempt to specify still more fully why a view of 'life' as 'that which includes all', advanced by Shelley, does not fall prey to mere vagueness. Here, the revisionist phenomenology of the late Michel Henry is especially helpful in opening out what the force of 'life' might be in Shelley's thinking. Henry, in an important essay on 'what science does not know' (to which I will return briefly in Chapter 1), lays out the corollaries of the methodological abstraction fundamental to modern science:

> In setting to one side the sensible qualities of the universe, the *blue* of the sky, the *green* of trees, the *serene* or menacing character of a landscape, the *sweetness* of odours, the *beauty* of forms – of old towns, or their horror in the monstrous suburbs of our time – [science] does not only eliminate the external aspect of objects that surround us but our very life. For it is indeed true, according to Descartes's brilliant intuition, that the sensations which result in the world giving itself to us under the appearance of a sensible world are not in the things but only in us, in our spirit. Things do not sense themselves, they are thus incapable of being hot, painful, sad, or serene. Only that which senses itself, that which internally feels itself can feel something such as heat or cold, suffering or joy. That which feels itself immediately, internally we call subjectivity or life – not biological life but life in the sense that everyone gives to this word in declaring, for example: life is short, life is sad, or, then again, as one of Maupassant's characters has it: 'Life is neither as good nor as bad as they say.'[17]

It is perhaps too infrequently recalled that, only a few sentences after making his notorious claim that '[i]f Shelley had been born a hundred years later, the twentieth century would have seen a Newton among chemists', Whitehead justly remarked that Shelley 'can simply make nothing of the doctrine of secondary qualities which is fundamental to [science's] concepts. For Shelley nature retains its beauty and its colour.'[18] Shelley holds this view in common, for instance, with Henry, and, in the above passage, what Henry wishes to recover from scientific reductionism is the meaning of a lived life rather than an objectified one. Accounts of life that miss out qualities such as these – and biology's understanding of life would, for Henry, be just such an account – are not really explanations *of life* at all. What Henry brings out, moreover, is that a description of life fully attentive to its shortness, sadness, goodness and badness will display a certain recalcitrance to settled definition. Life is fundamental – there is no available perspective outside of it, and it is thus prior to any understanding proffered by biology – but for that reason it can only provisionally be subjected to the kind of experimental objective scrutiny central to scientific investigation, since it is the foundation of such scrutiny. As Shelley puts it, life is, therefore, 'at once so certain and so unfathomable' (*SPP*, p. 505). This is not at all to say that Shelley simply came to reject the findings of the emerging life sciences; on the contrary, he was deeply excited and informed by them, as Ruston in particular amply testifies.[19] But it is to say that central to the kind of understanding of life that Shelley wishes consistently to pursue throughout his work is its indelibly qualitative nature. Life is always felt to be – one might as well say life is always lived as – good or bad or indifferent – and indifference itself is an irreducibly qualitative aspect of life.

Whereas Henry's work can sometimes read as a paean to life, despite the acknowledgement that it can be 'sad', Shelley's, for all those moments where life is held up to be celebrated, shared and perpetuated, evinces a very strong sense that life is worryingly wrong. It is this sense that has often been taken to predominate in Shelley's understanding of 'life'. Writing in 1900, for instance, W. B. Yeats suggested that Blake, 'who for all his protest was glad to be alive', should be contrasted with Shelley, 'who hated life because he sought "more in life than any understood"'.[20] The quotation is a slight misremembering of the line from the first stanza of Shelley's late *ottava rima* lyric, 'The Zucca', where the speaker recalls the 'infant Winter', 'when I, desiring / More in this world than any understand, / Wept o'er the beauty, which, like sea retiring / Had left the earth bare' (Hutchinson, pp. 664–5; ll. 2, 3–6). As the quotation from 'The Zucca' already intimates, despite Yeats's assertion of Shelley's hatred of life, Shelley does not just reject life out of hand but desires 'more' in it than is routinely or easily comprehended. Central to 'The Zucca' is not so much dissatisfaction with life as such but rather with the fact that what passes for life too infrequently or only fleetingly is understandable as life at all: it is only for a moment that the mysterious 'I know not what' that the speaker 'loved' (l. 20) is 'not forbidden / To live within the life which thou bestowest' (ll. 29–30). What Shelley mourns here is that life is bestowed without, as it were, being animated. Shelley's hatred, such as it is, is not for life but for life that does not live.

The character of Shelley's understanding of life, therefore, is much more nuanced than Yeats would appear to allow. Richard Eldridge has endeavoured to explore the ramifications of this more than purely negative hatred of life. He quotes Thomas Mann's delineation of the difficulties involved in analysing the 'psychic state' at work in the background to Goethe's *Die Leiden des jungen Werthers*. Mann writes:

> A discontent with civilization, an emancipation of emotions, a gnawing yearning for a return to the natural and elemental, a shaking at the shackles of ossified culture, a revolt against convention and bourgeois confinement: everything converged to create a spirit that came up against the limitations of individuation itself, that allowed an effusive, boundless affirmation of life to take on the form of a death wish.[21]

Sweeping as Mann's portrayal of the late-eighteenth-century European 'discontent with civilization' is, its insight into the paradoxical rejection of life motivated by an 'effusive, boundless affirmation' of it is nevertheless valuable. It is precisely because it is felt that life ought to be, in a word, good that its bad form is rejected. Perversely but understandably, under conditions in which life is not liveable, rejection of life comes to be the only authentically available action that is affirmative of life: 'it is all too plausible', comments Eldridge, 'that one might not only become melancholic but come to wish for nothing more than surcease, even to regard the taking of one's own life as the only possible creative act with a fixed endpoint, as the only meaningful act.'[22]

This specific rejection of life, rather than the otherworldly and general turn away from it diagnosed by Yeats, is strongly discernible in Shelley's writing. His concern with 'life' is as much a concern with what it ought to be as with what it is. For instance, at the height of one of those episodes of his life in which fraught emotion and high principle comingled – his quarrel with his erstwhile friend Thomas Jefferson Hogg over the latter's advances to Shelley's first wife, Harriet – Shelley wrote to Hogg, upbraiding his conduct and, significantly, arguing that life unqualified by certain ideals was not worth having:

> Prove to me satisfactorily that Virtue exists not, that it is a fabric as baseless as a school-boy's vision, then take life. I will no more with it. I would not consent to live to breathe to vegetate, if this vegetation simply went on to imbibe for no other end than it's [*sic*] own proper nutriment the juices which surrounded it. – Does the vegetable reason as to the good it does to the air when it absorbs azote, does the panther destroy the antelope for the public good, does the lion love the lioness for his sake or her own. Prove that Man too is necessarily this; my last act may be an act of this very selfishness but it would be an act of precluding the possibility of more of it, or I would leave the world to such as could bear to inhabit it's [*sic*] surface. (?14 November 1811, *Letters* I, pp. 179 80)[23]

Shelley perhaps insinuates that it is Hogg's infatuation with Harriet which is itself 'as baseless as a school-boy's vision', and thus as wretchedly unrealistic as the kind of onanistic fantasy that that phrase hints at. But the interest of this letter is more than merely biographical and lies rather in its description of a life unqualified by (here) 'Virtue' as frankly unliveable. The above passage successively downgrades the kind of existence conceivable were virtue indeed shown to be fatuous: 'I would not consent *to live to breathe to vegetate*, if this vegetation simply went on to imbibe for no other end than it's own proper nutriment the juices which surrounded it.' Life without virtue is aimlessly enduring vegetation, and those Shelley would leave behind were virtue not to exist would merely 'inhabit [the world's] surface', just eating and excreting like plants similarly rooted to the ground, their capacity to tolerate doing so the result not of a virtue such as forbearance but of inertia.

It is tempting to write off the episode of the break with Hogg as the tempestuous and faintly comical consequence for a highly charged adolescent friendship of ill-conceived moral experimentalism. We would be wrong to do so, however, if only for the reason that friendship, for Shelley, is one significant quality that makes life liveable. The imagination of true friendship as the mutually sustaining dissolution of two parties into one another is central to Chapter 4's consideration of the portrayal of the sorority between Ione and Panthea, which is performed on the most intimate level of the fabric of their speech. Without love, life becomes its own tomb, a tomb which does not merely contain what has gone dead but perpetuates it, horrifyingly, as a perverse form of living, for, as the essay 'On Love' has it, '[s]o soon as this want or power is dead, man becomes the living sepulchre of himself, and what yet survives is the mere husk of what he once was' (*SPP*, p. 504). The importance of this investment in friendship is also discernible, for example, in Shelley's translation of the *Symposium*. In a thorough overview of Shelley's 'mistranslations' from Plato's Greek and their consequences, Stephanie Nelson discusses Shelley's struggles with the contrast between *huperapothanein* and *epapothanein*, a contrast by which Diotima stresses that Achilles not only died for Patroclus in the way one might for a friend still alive (*huperapothanein*) but rather died for him even though Patroclus himself was already dead (*epapothanein*). Nelson's view of this translational difficulty is that 'Shelley's solution is to ignore the problem' and, instead, to emphasise that 'the gods honor Achilles because he dared not "to die for him merely, but to disdain and reject that life which he had ceased to share"'.[24] Yet, contrary to what Nelson suggests, it is not quite the case that Shelley simply sidesteps the particular conundrum for translation here; rather, what he chooses to call attention to is that Achilles comes to abhor a life that can no longer be characterised by the fact that it is shared with his friend. For Achilles, life has ceased to be liveable *for him* because it is no longer lived *by Patroclus*.[25]

What each of these examples – the letter to Hogg and the translation of Diotima's reflection on Achilles' sacrifice for his friend – brings into view is that life, for Shelley, is never straightforwardly or immutably life if it is just living on, if it is just, that is to say, mere enduring. His hatred of life, alleged by Yeats, is thus no simple rejection of life for the sake of something other than life. Shelley is an enemy of life for the sake of its realisation; he hates life, that is, lived under conditions of suffering, injustice and oppression. In particular, life exploited by tyranny and subservient to the demands of commerce is a life perverted into survival alone, and his work (as I show in Chapter 3 in particular) contains a sustained delineation of the forms of oppression under which life is rendered unliveable, a delineation that seeks to expose those conditions of injustice and forms of oppression as socially contingent rather than unchangeable.

One programme for changing oppressive social forms that was enormously influential on Shelley was, of course, that set out in William Godwin's *Enquiry Concerning Political Justice*. Toward the end of that book, Godwin appends a set of reflections on 'health, and the prolongation of human life', amongst which he offers a word in favour of the improvements to human health that he has been advancing:

> If the remedies here proposed tend to a total extirpation of the infirmities of our nature, then, though we should not be able to promise them an early or complete success, we may probably find them of some utility. They may contribute to prolong our vigour, if not to immortalize it, and, which is of more consequence, to make us live while we live. Every time the mind is invaded with anguish and gloom, the frame becomes disordered. Every time languor and indifference creep upon us, our functions fall into decay. In proportion as we cultivate fortitude and equanimity, our circulations will be cheerful. In proportion as we cultivate a kind and benevolent propensity, we may be secure of finding something to interest and engage us.[26]

This kind of argument may appear to be an elaborate version of the worldly wisdom that a healthy mind is a healthy body (and vice versa). Its abiding appeal, however, and the appeal of Godwin's thinking for Shelley, certainly, is in its insistence that we 'should remove ourselves to the furthest distance from the state of mere inanimate machines'.[27] I return to this aspect of Godwin's thinking later, in particular in Chapter 6, where I consider briefly the relation of poetry to the circulation of the blood, which interests Godwin in this late section of the *Enquiry*.[28] But here I want to emphasise Godwin's own contention that the expedients he recommends for remedying our infirmities are not chiefly aimed, in fact, at 'prolong[ing] our vigour' but rather at making us 'live while we live'. This revealing phrase suggests, as I have been arguing, that we may not, actually, be living while we live; and, as I have also been arguing, this condition of lifeless life is a central focus of Shelley's thinking – a focus which is matched, in Shelley's work, by a profound interest in what it is that might serve to make us live while we live.

It is worth digressing briefly here to acknowledge the influence on my reading of Shelley of a writer whose thoughts and turns of phrase I have been borrowing from intermittently throughout this introduction. Maureen N. McLane has, with some justice, suggested that '[a]t times [...] Shelley can read like Theodor Adorno *avant la lettre*'.[29] McLane offers this remark in the course of explaining the famously 'unacknowledged' status of the poet as being fundamental to 'a negative critique of the age even as he [the poet] best embodies its genius; his failure is symptomatic not of his own lack but of the deformations of the socio-political system and the literary-critical milieu'.[30] As might be expected, comparison of Shelley and Adorno in connection with other, additional concerns has proved fruitful, and many of the features of Shelley's work that I investigate in this book find an Adornian complement, so to speak: the refusal to accept that what passes for 'life' is really living; the sceptical critique of reason's dismissal of what it presumptuously takes to be irrational; the cognitive significance of art; and the importance of specific experiences of artworks to any consideration of art's capacities.[31] But these points of substantial contact notwithstanding, I do not take in what follows an 'Adornian approach'. Implicit in McLane's remark quoted above is the danger (although she does not, I think, succumb to it) that Adorno be read as a theorist from whom an infinitely portable critical framework may be derived, and, concomitantly, that the interest of any particular aspect of Shelley's work be only fully realised once it is shown to fit, one way or another, into that framework. Such an approach would both betray the character of Adorno's own thinking and smooth out precisely those points in Shelley's work that, I aim to show, make his particular understanding of 'the apprehension of life' remarkable.

This is by no means to say that figures who influenced Shelley himself, who were contemporary with him or who came long after his decease will not be addressed in what follows; it is to say that much of the burden of the argument of this book will fall on extensive attention to the consequences of specific expressions and choices of words in Shelley's works. For example, to begin to see what is involved, for Shelley, in a living life, it is necessary to focus precisely on what he says is lost in 'living on' in the statement that is the leitmotif for this book: '[w]e live on, and in living we lose the apprehension of life.' We lose, not life itself simply, but the *apprehension of* life. It is a central task of this book to examine what this perhaps rather cryptic phrase might mean, and, in conducting that examination, it is worth emphasising both *apprehension* and *of* because the latter, minuscule word is significantly ambivalent. Let us, for a moment, suppose that 'apprehension' means (as the *OED* says it means in one of its usages) something like the operation of grasping intellectually. If that is the case, then it is in living that we come to fail properly to recognise what life is. The loss of the apprehension of life is thus a cognitive deficit: we lose knowledge about life. But, at the same time, 'the apprehension *of* life' could be taken as a possessive phrase, and thus as indicating that what is lost is life's apprehension, which is to say its own ability to apprehend rather than, conversely, to be apprehended.

Both of these senses, to repeat, are present in Shelley's characterisation of what is lost in living on. The latter sense – that life loses its apprehensive power, so to speak, its capacity of apprehension – is reinforced as soon as we begin to examine the resonance that the term 'apprehension' might have had for Shelley. The particular nature of this resonance and, especially the association of apprehension with poetry, is a central topic of Chapter 5. It is necessary to point out here that 'apprehension' in a sense that comes down to Shelley suggests an operation that is at once intellectual and sensible, mental and bodily. The Latin *apprehensio*, from which the English term is derived, was employed by late medieval logicians, Duns Scotus the most prominent amongst them, who divided logic into apprehension, judgement and ratiocination, which were held to be the three fundamental operations of mind.[32] Although apprehension was thought to be the most basic of these operations, it was neither decisively separated from nor subordinated to higher powers of conscious thought. As Timothy C. Potts remarks, 'apprehension, which may be perceptory or intellectual, aims at truth, the world as it is; desire, which may be instinctual/emotional (the "passions" of the soul) or rational (will), aims at the good, the world as one would like it to be and, thus, at changing it'.[33] Significantly, the use of 'apprehension' to designate any kind of mental faculty or operation rather than to indicate the physical act of seizing or grasping (for example, a criminal), begins concertedly to gain currency in English around the end of the sixteenth century (despite having first appeared in 1398).[34] It was, for instance, used by Shakespeare in a number of specific contexts (one of which, Theseus's speech in *A Midsummer Night's Dream*, will be examined in Chapter 5 in order to illuminate the role of 'apprehension' in Shelley's poetics). Crucially for Shakespeare, 'apprehension' in this sense is far from being the lowest of the human mental faculties. Glossing Hamlet's estimation of man as 'like an angel in apprehension!', Terence Hawkes takes this term to be one of many deployed – admittedly, 'in a period not notable for precision in matters of nomenclature' – to designate the 'angelic faculty in Man'.[35] Yet it does appear significant that for Shakespeare this angelic faculty is precisely *in man*, which is to say that 'apprehension' designates the site, so to speak, where consciousness is enacted in sensation or, to put this another way, it designates a kind of sensation that is always already conscious. This accords with the fifth sense given for this term in the *OED*: '[t]he action of laying hold of with the senses; *conscious* perception' (my emphasis).[36]

I want in particular, then, to underline, first, the idea that apprehension is both sensible and intellectual, and, second, that it is especially characteristic of, as Hawkes's gloss of Hamlet's remark would imply, human life. To lose the apprehension of life is to lose something vital about life itself, and, therefore, the restoration of apprehension is a necessary task which, crucially, Shelley ascribes to poets. With these points especially in view it is possible to return to some of the key tenets of Shelley's poetics afresh. Thus, in 'A Defence of Poetry', he famously claims of the language of poets that it is 'vitally metaphorical; that is, it marks the before unapprehended relations of things, and perpetuates their apprehension' (*SPP*, p. 512). Poetry, then, is specifically concerned with fostering apprehension, since, again, 'to be a poet is to apprehend the true and the beautiful, in a word the good which exists in the relation, subsisting, first between existence and perception, and secondly between perception and expression (*SPP*, p. 512). The good, the true and the beautiful here might suggest that what the poet is concerned with is a purely intellectual endeavour, and yet the mention of the relation of perception to existence might conversely be taken to evoke a more sensory operation. In fact, apprehension is placed in between the intellectual and the sensible, for its purpose is to see the good in the relation between perception and existence.

This sketch of the meaning of 'apprehension' has the following significant consequence in particular. First, poetry's association with apprehension is an association not with an anti-intellectual realm of mere feeling, of a vague domain of sheer unqualified life, but rather with a living capacity or experience that is at once intellectual and sensible. However, it might still be thought, given that 'the apprehension of life' is opposed to 'living on', that Shelley conceives of this opposition as one between a mere flash of momentary insight and enervating endurance. Shelley is frequently tempted by the allure of the moment, but, nevertheless, poetry is not just, for him, to supply a kind of transcript of momentary apprehensions and flashes of insight; rather, it both perpetuates them and, moreover, 'awakens and enlarges the mind itself by rendering it the receptacle of a thousand unapprehended combinations of thought' (*SPP*, p. 517).[37] Poetry's role in awakening and enlarging the mind means that Shelley dissents from the view that poetry is intellectually nugatory (however aesthetically beguiling) for any enlightened philosophy. To make this claim is to put a significant burden on the readings of Shelley's poems advanced in this book. Discussion of semantic variety and musical felicity in Shelley's works does not serve as illustration of a thesis established prior to that discussion. Rather, the theoretical ambitions of the account offered here are precisely dependent upon the dynamics of poetic composition to which I wish to draw particular attention.

That it is poetry, for Shelley, that fosters 'apprehension' is one of the fundamental arguments of this book, therefore. In a pertinent statement for my purposes, the anthropologist Veena Das has remarked that '[s]ome realities need to be fictionalized before they can be apprehended'.[38] Das's work is focused in part on the role of fiction in coming to terms with traumatic experience, and her use of 'apprehend' here indicates an experience that is cognitive but, at the same time, more than merely mental (at least in so far as 'the mind' is often understood). For Shelley, as I discuss in Chapter 4's consideration of the thought experiment in 'On Life', where 'a poet' is envisaged as having created the universe, it not already existing, the habitual blunting of life entails that reality needs poetry in order to be apprehended.

But Das's remark is also significant in its implication that the process of fictionalisation – as opposed to whatever can be extracted from fiction – is cognitively significant. Comparably, recent work in philosophical poetics has sought to claim a more fully and specifically philosophical role for just those aspects of poetic practice often overlooked as secondary to intellectual content. Susan Stewart, for example, offers the following striking suggestion in this regard:

> [T]he knowledge that we are alive is a kind of knowledge that poetry seems particularly equipped to offer us [...] The physical qualities of poetic composition convey knowledge of ourselves as living beings among other living beings; they also provide relief from the suffering of disembodiment that gives rise to such a question in the first place.[39]

The three central aspects of this suggestion are essential to this book: poetry knows life in a way not routinely available to us; poetry bears (and, as Stewart claims, 'conveys') this knowledge not in theses or world views extractable from it, but in its 'physical qualities', in, in particular, the sounds of its words and letters; and, since this knowledge is concerned with us 'as living beings among other living beings', it is in no way separable from ethical and political concerns.

These three aspects of poetry's claim, and their indissoluble interrelation, have been brought to the fore in some prominent recent work in Romantic studies. (This work, incidentally, has been written by critics who I do not pretend would always agree with one another, but who, nevertheless, have been essential to the formation of this book's thinking about life, poetry, knowledge, and their vital relation.) In order to think about the 'physical qualities' of poetry in this way, it has been necessary, first of all, to stop insisting that, as Susan Wolfson has put it, 'literary form can register the pressure of historical conflicts and contradictions only when it ruptures or collapses', to stop, that is, positing the breakdown of everything gathered under the heading of 'poetic form' as the condition of possibility for poetry's opening onto a knowledge that it could never, *as poetry*, contain.[40] On the contrary, as Wolfson claims, '[a]ny view of poetic artifice that perceives only its power to occlude and mystify misses [...] the capacity of poetry to strengthen critical understanding by engaging attention with its constructedness'.[41]

Certainly, poetry's capacity 'to strengthen critical understanding by engaging attention' is essential to its thinking. This way of putting the matter, though, especially when read out of the context of Wolfson's argument as a whole, might be taken to suggest that poetry's forms are a kind of provocation to thinking for the reader, grist to the critical mill.[42] But what if there is a thinking that takes place in, and has as its very condition of being, the physical qualities of poetry? Might there be a musical or a poetic thinking? Shelley seemed to think that there is. Explaining his choice of 'the stanza of Spenser' in the preface to *Laon and Cythna*, and after having remarked that blank verse offers 'no shelter for mediocrity', he makes the following remark: 'But I was enticed also, by the brilliancy and magnificence of sound which a mind that has been nourished upon musical thoughts, can produce by a just and harmonious arrangement of pauses in this measure' (*Poems* II, p. 42).

But what does 'musical thought' mean? Can thinking really be 'musical' – rather than, say, clear or obscure, perspicuous or dull? Simon Jarvis has argued that in expressing his desire to write a 'philosophic song', Wordsworth suggests 'not that philosophy gets fitted into a song – where all the thinking is done by philosophy and only the handiwork by verse – but that the song itself, *as song*, is philosophic'.[43] He argues likewise that for Blake, Shelley and, again, Wordsworth, 'thinking was not something which naturally first of all happened in prose, and which then had somehow to be put into verse. It was instead something which could happen in verse too, and would happen differently if it did.'[44] If that is so, if thinking 'would happen differently' were it to happen in verse, then 'thinking' must come to mean something quite other than what it means when it is assumed that it 'naturally first of all happens in prose' – where prose is understood as the pellucid making-explicit of thinking to itself. What, then, if thinking is other than making explicit? In the following passage, the connection between thinking and living is as intimate as can be. It is not simply that I might think that I am alive, but that in thinking I have evidence that I am alive:

> [w]hat grounds my being is not reflection, knowing that I know, thinking that I think, and it is thus not at all anything emptied of affectivity; it is rather the primordial fact of affectivity itself in so far as I am affect. The feeling of thinking, as the feeling which *I – am*, and not thinking about thinking.[45]

Thinking is not, in such an account, reliant on the primary deletion of everything not credited with the clarity of reflection. Any such deletion, in fact, would fail properly to understand 'the process of thought', as Adorno argued:

> [T]he demand for intellectual honesty is itself dishonest. Even if we were for once to comply with the questionable directive that the exposition should exactly reproduce the process of thought, this process would be no more a discursive progression from stage to stage than, conversely, knowledge falls from Heaven. Rather, knowledge comes to us through a network of prejudices, opinions, innervations, self-corrections, presuppositions and exaggerations, in short through the dense, firmly-founded but by no means transparent medium of experience.[46]

Read one way, Adorno's account might seem like a dispiriting enumeration of the obstacles that lie in the way of any exposition of thought whatever: with thought, nothing is ever as straightforward as it seems. But alternatively, those obstacles turn out, in fact, to be intellectually significant in a way not routinely recognised by putatively direct exposition. And I would wish to stress that to Adorno's list – 'prejudices, opinions', etc. – we may add the chimes, euphonious and dissonant, the verbal play, the small changes of letters and sounds across words that are the being of poetry. For poetry too is 'dense, firmly-founded but by no means transparent', and it is in its indissoluble density that its very thinking occurs.

Shelley holds, then, and as I have already suggested above, that poetry is capable of a restoration of thinking and feeling, since if the thinking which is feeling outlined by Jarvis above were somehow lost or diminished – this thinking that I would want to call 'the apprehension of life' in both of the senses that I sketched for this phrase above – then living itself is lost or diminished until restored. Such restoration is itself necessarily vulnerable, and in need, in time, of its own restoration. But above all, if thinking is not primarily or only a mode of making-explicit, of spelling-out, then that which in poetry is irreducible to its paraphrasable content is capable of it.[47] The sound of poetry, which has received renewed attention in some excellent recent discussions of Romantic poetry, is therefore central to this book's consideration of Shelley's view of poetry's claim to restore 'the apprehension of life';[48] in Chapter 5, in particular, I take Shelley's defence of poetic 'enchantment' against rational demystification of it to be predicated in large part on something like the understanding of the potentialities of poetic sound that has emerged from the account of 'poetic thinking' that I have been outlining, but in each of my readings of Shelley's verse I aim to take as seriously as possible the capacity of poetry to foster the apprehension of life, not through its statements merely, but through the physical qualities which are its being as poetry.

There are two qualifications to this emphasis on sound that ought to be entered here. First, poetry has more physical qualities than its sounding alone. Though this book, in considering these qualities, does largely focus on the importance of sound to Shelley's verse and on the complexities of enunciation in reading, it should be acknowledged that graphic phenomena – letters, punctuation marks and, importantly, blank spaces – are also to be numbered amongst the physical qualities of poetry. Even if they need not always characterise the materiality of poetry – in the oral performance and auditory reception of poetry, for example – they are at least potential physical qualities of poetry by the time that Shelley is (after all) writing. Peter de Bolla has remarked in a recent consideration of Wordsworth's *Lyrical Ballads*, for example, on the need 'to weigh within the balance of our own experience of language the forms of writing in their most material guises. In their look, shapes, and geometries.'[49]

But, of course, sounding and writing are not so neatly separable as this mere acknowledgement of poetry's graphic being may be taken to suggest. The sounding of Shelley's poetry is the complex and indirect result of a reading of his writing. Eric Griffiths has written of the 'doubts and difficulties' that beset this relationship, and of the pleasures that it yields as well:

> Print does not give conclusive evidence of a voice; this raises doubts about what we hear in writing but it also gives an essential pleasure of reading, for as we meet the demand a text makes on us for our voices, we are engaged in an activity of imagination which is delicately and thoroughly reciprocal [...] All writing is dramatic, though not all writing is theatrical. 'Dramatic' in the sense that writing is an act of supplication to an imagined voice. Sometimes, the voice writing asks is baffled, choked, actually unvoiceable

> by any physical voice, so many-angled and disparate are the things which written words may be saying all at once. But even to know one has lost one's voice, or that one's voice can do no good at some point, is an effect of voice, something that only those who have a voice, and listen to others' voices, can feel.[50]

I want to imagine the tense reciprocity obtaining between poem and reader as their 'interanimation', in the sense that the poem only lives in the reader's reading, but that, at the same time, the reader is brought more fully to life by the poem. One dramatisation (which, in fact, may or may not be thought of as 'theatrical')[51] of this interanimation is to be found in the mutual dissolution of Panthea's and Ione's speeches in *Prometheus Unbound*, to which I return in Chapter 4.

It is by now necessary, having outlined the main claims of this book, to give some indication about how those claims are organised. Shelley's work, as I mentioned above, evinces a critique of *mere* life – life as it is when, often for socially, politically and economically specific reasons, we do not feel that we are alive at all – and, at the same time, an attempt to foster 'the apprehension of life' that is missing from life in its reduced condition. This critique and fostering are intimately interwoven in Shelley's work and thence throughout *Shelley and the Apprehension of Life*; it is nevertheless necessary first to elaborate Shelley's critique of what passes for 'life', which is the burden of Chapters 2 and 3 in particular, before moving on to examine his emphatically poetic response to that critiqued life, which is the focus of attention in Chapters 4, 5 and 6. But since Shelley's approach to thinking about life demands fuller consideration than has been possible in this introduction, Chapter 1 begins the main development of the book's argument by renewing some of those questions about attempts to situate Shelley's work in relation to theories of life sketched above. In particular, since the argument I go on to develop is that Shelley's poetry is the record of his thinking of life, I attempt to establish at the outset his resistance to the prospect of rendering a definable *theory* of life in his work. Part of the reason for that resistance is the frustration by life itself of putatively anticipatory conceptions of it.

Having argued that life cannot be known in advance of its living, I turn in Chapter 2 to Shelley's reception of British empiricism, not in order to conjure, yet again, the sceptical atmosphere in which Shelley's work subsists but rather to explore quite specifically the sense he inherits from, in particular, Locke and Hume that life turns out not so much to be grasped in, but rather eroded by, its living.[52] It is shown that, for Shelley, the Humean 'custom' through which life is rendered mechanically habitual is an ineluctably political category. Chapter 3 thus develops the explicitly political and social dimension of this discussion by showing how, for Shelley, tyranny is chiefly understood not as the power to inflict death but rather as the exploitation of life.

It is between Chapters 3 and 4 that, in so far as they are separable, the accounts of Shelley's critique of mere life and his claim for poetry's capacity to revive life in its apprehension are hinged. Part of Chapter 3's discussion of tyranny necessarily involves an account of Shelley's understanding of slavery, and I begin the turn to Shelley's poetics by investigating whether artworks are for him, as it were, the mere vassals of their creators. In particular, this is in order to focus the question of whether the materials of artworks are simply invested with animation by the agency of the artist, or if, instead, that material is essential to the constitution of art's animation. This exploration concludes by focusing on a single word in the 'Ode to the West Wind' as the culmination of this investigation into the tension between the artist and his materials, and it is to the exact understanding of the sounds of words in Shelley's poetics that Chapter 5 turns. As I pointed out above, Shelley is resistant to the rationalist demystification of poetry, not because he simply wishes to restore enchantment irrationalistically to power but instead because he thinks that rational demystification is, in many of its guises, itself mystifying. Like the rethinking of thinking outlined above, necessitated when we allow ourselves to consider whether poetry may indeed be a bearer of knowledge, this resistance to the limitations imposed by self-proclaimed reason requires a rethinking of reason itself. The final chapter returns to the book's initiating consideration of the relation of poetry to theory and aims to bring together its related considerations of the workings of poetry, its relation to knowledge and life. Poetry's refusal to put forth a theory of life is the necessary condition for the life of theory in it. In conclusion, I turn to a potentially suppressed possibility for the understanding of 'apprehension' in Shelley's usage and argue that Shelley finally posits no simple opposition between 'living on' and 'the apprehension of life' but hopes rather that onward life may become liveable.

CHAPTER ONE

Poetry and the theory of life

The index entry for 'life' in Jasper Griffin's book *Homer on Life and Death* reads 'Life, *see* death', and only then gives a somewhat diminutive handful of references for 'life, Homeric vision of'.[1] Griffin's initial redirection of the reader interested in Homer's vision of life to the much fuller set of references to his view of death is revealing. First, although Griffin's book contains ample testimony to Homer's various ways of describing life in contrast to his consistent portrayal of death as emptiness, it can often seem that what is called life is fundamentally insubstantial, just a version of death's emptiness.[2] What is called life might scarcely seem worth the living. This suspicion of life's ultimate deathliness, as suggested by Griffin's index, is a major feature of Western (and Eastern) thought and culture from antiquity to the present. But Griffin's redirection also hints at the difficulty of saying directly what life is – as, in fact, does the multiplicity and figurativeness of Homer's attempts to encapsulate the state of living. Death, for Homer at least, is definable because it is nothing; life escapes definition because, so it would seem, it is everything. That is not to say, of course, that Homer's ways of imagining life are merely evasions of the central question as to what life really is. Life does at least include 'seeing the light of the sun' and 'having one's limbs full of movement'.[3] But it is to say that life is also being in the dark and sitting still, and it is that multitudinous character of life which means that fittingly encapsulating figures for it prove extraordinarily hard to hit upon.

This chapter is concerned with Shelley's relation to attempts to resolve this proliferating variety of life into theoretical coherence and hence with the relationship of his poetry and poetics to the idea of 'theory' more generally. Often, Shelley appears to hold theory in much higher esteem than he does poetry. Writing to Hogg early in 1811, for example, Shelley states that 'I confess that I think Pope's "all are but parts of one tremendous whole" something more than Poetry, it has ever been my favourite theory'

(3 January 1811, *Letters* I, p. 35).[4] Immediately before this assertion, Shelley discourses on the mischief caused by the deployment of the 'word "God"' and, in doing so, reveals that his 'favourite theory' is not the result of the provision of proofs but, rather, of a kind of argument quite distinct from the explicit assertions that comprise a theory. The term 'God', he writes,

> does not imply 'the Soul of the Universe the intelligent & necessarily beneficent actuating principle' – This I believe in; I may not be able to adduce proofs, but I think that the leaf of a tree, the meanest insect on wh. we trample are in themselves arguments more conclusive than any which can be adduced that some vast intellect animates Infinity. (*Letters* I, p. 35)

The disavowal of adducing proofs here sits oddly with the assertion of his 'favourite theory' that Shelley is about to make. What is especially notable is Shelley's sense that the leaves and insects, which habitually escape our notice, are 'themselves arguments more conclusive than any which can be adduced'. Although it would be tempting to write this off as a straightforward assertion of faith (however heterodox) based on something like the so-called argument from design, it is significant that the minute phenomena of the natural world are not, in fact, recruited to some theoretical framework – they are explicitly not arguments that 'can be adduced' – but are taken rather in themselves to be 'conclusive'. What is attested to here then, immediately before the implicit statement of preference for 'theory' over 'Poetry', is the cognitive significance of para-theoretical areas of experience.

I want to begin to develop the rather fleeting suggestion contained in this early letter by, in particular, examining attempts to account for the influence of a particular body of theory – the life sciences emerging in the early nineteenth century – on Shelley's work. As I suggested in the introduction, while Shelley was deeply interested in scientific explanations of the phenomena and, indeed, essence of life, explanation of his poetry in light of his interest in the life sciences runs up against his refusal, in the preface to *Prometheus Unbound*, to provide in his poems 'a reasoned system on the theory of human life' (*Poems* II, p. 475). Of course, the kind of 'reasoned system' from which Shelley distances his poetry here is the kind of political and moral polemic productive of 'didactic poetry' (as that category had come to be understood by the time Shelley was writing), rather than systematic scientific thinking about the nature of life.[5] Moreover, *Prometheus Unbound* itself is undeniably informed by scientific thinking, as has been revealingly explicated.[6] The impression that what is announced in the preface to *Prometheus Unbound* is, then, a specific rejection of moralising poetry is reinforced if we recall Shelley's account of the state of tragedy in 'periods of the decay of social life', when it becomes 'a weak attempt to teach certain doctrines, which the writer considers as moral truths' (*SPP*, p. 520). Shelley is in no doubt of the unsuitability of poetry to ends like these: 'To such purposes', he writes, 'Poetry cannot be made subservient. Poetry is a sword of lightning, ever unsheathed, which consumes the scabbard that would contain it' (*SPP*, p. 520). He is concerned to keep poetry from being 'contained' – which is not say, it might be claimed, that he forbids poetry from containing, for instance, the findings of advanced scientific thinking.

Yet, as soon as poetry is itself viewed as primarily a receptacle – as the scabbard, rather than the sword – it has come to be defined by what we find within it. Containing and being contained thus come to the same thing: despite his explicit concern in both the preface to *Prometheus Unbound* and 'A Defence of Poetry' with poetry (or what is allowed to pass for poetry) subserving feeble moralising, Shelley in both places does imply a commitment to poetry's resistance to the teaching of 'doctrines' of any kind. This resistance is twofold. Clearly, in the preface and in 'A Defence of Poetry', Shelley is emphasising what has come to be called poetry's autonomy: its ultimate independence from doctrinal purpose. But this defence is matched, in fact, in Shelley's work by a profound scepticism about whether any theory of life may be tenable. In particular, the questioning in Shelley's work of the possibility of theory having an effect on life and, more radically still, of the possibility of knowing what life is at all is one of the main concerns of this chapter. Emphasising Shelley's scepticism with regard to theories of life is not, however, in turn to say that his poetry halts, as it were, at that scepticism. That it is in some of his best, most highly wrought verse – however fragmentary in some instances it may be – that Shelley expresses this scepticism means that his verse practice itself articulates a way beyond altogether despairing of life.

Shelley's 'lyricised science'?

As I mentioned in the introduction, discussions of Shelley's relation to science occupy important places in the history of commentary on his work. Evaluating the role of scientific thinking in Shelley's work was already long established as a way of addressing the challenge posed by F. R. Leavis's assessment of the poet by the time that Roy Fuller, during his tenure of the Professorship of Poetry at the University of Oxford in the early 1970s, concluded one of the lectures given in fulfilment of that position by asking who could doubt that 'it is high time that young poets attempted interpenetration (as the phrase goes) not only with the natural sciences but also, and consequentially, with a wider and realler world?'[7] One reason why Fuller might have expected few to doubt the need for poets to engage with the natural sciences is because, despite his apparent assumption that they are not in the habit of it, such engagement has in fact long been an important feature of the work of many poets. Nevertheless, Fuller wants poets to pay proper attention to science because science, the implication is, allows privileged access to a world 'wider and realler' than that otherwise open to poetry. He writes, for instance, of 'the reality that science was making even more real' during the early part of the nineteenth century, when poets like Wordsworth and Keats were deplorably wary, in his view, of the effects of science on rainbows and suchlike.[8] But Fuller begins his lecture with a discussion of Shelley, who, he acknowledges, was not only deeply interested in scientific discovery – the same might be said (and has often been said, though Fuller does not acknowledge it) of the medically trained Keats – but whose poetry is in fact only really explicable through recourse to specific scientific insight. Fuller rehearses the already (by 1971) canonical Leavisian criticism of the alleged vagueness of 'Ode to the West Wind' and the riposte delineated by Desmond King-Hele in *Shelley: His Thought and Work*. Approving of the efforts of King-Hele to show that, counter to Leavis's charge, Shelley's description of clouds in that poem is actually remarkably astute and based, what is more, on an advanced grasp of meteorology, Fuller all the same ultimately finds himself to some extent in accord with Leavis's view, for

> generally speaking Shelley's power of employing reality in his verse is uncertain, as his use of scientific notions is faint and damaged by the peculiarities of his vocabulary and narrative style. We must feel that had his knowledge and practice of the discipline been more profound or systematic his poetry would have been greatly improved.[9]

It is rather taken for granted by Fuller (in agreement with Leavis) that uncertainty about reality is always a vice in poetry and that (unlike Leavis) this can be corrected by a properly informed grasp of science. There is also a troubling vacillation discernible in Fuller's insistence that 'we must feel' Shelley's poetry is marred by its insufficient basis in a 'discipline' (putatively) not reliant upon individual feeling but, instead, on 'notions'. On the one hand, feeling is disavowed, to be replaced by scientific discipline; on the other, we must feel that this would be for the best. In the end, it is clear that Fuller is not calling for 'interpenetration (as the phrase goes)' between poetry and natural science at all but rather for the tutelage of poetry by science, whose access to the real is incomparably greater than poetry's could ever hope to be.

Whatever the questions begged by Fuller, his lecture's publication in the *Times Literary Supplement* drew a number of articulate responses pertaining to the reading of Shelley offered in it, two of which in particular are worth attending to here. First, Leavis himself wrote, predictably enough,[10] to correct the suggestion that were only Shelley's understanding of science better the criticism that his poetry evinces a 'weak grasp upon the actual' would be answered.[11] Leavis's rejection of the solution implicitly proposed by Fuller to Shelley's alleged difficulties is not only owing to his apparent suspicion of science.[12] For Leavis, King-Hele's demonstration of Shelley's scientific knowledge is wholly beside the point because 'imagery which has to be explained in this way does not owe the persuasiveness it has had, and can still have, for lovers of Shelley to the kind of felicity the meteorological specialist elucidates here'.[13] Those 'lovers of Shelley' have not primarily been drawn from the community of meteorologists impressed by the poet's knowledge; rather, those persuaded of Shelley's merits are 'not enjoying delicately precise and felicitous observation, but paying implicit tribute to the Shelleyan hypnoidal power, which precludes the kind of actively intelligent attention Mr. King-Hele's defence required of him'.[14]

William Keach once remarked that '[o]ften in his writing about Shelley, Leavis gets hold of the right point in the wrong way', and that certainly seems to be the case when recalling and explaining his earlier critique of Shelley here.[15] Leavis rightly sees that the scientific explanation, valuable as it is, does not explain away the fault he finds in Shelley's poetry. But where both he and King-Hele alike err is in their implicit refusal to acknowledge that poetry has sources of merit other than precise attention to a reality assumed, moreover, always and ultimately to yield to 'actively intelligent attention'. Responding to Leavis's letter with a stern acuity of which Leavis himself would have been proud, J. H. Prynne – at that date, one of the 'young poets' to whom Fuller appealed, and already a writer hardly averse to poetry's 'interpenetration' with the natural sciences – both accurately describes and then dismantles Leavis's objection to Shelley's use of language in poetry. First, Prynne notes that Leavis's reading identifies in Shelley a propensity for the initial ground of a sequence of metaphors or similes to lose its primacy to the subsequent development of that sequence and that, according to Leavis, this propensity is ascribable to feeble-mindedness, no matter with what intelligence Shelley might otherwise be credited. Prynne, taking into account the response to this charge offered by King-Hele and others, does not doubt that, '[w]hatever interesting detail is unearthed about the hitherto less closely observed niceties of scientific reference in Shelley's vocabulary', the first of Leavis's insights is just. He goes on to question, however, whether the second of these points holds. For Prynne, it does not, because

> the variable transfer of the criteria for imaginative coherence from the grounds of figurative language to the forms of language resulting from overlapping figurational transformation is a major source of excitement and energy in Shelley's writing. And [...] at its best, this produces a power and vigour of creative intelligence in the working out of ideas astonishingly disregarded at the present time.[16]

I have spent this long discussing what might appear simply to be a spat in the letters pages of the *TLS* in 1971 because, in fact, Fuller's lecture and the responses of Leavis and Prynne to it crystallise an important moment in the twentieth-century reception of Shelley and also, moreover, because they bring into view a set of concerns especially pertinent to the more recent interpretation of his work in the light of his understanding of the emerging life sciences. In the book on which Fuller draws in order to offer a (limited) riposte to Leavis, King-Hele opened his chapter on Shelley's grasp of science by stating that 'December 1819 saw the completion of the fourth and last act of *Prometheus Unbound*, which was written in a remarkable new style, best described, perhaps, as "lyricized science".'[17] Notwithstanding King-Hele's own caution about this description (that 'perhaps', those scare quotes), it is clear that the 'remarkable new style' is of ultimately secondary importance to what it merely stylises. And it is notable that subsequent readings of Shelley's relation to scientific thinking are, despite their more nuanced attention to what Shelley's 'remarkable [...] style' might entail, still willing to cite King-Hele's description of the last act of *Prometheus Unbound* without comment either way.[18]

The difficulty with designating Act IV of *Prometheus Unbound* 'lyricised science' is that it implicitly overlooks the constitutive differences between science and poetry, viewing the latter as a repository for the findings (duly established as doctrine) of the former.[19] For example, in her discussion of the role played in Shelley's work and thought by the vitalist controversy carried on between John Abernethy and William Lawrence, Sharon Ruston usefully aims to dismantle the '"two cultures" model of science and literature', which, in the Romantic period, 'simply did not exist'.[20] But, in the process, it is made to seem precisely indifferent to theories of life 'whether [they are] expressed in lectures to the Royal College of Surgeons or in poetry'.[21] What is revealed by a statement such as this is that the process of 'lyricising' science has no significant effect on the thinking that science is always already taken to have set forth; at most, poetry can realise the 'imaginative potential' which is, again, already latent in scientific theories of life.[22] Lyricising is thus far removed from the operation of the 'creative intelligence' that Prynne discerns in Shelley, not least because on such a view as that intimated by King-Hele, poetic creativity is not really intelligent, since intelligence is reserved for science. Furthermore, 'creative intelligence' as understood by Prynne is also significantly distinct from the 'actively intelligent attention' (by which is meant accurate observation of perceptible reality) that Leavis finds to be lacking in Shelley and also from the 'remarkable intelligence [...] that he used [...] to acquire a great deal of varied knowledge' which Leavis is willing to acknowledge is evident in Shelley (even if he does not concede that Shelley's knowledge of science acquits him of the charge of mental weakness).

Crucially, the distinctively creative intelligence invoked by Prynne need not be inimical either to the precision demanded by Leavis or the information unearthed from Shelley's poems by interpreters keen to show his scientific learning. Yet the danger of the view represented by the latter is that science is credited with thinking, which is done in advance, while the poet prettifies. For Shelley, on the contrary, a theory of life is radically dependent on the bringing-to-consciousness to which, in his view, poetry is essential – as he argues, again, in the preface to *Prometheus Unbound*:

> But it is a mistake to suppose that I dedicate my poetical compositions solely to the direct enforcement of reform, or that I consider them in any degree as containing a reasoned system on the theory of human life. Didactic poetry is my abhorrence; nothing can be equally well expressed in prose that is not tedious and supererogatory in verse. My purpose has hitherto been simply to familiarize the highly refined imagination of the more select classes of poetical readers with beautiful idealisms of moral excellence; aware that until the mind can love, and admire, and trust, and hope, and endure, reasoned principles of moral conduct are seeds cast upon the highway of life which the unconscious passenger tramples into dust, although they would bear the harvest of his happiness. (*Poems* II, p. 475)

As I acknowledged above, although *Prometheus Unbound* is clearly informed by a wide range of Shelley's scientific interests, especially in the fourth act, Shelley does not seem in the preface to have the sort of 'theory of human life' being elaborated by natural scientists such as John

Abernethy, William Lawrence and others principally in mind; the influential theories of human life advanced by Thomas Malthus and William Paley – and theoretical ripostes to them – are what are chiefly at issue instead. But, as I also argued above, the point about what his poetic compositions might or might not be 'dedicated' to certainly does pertain to theory, including science, in general – and, moreover, for Shelley, the scientific debate concerning human life is not at all neatly separable from the kinds of social and theological thinking advanced by Malthus and Paley.[23] Worthwhile as such theories of human life – or rival theories countering them – might be, it is not the task of *Prometheus Unbound*, at least, to put them into verse.

This is not, crucially, to sever poetry from theory irreparably. Despite Shelley's rather ardent rejection of 'didactic poetry' to which it builds, the passage quoted above in fact suggests that poetry is not to be implacably distinguished from 'reasoned principles of moral conduct'. In his *Academical Questions*, a crucial influence on Shelley, William Drummond is sceptical of rationalist attempts to argue for the worth of virtue. But Drummond does not advocate an at once irrational and amoral rejection of virtue as such:

> If you wish to make men virtuous, endeavour to inspire into them the love of virtue. Show them the beauty of order, and the fitness of things. Seek to elevate the mind to the contemplation of divine perfection, in which alone is assembled whatever is most excellent in intellectual nature. Represent vice, as indignant virtue will always represent it, as hideous, loathsome, and deformed. But do not hope that your precepts can avail you, if you forget, that will cannot be changed, while sentiment remains unaltered. There is no power, by which men can create, or destroy their feelings. Sensation alone overcomes sensation.[24]

What is crucial about Drummond's insistence that the character of the representation of vice and virtue is no merely extraneous matter is the refusal to countenance an emphatic separation between what the mind may contemplate and what it may love: 'endeavour to inspire into them the love of virtue [...] Seek to elevate the mind to the contemplation of divine perfection.'

Shelley, likewise, considers love a part of what the mind must do, and, thus, the description of the relation subsisting between poetry and the theory of human life in the preface to *Prometheus Unbound* is more nuanced than might at first appear. To be sure, Shelley says that he does not 'dedicate my poetical compositions *solely* to the *direct* enforcement of reform'. This provisional statement contrasts with the markedly more emphatic vein in which, however, he continues: he does not 'consider them [his poetical compositions] *in any degree* as containing a reasoned system on the theory of human life'. The shift from a qualified statement of poetry's involvement in the enforcement of reform to an emphatic rejection of the idea that it contains a theory of human life is to be accounted for by the fact that poetic compositions, by enabling their readers to love, admire, trust, etc., may contribute to reform even if that is not their immediate aim, whereas the theory of human life would be a set of guidelines for life's conduct. As Drummond had suggested, actual humans, as yet incapable of love, etc., would consequently be incapable of putting such a reasoned programme into practice.

The passage from the preface to *Prometheus Unbound* has attracted comment on the audience for his poetry that Shelley envisages in it and, in particular, on whether the fact that he sees his poetry as addressed to 'the more select classes of poetical readers' shows that he gives up the idea of reaching a popular audience.[25] Comparably perhaps, when examining Jesus's saying in the Sermon on the Mount, 'Sufficient unto the day is the evil thereof' (Matthew 6:34), Shelley warns that '[i]f we would profit by the wisdom of a sublime and poetical mind we must beware of the *vulgar* error of interpreting literally every expression which [it] employ[s]'.[26] I do not wish to adjudicate the question of Shelley's imagined audience in *Prometheus Unbound* other than to remark that Shelley's 'highly refined' and 'select' readers are nevertheless presumably unfamiliar, prior to reading his works, with the idealisms of moral excellence with which they are to be familiarised; in fact, they are also figured as 'unconscious passenger[s]' on 'the highway of life', and, thus, rather than morally superior, are in fact striking anticipations of the 'great stream / Of people', ignorant of its goal, origin or reason for being, in 'The Triumph of Life' (*SPP*, p. 485; ll. 44–5). Crucially, then, love, admiration, trust, hope and endurance are not themselves sub-theoretical capacities, so to speak, filling in for the disavowed 'theory', but are part of consciousness itself. The mind unequipped with these capacities is, according to Shelley, unconscious. Poetry is therefore not indigent with regard to a theory of human life but is rather its very condition of possibility.

True theory/living death

The passage from the preface to *Prometheus Unbound* is a central statement of Shelley's poetic theory, and we will need to return, in particular, to his insistence on poetic imagination (or 'beautiful idealisms') as indispensable to the acceptation of 'reasoned principles' later on in this book. For now, I want to further the investigation of Shelley's view of the use and uselessness of theory for life. So far, I have been outlining how the expression of reticence concerning the provision of a 'theory of human life' in the preface to *Prometheus Unbound* is, in fact, allied to a view of poetry as the very condition of the possibility of any theory at all, which is to make a claim for the intellectual significance of poetry in its own right rather than as a vessel for already established theoretical thinking. Again as we have seen, the question of the provision of a theory of human life, therefore, is hardly just a theoretical one, although its practical impact on life is radically dependent on the proper exercise of the capacities, in particular, of love.

Having intimated that, for Shelley, poetry is itself cognitively significant, without being dependent for that significance on the 'doctrine' it might contain, I want to turn now to consider those moments in Shelley's verse where he evinces what appears in fact to be a profound scepticism regarding the potential relevancy of theory for life at all. The putative effect of theory on whether life may be liveable is of central concern in 'Julian and Maddalo'. Julian insists that

> We know
> That we have power over ourselves to do
> And suffer – what, we know not till we try;
> But something nobler than to live and die –
> So taught those kings of old philosophy
> Who reigned, before Religion made men blind
> (*Poems* II, p. 673; ll. 184–9)

The problematic relation between knowing and not knowing that is in evidence here – we know that we can direct ourselves, but whither, we do not know – entails that, despite the confidence with which Julian expresses his position, knowledge in itself is insufficient to the achievement of certain ends. And what those ends are is equally significant. We know, that is, that we are capable of doing 'something nobler than to live and die', but Julian doubts whether, in the absence of that knowledge, we even live at all. This is the recalled exchange between him and Maddalo, beginning with Maddalo's response, which follows the lines above, and in which these problems of what it is that Julian thinks we know, what its effect on life might be and whether without it we can really be said to live at all, are pivotal:

'My dear friend',
Said Maddalo, 'my judgment will not bend
To your opinion, though I think you might
Make such a system refutation-tight
As far as words go. I knew one like you
Who to this city came some months ago
With whom I argued in this sort, and he
Is now gone mad, — and so he answered me, —
Poor fellow! but if you would like to go
We'll visit him, and his wild talk will show
How vain are such aspiring theories.'
'I hope to prove the induction otherwise,
And that a want of that true theory, still
Which seeks a "soul of goodness" in things ill,
Or in himself or others has thus bowed
His being — there are some by nature proud,
Who patient in all else demand but this:
To love and be beloved with gentleness,
And being scorned, what wonder if they die
Some living death? This is not destiny
But man's own wilful ill.'

(*Poems* II, p. 674; ll. 191–211)

Commenting on this passage (and, according to convention, taking Maddalo to be based on Byron, Julian on Shelley), Earl Wasserman aptly drew attention to Byron's subsequent declaration of the nullity of life in *Don Juan*, where he claims that, amongst others, Machiavelli, La Rochefoucauld, Plato and Rousseau all 'knew this life was not worth a potato'. This scorn gives way to a degree of reticence – 'We live and die, / But which is best, you know no more than I' – only to be reprised when it is asked, 'Must I restrain me, through the fear of strife, / From holding up the Nothingness of life?'[27] As well as asserting life's essential worthlessness, Byron is also scoffing here, of course, at the pretensions of theory, since all that some of its most eminent representatives have managed to show is life's equivalence to a starchy tuber. In the passage from 'Julian and Maddalo' above, Maddalo's rejection of optimism is equally stern, but, unlike the Byron of *Don Juan*, he makes recourse to no external authority deriving from the philosophical tradition, preferring instead to strike at the very foundation of Julian's argument in articulate language. Maddalo, that is, is happy to grant that Julian's 'system' is 'refutation-tight / As far as words go', but words will not persuade him. One reason for this refusal to be convinced is suggested when Maddalo describes the Maniac to Julian and proposes that the pair visit him. The Maniac, he claims, will disabuse Julian of his 'aspiring theories', not through argument but, conversely, through 'his wild talk'. Julian is not so easily put off, and he responds in turn, this time by giving a slightly greater sense of what the 'something nobler than to live and die' of which we are capable might be. Again, this is put in terms of life and death, for the 'true theory' that Julian suspects the Maniac must lack is one that enables the adherent of it 'To love and be beloved'. For those lacking that capacity, he adds, 'what wonder if they die / Some living death?'

It is worth lingering over the central points of contention in this exchange, since they have considerable consequences for the understanding of theory, life and their relation, not just in 'Julian and Maddalo', but in Shelley's work more generally. First, Maddalo's suggestion that Julian will be undeceived by the Maniac's 'wild talk' rather than by any argument is developed in unexpected directions through the poem's interest in the mode, rather than the content, of speech: the sound of the voice rather than what it says. Thus, reporting another excoriation on the part of Maddalo concerning what is putatively 'eternal and divine', Julian declares, 'I recall / The sense of what he said, although I mar / The force of his expressions' (*Poems* II, p. 670; ll. 130–2). It would seem that it is a shame that the force of Maddalo's expressions has been marred, for, as Shelley's prefatory note to the poem has it, 'His more serious conversation is a sort of intoxication; men are held by it as by a spell' (*Poems* II, p. 661). Julian's memory serves him better when introducing the Maniac's soliloquy, because, despite the 'loud and gusty storm' from which the Maniac's auditors must steal 'his accents', he says, 'I remember what he said / Distinctly: such impression his words made' (*Poems* II, p. 679; ll. 298–9). Julian means that he remembers precisely what the Maniac said and not merely its 'sense' or gist as in the case of Maddalo's speech earlier. But he is also drawing attention to the 'impression' made by the words, which is other than their sense, even as it is fundamental to the recollection of that sense.

Rather like Maddalo's 'serious conversation', the Maniac's voice can be transfixing, for when Julian and Maddalo arrive at the asylum, they are met with 'fragments of most touching melody', 'sweet sounds' (*Poems* II, p. 675; ll. 221, 228), the source of which Maddalo explains: 'And those are his sweet strains which charm the weight / From madmen's chains, and make this hell appear / A heaven of sacred silence, hushed to hear' (*Poems* II, p. 677; ll. 259–61). The intricate musical interlacing of these lines is especially notable, since what they record is the music of the Maniac's 'sweet strains' – which they record, therefore, both in description and echo. Yet, although Julian seems better able to recall the impression made by the Maniac's words, in contrast to the force of Maddalo's, which he mars, he is nevertheless also able later in the poem to remember precisely one apothegmatic statement of his friend's when describing again, significantly, the quality of the Maniac's language:

> The colours of his mind seemed yet unworn
> For the wild language of his grief was high
> Such as in measure were called poetry,
> And I remember one remark which then
> Maddalo made. He said: 'Most wretched men
> Are cradled into poetry by wrong,
> They learn in suffering what they teach in song.'
> (*Poems* II, p. 691; ll. 540–56)

The Maniac's language is wild, but also, like Prometheus's, high, and both linguistic wildness and elevation point to the undiminished vibrancy of his mind, however fractured it may be. In the context of Julian's description of the Maniac's language, Maddalo's statement about what poetry teaches – a statement which, in any case, is perhaps rather unexpected, given that Maddalo is sceptical at least of the kind of teaching Julian advocates – must be taken not simply to refer to the content of poetry. Rather, just as the lessons of suffering are not coherent theories, so the teachings of song take place underneath, beside and above the lexical sense of language. We will examine in detail the importance of sound in Shelley's verse in Chapter 4; for now, it is important simply to stress that this focus on the quality of the Maniac's voice, rather than necessarily or exclusively on what he says, entails that 'wild talk' might not be mere gibberish and that what is not strictly argument (theory, true or false) is not merely nugatory. The teaching of 'song' is still teaching, even if it sets out no theory.

The initial disagreement between Julian and Maddalo, as well as hinging on a differing vision of linguistic communicability, also brings into view the treacherousness of one term in particular: 'life'. Maddalo's gruff anti-utopianism appeals in general to the routinely recognised facts of life in opposition to the hopeful ideal that we might be capable of 'something nobler than to live and die'. What life means is acutely – and painfully – undecided in 'Julian and Maddalo', caught on the horns of the friends' disagreement but also evident, for example, in Julian's Coleridgean claim concerning the jilted that, 'being scorned, what wonder if they die / Some living death?' (*Poems* II, p. 674; ll. 209–10). The vague 'Some' is open-ended, hinting at the possibility that each 'living death' might be as uniquely individual and impossible to characterise in advance as each life. But note also that this living death is not lived but, curiously, died. As soon as we attempt to grasp what this might entail, the contradictions mount up, such that the question of whether the condition of neither loving nor being loved would be more like life or death becomes dizzyingly indeterminable: it is a death, but a living one, which is nonetheless died, rather than lived, but then again it must, if it is living, somehow be lived – and so on, ad infinitum. And what is yet more, if a living death is died (not lived) then might not the death of death suggested by that entail in turn, and surprisingly, life? The terror of the condition imagined here is precisely in its maddening irresolution not so much *between* life and death but *in* them both at once.

Thought of life

The suspicion in 'Julian and Maddalo' of whether life lives and interrogation of the potential impact of 'true theory' on that question are echoed throughout Shelley's work. Like 'Julian and Maddalo', with its reworking of the far-from-straightforward relationship of Shelley and Byron, the nine-line poem of a year previously, 'Alas, this is not what I thought life was', is also amenable to biographical explication. Apparently drafted in dejected response to criticism in the *Quarterly Review* (of which Shelley had been informed by Peacock), the poem is, moreover, one of Shelley's most sceptical statements concerning the usefulness or otherwise of correct thinking as a preparation for life:

Alas, this is not what I thought life was –
I knew that there were crimes and evil men,
Misery and hate – nor did I hope to pass

Untouched by suffering through the rugged glen.
In mine own heart I saw as in a glass
The hearts of others … so [ ] and when

I went among my kind, with triple brass
Of calm endurance my weak heart I armed
To bear scorn, hate and fear, a woeful mass
(*Poems* II, pp. 416–17)

The poem gives a brief account of the speaker's disappointment at life's having turned out otherwise than he had anticipated – even though that anticipation was hardly optimistic. Yet from what vantage point is it possible to *anticipate* anything about life at all? As Eric Lindstrom has put it, remarking on Shelley's concern in 'On Life' with 'Life – that which includes all', '[t]he inclusive nature of Shelley's attitude toward life leads to the uncanniness of any view outside it'.[28] Moreover – and somewhat more emphatically, in the sense that he holds a view outside of life not to be uncanny but rather impossible – Michel Henry has written that the life of which we might complain in the way that Shelley does 'is not a thing (as is the case with biological life, for example) but is precisely a knowledge [*un savoir*], the first and the most essential of all, that which all the others presuppose'.[29] Because life is not a thing, it cannot be submitted to the same regimes of weighing, measuring and experimentation to which things may be submitted, for, Henry asks, 'who has ever seen his life, his boredom [*ennui*], his joy, his anguish?'[30] And yet, without this invisible life which is the basis of all possible knowledge, it would be impossible to anticipate anything at all.

But perhaps, in the case of this poem, these convictions about the uncanniness or even impossibility of a view outside of life, and therefore of any anticipation of life, might be defused by saying that what is meant by 'life' here is something like adult life, or life that has come to have a public as well as a merely private dimension, the life, say, of a published author, as opposed to that of his formerly obscure self. Again, though, even the distinction between life understood in those terms and the perspective from which the speaker thought that life might be quite otherwise is not securely tenable, because the speaker, before embarking on any supposed adult or public life, already knew that 'there were crimes and evil men', and he cherished no false hopes for special treatment. He thus already had the advantage of experience of dealings with the world. Developing Freud's insight that the 'attributes of life were at some time awoken in inanimate matter by the action of a force *of whose nature we can form no conception*', Cathy Caruth has written that '[l]ife itself [...] is an imperative to awaken that precedes any understanding or consciousness and any possible desire or wish'.[31] This imperative to live, that is to say, is neither conceptually nor volitionally formed, and so it is, as it were, radically imperious, in that there is no agency that might choose to answer or ignore it. Life, therefore, is neither the result of a desire or wish nor (and this is the crucial point in this context) does it conform to a pre-established idea of it.

Overall, then, the poem would appear to confirm the nullity of preparatory conceptions of life. Indeed, this point seems to be echoed on a formal level, by the rhymes – both terminal and internal – of the initial stanza. First, it is striking that the *a* rhyme (on 'was', 'pass', 'glass' and so on) in fact also recalls the poem's very first word, 'Alas'.[32] It might then be tempting to view this echo of the terminal rhymes with the poem's initial word as suggesting, contrary to the poem's argument that preparatory initiation is doomed to fail when faced with life, that the poem's form is actually instantiated with its very first word and thus that there is a sequential development from the start: all of the rhymes, that is to say, are not only established at the end of the first line but already at its beginning, in its first word. But on closer inspection, this pattern is not as literally straightforward as it appears. The first terminal rhyme word, 'was', sits uncomfortably with the rhyme words that follow it – 'pass' in the first stanza, 'glass' in the second, and then 'brass' and 'mass' in the third – and with the initial 'Alas', with which those words do chime. This sonic discomfiture, of course, is not apparent straightaway with the enunciation of 'was' itself but only once that word has met its mismatch in 'pass'. Like the inaccuracy of the anticipatory thought of life, the unsuitability of the rhyme scheme's initiation is only apparent once it has irrevocably gone by. Preparatory conceptions turn out to fit ill with what they prepare for.

Furthermore, it might be added that these glitches in the poem's patterning portend a general scepticism concerning the ability to articulate any response to life at all. That scepticism extends to the explanatory power of language itself. At the poem's beginning and end, language appears to teeter close to the condition not of articulated complaint but of dejected exclamation. To begin with, 'Alas' is formed from *lasse*, meaning wretched or weary (ultimately from Latin *lassus*), and the interjection 'ah'.[33] Its components are a word and something that is not quite a word but rather a cry or moan. That formation may seem to indicate the power of language to recruit what is otherwise sub- or para-linguistic to lexis. But the half-echo of 'Alas' at the poem's conclusion in 'a woeful mass' might actually intimate otherwise. The proximity in sound of this phrase to 'oh awful mass' hints instead at the potential collapse of descriptive designation – 'a woeful mass' – into plaintive exclamation.[34] Language's ability to articulate regret is close to being overwhelmed at the beginning and end of this poem by the cries of despair.

I will return to the question of this poem's sonic texture below, because (and I say this tentatively, since taught by this poem I do not wish to anticipate too much) I am not convinced that the argument I have just advanced – that the poem both semantically and formally refuses any thought of life whatsoever – is the only account that might be developed of what this poem's musical articulation is doing. But I want to concentrate for now on what we might call the poem's narrative and especially on its relation of what became of the speaker's thought of what life might be. That thought, it seems, is now, at the beginning of the poem, a thing of the past, and this is emphasised by the abbreviation of 'would be' ('this is not what I thought life would be') in 'was'. It is as if the failure to meet the conditions imagined in the conditional statement renders that statement's conditionality simply a past mistake, as if, that is, what might have been was, all along, never going to be. After this opening lament, the poem turns in its second line to give the reasons for that lament. The poet's 'Alas' would appear to betoken both his misfortune in life and also his disappointment at the fact that what he thought life would be has turned out not to be the case, no matter how worldly and disillusioned that thought was. It becomes clear, though, that the poem's short narrative is not going to provide an explanation of why the thought of life has turned out to be wrong after all – an explanation that is surely required since that thought does appear to have anticipated the hardly trifling range of evils that might quite justifiably have given rise to a complaint such as this poem is. What we are especially entitled to expect after the initial complaint, then, is an account of the contrast between the thought of life and the ills that it foresaw, on the one hand, and the facts of life which have nevertheless exceeded even its dire prognostication, on the other.

Such an account we emphatically do not get. In addition, one may point out that, strictly speaking, the second line is concerned not, in fact, with what was thought of life but rather with what was known of it. One might emphasise at this point the distinction between thought and knowledge that Immanuel Kant's philosophy had stressed shortly before this poem was written: thought is distinguished from knowledge in that we may think what we like but only ever know what is actually the case. Yet the distinction between thought and knowledge is precisely blurred here, because, as the poem turns from the complaint of its first line, we learn not what the poet thought of life but rather that some of this thought was in fact knowledge that has not been refuted but instead confirmed (and some) by life: 'I knew that there were crimes and evil men.' It is worth saying again that this is precisely not the knowledge that the opening line encourages us to expect: what we expect to learn is how the poet's thought was mistaken, but we learn instead how it was, in fact, accurate. For this to be a straightforward narrative of disappointment, we should be told here that the speaker thought life was a bed of roses but we learn instead that he knew it was a vale of tears all along.

The poem bemoans the fact not so much that life has failed to live up to the expectations of the one living it, therefore, but rather that it has turned out all too much as expected, full of crimes, evil men, misery and hate. At no point do we, in fact, learn what part of the pre-existing thought of life has been disproved or, at least, shown to be a radical underestimate of life's ills, by life itself; at no point do we hear of any conception of life that would not be gleaned from the experience of life itself anyway and thus established, precisely, as knowledge. Such knowledge here is surreptitiously cast back onto an original, pre-animate state of which we here learn nothing – rather as Shelley's youthful attempt to elicit information concerning the Platonic world of forms from the newborn baby of an Oxford woman did not get very far.

Once again, it turns out that a theory of life is remarkably hard to come by, either because life turns out never to confirm mere thoughts about it, or because such thoughts are irrecoverable once one is in life, or because there never was, in fact, a vantage point prior to life from which any thought at all would be possible. If the hope that there might be a plausible thought of life in advance of life itself is always frustrated, then perhaps there is, nevertheless, hope of obtaining a theoretically privileged position, so to speak, after death. Shelley is, however, equally sceptical of this prospect, especially in a sonnet subtly concerned with the propensity for life to seek its rationale in its opposite:

> Ye hasten to the [grave]! What seek ye there,
> Ye restless thoughts and busy purposes
> Of the idle brain, which the world's livery wear?
> O thou quick Heart which pantest to possess
> All that pale Expectation feigneth fair!
> Thou vainly curious mind which wouldest guess
> Whence thou didst come, and whither thou must go,
> And all, that never yet was known, wouldst know;
> O whither hasten ye, that thus ye press
> With such swift feet life's green and pleasant path
> Seeking alike from happiness and woe
> A refuge in the cavern of grey death?
> O Heart and Mind and Thoughts, what thing do you
> Hope to inherit in the grave below?
>
> (*Poems* III, pp. 726–7)

The Longman editors record that no draft of this poem exists, though it was first published in *The Literary Pocket-Book* for 1823 and an intermediate fair copy in Shelley's hand is extant (*Poems* III, pp. 725–6, headnote). Of course, Shelley's texts are remarkably unstable in general, and the kind of textual questions in evidence in this case is therefore hardly rare, and it is perhaps curiously apt that only more or less completed versions with little trace of their genesis remain for a poem sceptical of the mind's rush to the completion of life. The word 'grave' in brackets seems, however, especially textually uncertain, with the intermediate copy of the poem undecided between 'dead' and 'grave' (*Poems* III, p. 726, n. 1). The editors' explanation for Shelley's various cancellations, restorations and smudgings of this word is that he 'may have been uncertain about anticipating the word [i.e. "grave"] in the final line' (*Poems* III, p. 726, n. 1). This is an intriguing speculation, since the poem is about the uncertainty of anticipation, on the one hand, faced, on the other, with the certainty of ultimate arrival in the grave. The smudge of 'grave' above the cancelled 'dead' in the intermediate copy thus eloquently expresses the poem's fascination with the grey areas of the human mind and, in particular, the uncertain consequences of certain death. The indefinable potential of the grave, cautiously held not to be worth realising in 'Ye hasten to the grave', was developed to quite other, and striking, effect in Shelley's sonnet of three years earlier, 'England in 1819'. Whereas 'Ye hasten to the grave' views the apparent hopes of its death-driven addressee sceptically, Shelley's great sonnet on the various ills of English society sees those ills not just as perpetuating death but as generative of a revolutionary change for which they are the merely empty basis. 'An old, mad, blind, despised and dying King; / Princes, the dregs of their dull race', and so on, for another ten lines, 'Are graves from which a glorious Phantom may / Burst to illumine our tempestuous day' (*Poems* III, pp. 190–2; ll. 1–2 and 13–14). Far from monumentally entombing the members of the English establishment and hermetically sealing them off from their abused people, graves dramatically open here at the close of this poem, potentially releasing the revolutionary transformation of society for which Shelley wished.[35] Shelley's tentativeness, even nervousness, about the use of the word 'grave' at the start of 'Ye hasten to the grave' concerns, then, not just the repetition of the word but may also arise from his sense of the possibility that the uncertain inheritance of the grave may actually be something worth hoping for.

'Ye hasten to the grave' is itself, therefore, predicated on the not-altogether-secure distinction between life and the grave. The poem's consideration of this distinction is extended in its consideration of the yet-more-intractable difference between 'restless thoughts and busy purposes', on the one hand, and 'the idle brain', on the other. Restlessness and business are symptoms of the 'vainly curious mind', which is thus 'idle' in the sense that its powers, like those of an idling engine, are directed to no specifiable or achievable end.[36] This discrepancy between the outward appearance of life – what the text of this edition has as 'the world's livery', but which *The Literary Pocket-Book* in fact had as 'the world's living' (*Poems* III, p. 726, n. 3) – and underlying torpor or weakness is ingeniously developed in the following lines: 'O thou quick Heart which pantest to possess / All that pale Expectation feigneth fair!' First, deploying a double meaning of which Shelley was fond, the heart is 'quick' both in the sense that it is alive and also because it beats quickly. But its speed, while on the one hand betokening its vitality, also threatens, as it were, to outpace its life, causing the heart to pant. This tendency to atrophy is evident also in the fact that the heart's desire is described as 'pale Expectation' and, moreover, in the particular modulation of the breath in enunciating the phrase 'feigneth fair'. The initial fricative consonants of the phrase's two words susurrate, thus contrasting with the four more emphatic plosives of the preceding line and a half, and in having to enunciate these fricatives in combination twice with almost identical vowel sounds the breath is exhaled twice with little opportunity for inhalation in between. Indeed, the repetitive sonic character of 'feigneth fair' at the line's end brings its movement to a literally exasperated, rather than resounding, conclusion. And, moreover, the word for a breathless swoon, 'faint', is itself echoed – felicitously faintly – in 'feigneth'.

It might be concluded that 'Ye hasten to the grave' counsels adherence to the certainties of life, such as they are, rather than fondly seeking after greater knowledge in the mysterious realms of death. Asking 'what thing do you / Hope to inherit in the grave below?' both cruelly plays on the fact that it is not the dead, but the living, who may hope for any sort of inheritance and also renders the hoped-for inheritance as featureless as can be: it is a 'thing' without further specification – quite unlike, for instance, the finally fulfilled inheritance envisaged for the noble dead in *Adonais*:

> The inheritors of unfulfilled renown
> Rose from their thrones, built beyond mortal thought,
> Far in the Unapparent. Chatterton
> Rose pale, his solemn agony had not
> Yet faded from him; Sidney, as he fought
> And as he fell and as he lived and loved
> Sublimely mild, a Spirit without spot,
> Arose; and Lucan, by his death approved:
> Oblivion as they rose shrank like a thing reproved.
>
> (*SPP*, pp. 423–4; stanza XLV, ll. 397–405)

In contrast to the vague 'thing' hoped for by the examinee in 'Ye hasten to the grave', 'unfulfilled renown' is the inheritance properly due to Chatterton, Sidney and Lucan. Here, it is not inheritance that is 'a thing' but, rather, 'oblivion', now reproachfully reduced to the indistinctness to which it would condemn those deserving of recognition. The tentative return to life of the young dead poets is delicately evoked in these lines. The phrase 'Chatterton / Rose pale' imagines the pallid complexion of the youth as he comes back to the life that he had relinquished, and yet, especially thanks to the pause effected by the line ending, it also allows for the metaphorical imagination of him as a 'Rose pale', whose blush is just about returning, or, rather 'had not / Yet faded'. Similarly putting to effect the line ending at its centre, the description of Sidney as 'a Spirit without spot, / Arose' again fleetingly imagines the earlier poet as 'a rose', not least, furthermore, because of the echo of 'Arose' with the nominative 'a Spirit'. This coming to life is performed at an almost imperceptible level in the drift between syllables and across line endings – which is fitting, since it takes place 'Far in the Unapparent'.

The gently budding life performed in the subtly developed horticultural metaphor of these lines from *Adonais* contrasts still further with the evocation of the verdancy of life in 'Ye hasten to the grave'. Like the rather vacuous 'thing' hoped for in the grave, the poem's view of life itself is also weakly specified. The description of life as a path and, what is more, as 'green and pleasant' is, by 1821, already the most stockish of stock characterisations. Where *Adonais*'s imagination of the coming to life of its fallen poetic heroes was so subtle as almost to be imperceptible, this description of life is immediately, banally recognisable. Wherever life is announced to be a green and pleasant path, it has been trodden into the mud. Even in the terms of the poem itself, that description is not straightforwardly acceptable, for 'green and pleasant' is balanced (or cancelled) out in the following line by 'happiness *and woe*'. It is not that life can safely be envisaged as uniformly cheerful in contradistinction to the greyness of death; it is that the speaker of this poem cannot characterise life consistently at all.

Triple brass

Is it, then, that the thought of life was a chimera all along? Is any attempt to think of life otherwise than as it is, impossible? This second question in particular brings into view the potentially malign consequence of the fact that there is no perspective outside of life from which to think of it: if life is the basis of all knowledge, then would it not be impossible to think of life as somehow different? Must life as it is simply be accepted for what it is?

Both of the poems discussed in the previous section, 'Alas, this is not what I thought life was' and 'Ye hasten to the grave', do seem to despair (morosely in the case of the former and cynically in the case of the latter) of the possibility that life might consistently be thought otherwise than it is. But I want to return now to the earlier poem to ask whether that is all there is to its thinking of life. And I want to argue that it is not that the thought of life is simply lost in an absent past, covered over by a knowledge of what life in fact is; rather, the possibility of the difference of this thought from what we know of life does not only fail to grasp life in its origin but instead opens up a different future for life.

The poem's imagination of poetry's relation to life and to the possibility of a thought of life is significantly influenced by whether or not the poem is fragmentary. The fragmentariness, that is, of an attempt to address life might be the consequence of life's supervening on that attempt, since the demands of life come to trump, in this case, the demands of poetic artifice. The Longman edition follows established editorial opinion concerning this poem, calling it 'the present fragment'.[37] But is that fragmentariness complete in its refusal of completion, on the one hand, and what sorts of completion might the lines wish for, on the other? Terza rima, the form in which the poem is written, like blank verse (into which Cary, for instance, translated the terza rima of Dante's *Commedia*)[38] or heroic couplets (the verse form of 'Julian and Maddalo'), presents a challenge to completion because the scheme of its interlinking tercets, *aba/bcb/cdc*, is potentially infinite. Yet it is also important to recall at the same time that terza rima is unlike blank verse or heroic couplets, since these forms move perpetually onward, whereas the second line of every terza rima stanza rhymes with the first and third line of the preceding stanza, so that, for every two steps this form takes forward, it takes one back.

These features of terza rima may be familiar enough, but note that the usual scheme of that form (*aba/bcb/cdc*) is not, in fact, the scheme of 'Alas, this is not what I thought life was'. Rather than passing the bracketing rhymes of the preceding stanza on to the following one, the rhymes of the first and third line of the final stanza instead return here to the rhymes of the very first tercet so that the scheme of this poem is *aba/bab/aca*. Needless to say, the scheme of that final tercet does not identically repeat that of the initial stanza, since its middle line does not rhyme with the middle line of the earlier tercet.

Having made these observations, what I want to consider more fully is the degree to which it is right to think of this poem as fragmentary. The manuscript evidence ought, first of all, to be examined here. There are two attempts at this poem, the first of which is considerably rougher than the second (as might be expected), does not include the final tercet and has no visible break between its two tercets. It is, in fact, little more than a sketch, especially of its final three lines. Importantly, in the second attempt, the last tercet is still somewhat doubtful, with the return in the rhymes of that tercet to those of the first only established after the deletion of a terminal word that would have introduced a new set of rhymes and thus presented the possibility that the poem's terza rima would continue on in the expected way. This is the transcription of the final tercet:

> I went among my a/kind, I armed
> with triple brass
> Of calm endurance I ~~did girt/d my heart~~
> my weak heart I armed
> To bear scorn hate & fear, a woeful mass
> (*BSM* XVIII, 28/31)

How are we to interpret these deletions and revisions? On the one hand, it might be thought that the poem was left at a mere three tercets because it was simply abandoned, Shelley having rejected one possible, new set of rhymes, only to have had recourse, unsatisfactorily, to the rhymes already used in the opening tercet. But it is perhaps worth noticing that 'armed' is not, in fact, altogether rejected, even though it is moved to a position where it becomes the only terminal word in the poem not to find its rhyme with another terminal word (although 'armed' certainly is anticipated in the line that it ends, by 'calm', or, in fact, by the glissade of '*calm end*urance'). Therefore, in view of this transposition, the rhyme of 'brass' and 'mass', and thus the repetition of the *a* rhymes of the first tercet, may be viewed, not as a floundering resort to an already used rhyme but instead as integral to the poem's completed artifice.

The poem is not a fragment in the sense that it lacks completion at its end, either because its attempted completion is only provisional, and hence strained, or because it tails off into infinity in the absence of an arbitrary decision to bring it to a conclusion. The numerical character of the poem is, on the contrary, quite definite: its three stanzas each of three lines are formed in order to bear the three misfortunes of 'scorn, hate and fear'. The poet, indeed, declares that 'with triple brass / Of calm endurance my weak heart I armed'. The poem's 'triple brass' is its three stanzas and its terza rima form. The patterns of sound in this poem are not just indices of the collapse of the descriptive power of language into sub-linguistic complaint but are rather the means by which anticipation and recollection interact at all. If the narrative critique of the poem exposes anticipation as mistaken and recollection as merely the reminder of that past error, that critique takes place alongside and within a verse form which in this particular instantiation at once seals itself by returning to its inauguration and remains open to a potentially infinite development.[39] Life may have refuted its anticipation in thought, but the recuperative openness of the poem's form refuses to allow life to curtail its own possibilities.

The poem's 'triple brass' allows it to resist intimidation by the vagaries of life. But that phrase does more than name the distinctive features of the poem's formal texture; it places the poet in a different community from that of 'evil men' – the community of poetic tradition. The phrase does not originate with Shelley but with the *aes triplex* of Horace's ode, I.3, where it is remarked that 'Sure oak and triple brass were bound / That hardy mortal's breast around / Who first dar'd Ocean's unknown depths to brave'.[40] The context for the phrase in the ode – of indomitable character faced with an overwhelming challenge – is, of course, appropriate to the use that Shelley makes of the phrase, but, moreover, 'triple brass' had by the time Shelley uses it become a piece of the poetic tradition. So, for instance, it is used in numerous translations of classical epic, including, for example, in William Cowper's description in his rendering of book II of the *Iliad* of how Diomedes' spear, aimed at Hector's head, 'Glanced wide, for he had cased his youthful brows, / In triple brass, Apollo's glorious gift'.[41] Very different from the use of the phrase to evoke an antique martial heroism is Edward Young's complaint in *Night Thoughts* regarding how 'War, Famine, Pest, Volcano, Storm, and Fire, / Intestine Broils, *Oppression*, with her heart / Wrapt up in tripple Brass, besiege mankind.'[42] It is perhaps the deployment of this phrase in Young's poem (which Shelley knew) to characterise the multitudinous ravages to which 'Millions' are subject that is closest, by way of contrast, to Shelley's opposite usage of it to evoke the defence with which he arms himself against comparable (even if markedly less apocalyptic) buffets and disappointments of the world.

The key point to emerge from this brief tracing of the uses of the phrase 'triple brass' is that Shelley's description of his means of resisting a hostile world is itself a piece of poetic tradition. Inserting himself in that tradition by recalling that phrase, Shelley thus joins his 'kind' in order to resist the suffering inflicted by life. '[I]t is in the allusive history of figuration', John Hollander has argued, 'that poets write. The revision of prior metaphor', he continues,

> the quickening of old images that have frozen into statues or bric-a-brac, the rebuilding from echoing clay of new living figures, animated by the present breath of voice – this is the allusively originating role of transumption. The kind of figure that gets its strength from the way it both recalls

> and transcends a prior one is by no means the same as a mere modulation of a *topos* or commonplace.[43]

In this way, Shelley's insertion into tradition is also a reanimation of it and, moreover, a refusal to relinquish the possibility of the thought of life as it might be, rather than how it (disappointingly) is. This is especially so, since, similarly to how Hollander accounts for the 'transumption' of 'old images', this phrase is not simply recalled and deployed but transformed and set in motion, so to speak, by its implicit identification with the poem's terza rima itself and by its position, at the line end, in what is here the emphatically circling motion of that form.

Shelley's use of the resources of poetic form and tradition for rethinking what life might be is one of the central concerns of this book. But, before I turn to investigate Shelley's commitment to the poetic animation of life (as I will in Chapters 4, 5 and 6), we need first to further our investigation of his insight into how and why life, in the very process of its living, goes dead. The following chapter argues that Shelley drew on and developed the often implicit account in British empiricist thought of the effect of accumulated experience (what he follows Hume in calling 'habit' or 'custom') on living sensation, while Chapter 3 goes on to show how an understanding of tyranny as the exploitation of life, rather than the infliction of death, shaped Shelley's sense of the ills of contemporary commercial society. Equipped with a fuller sense of Shelley's critique of what we might call wrong life, we will then be in a position to return to his attempt to articulate poetry's claim to right it.

CHAPTER TWO

Living losing life

The curse of this life

In book II, chapter 10, of the *Essay Concerning Human Understanding*, Locke describes the operation of memory, or 'retention'. It is, so to speak, a vulnerable faculty, in need of regular renewal:

> But yet there seems to be a constant decay of all our *Ideas*, even of those which are struck deepest, and in Minds the most retentive; so that if they be not sometimes renewed by repeated Exercise of the Senses, or Reflection on those kind of Objects, which at first occasioned them, the Print wears out, and at last there remains nothing to be seen. Thus the *Ideas*, as well as Children, of our Youth, often die before us: And our Minds represent to us those Tombs, to which we are approaching; where though the Brass and Marble remain, yet the Inscriptions are effaced by time, and the Imagery moulders away. *The Pictures drawn in our Minds, are laid in fading Colours*; and if not sometimes refreshed, vanish and disappear.[1]

Locke's writing here attempts to militate against the very characteristic of memory that he describes. The aphorism '*The Pictures drawn in our Minds, are laid in fading Colours*' is commended to memory with its italic print (perhaps less likely to wear out?) and, even, with the chime of '*laid* in *fading* Colours'. Nevertheless, Locke argues that no matter how striking the original ideas we wish to remember, and no matter how retentive the mind, memory fades. His account of that fading is peculiarly maudlin, and not just because of the comparison of the death of ideas in the memory with the pre-decease of one's children. Locke remarks that the mind is like a tomb where the memorial inscription has faded, though the field for that inscription and the actual structure of the mind ('Brass and Marble') remain. For Locke, of course, those remnants are no consolation for the loss of what was once inscribed upon them.[2] But the proper functioning of memory only slightly lifts the deathliness that characterises the remembering mind: memory is still a tomb, whether the inscriptions on it are, from time to time, refreshed, or whether they are effaced. Locke suggests in the comparison of the ideas and the children of our youth that it is only when memory fails that the ideas of youth die, but his image of the mind as a tomb implies instead that, whether memory works or no, what it contains is, either way, dead: the mind-as-tomb contains ideas, and either clearly adverts to them in its memorial inscription, or fails to give notice at all of what is sepulchred within.

The paucity of recollected experience when compared with what Locke might have called fresh experience is a common motif of the British empiricist philosophy in which Shelley was steeped. It is, for instance, also fundamental to Hume's important discrimination between impressions and ideas in the second section of his *Enquiry Concerning Human Understanding*, 'Of the Origin of Ideas'. But whereas Locke, rather despite himself, had emphasised the inescapable deathliness of memory, even in its proper functioning, Hume attended to a different quality of memory and imagination in contrast with immediate sensation, namely, its shadowy, diminished life:

> Every one will readily allow, that there is a considerable difference between the perceptions of the mind, when a man feels the pain of excessive heat, or the pleasure of moderate warmth, and when he afterwards recalls to his memory this sensation, or anticipates it by his imagination. These faculties may mimic or copy the perceptions of the senses; but they never can entirely reach the force and vivacity of the original sentiment. The utmost we say of them, even when they operate with greatest vigour, is, that they represent their object in so lively a manner, that we could *almost* say we feel or see it: But, except the mind be disordered by disease or madness, they never can arrive at such a pitch of vivacity, as to render these perceptions altogether undistinguishable. All the colours of poetry, however splendid, can never paint natural objects in such a manner as to make the description be taken for a real landskip. The most lively thought is still inferior to the dullest sensation.[3]

Hume's description of impressions and ideas in terms, on the one hand, of 'force and vivacity', and of mere 'vigour' or a 'lively [...] manner', on the other, have attracted considerable commentary.[4] Much (if not all) of this commentary has endeavoured to read 'force and vivacity' and 'liveliness' not as indicating relative degrees of the strength, or, better, animation of sensation but, rather, as signalling greater or lesser degrees of verisimilitude. Thus, Hume is said to use 'vivid' and 'vivacious' not to mean 'animated' or 'active' but rather 'lifelike' or 'clear'.[5]

Such an interpretation views Hume's concern as having above all to do with the *likeness* or otherwise of ideas to impressions rather than with the relatively reduced *animation* of the former in comparison with the latter. Yet, for Shelley, the difference in the degrees of life between what Hume called impressions and ideas was, contrary to the interests of later commentary, a central concern – note, for instance, the important contention in his 'Speculations on Metaphysics' that thoughts differ not in kind but rather in force (*Works*, VII, p. 59). The focus of this chapter is Shelley's abiding worry about the apparently inevitable diminution over time of the life of experiences, sensations and memories – a diminution that does not result in death but that characterises the deadening of the life we have as 'we live on'. As I argued in the introduction, Shelley's statement that 'we live on, and in living we lose the apprehension of life' means that the loss that afflicts life is specifically a loss of life even as it is lived. Life, on such a view, is just the inevitable process of its own effacement, mouldering, decay and vanishing. This chapter aims to set out more fully Shelley's account of that process, turning, in its final section, to the political and ethical questions that arise when it is realised that the erosion of life as it is lived need not, perhaps, be ineluctable but may rather be the consequence of historically particular social forms and institutions, a possibility that is taken up more fully in the following chapter.

Shelley's insight into the relation between life and its own diminution in the course of its living was informed by his attentive and repeated reading of Locke and Hume. Moreover, his concern with this view of life extends right across his writing. For example, shortly after his arrival in Milan in April 1818, Shelley wrote to his friend, Thomas Love Peacock, who remained in the Buckinghamshire town of Marlow recently quitted by Shelley. The letter opens with the following paragraph, which both explores the vicissitudes of memory and the uncanny tenacity of experiences that are both more and less than living:

> I had no conception that the distance between us measured by the time in respect of letters was so great. I have but just received yours dated the 2^d^ & when you will receive mine written from this city somewhat later than the same date I cannot know. I am sorry to hear that you have been obliged to remain at Marlow, a certain degree of society being almost a necessity of life: particularly as we are not to see you this summer in Italy. But this I suppose must be as it is. I often revisit Marlow in thought. The curse of this life is that whatever is once known can never be unknown. You inhabit a spot which before you inhabit it is as indifferent to you as any other spot upon the earth, & when, persuaded by some necessity you think to leave it, you leave it not, – it clings to you & with memories of things which in your experience of them gave no such promise, revenges your desertion. Time flows on, places are changed, friends who were with us are no longer with

us, but what has been, seems yet to be, but barren & stript of life. See, I have sent you a study for Night Mare Abbey. (20 April 1818; *Letters* II, p. 6)[6]

Shelley's letters to Peacock frequently indulge in a kind of amicable jocular banter, but despite the flip at the end of this passage, there is a gloom that clings to Shelley's reflection on reminiscence here.[7] Life, he thinks, is cursed. Contrary to T. E. Hulme's claim that '[w]e may define Romantics [...] as all who do not believe in the Fall of Man', our situation, in Shelley's view, is precisely fallen in the sense that we have knowledge of which we would rather be rid: 'whatever is once known can never be unknown'.[8] This is a fall salvation from which is hard to envisage, since this is the curse of '*this* life', but the knowledge once acquired in it 'can *never* be unknown'. Even the consolation of the prospect of extinction is nowhere to be found here. The curse of this life is not so much, then, its ephemerality, not so much, that is, the fact that 'friends who were with us are no longer with us', but rather the very fact of a moribund persistence: 'what has been, seems yet to be, but barren & stript of life'. The determination of what had appeared unpromising nevertheless to cling to us contrasts with the fact that life has been stripped from it. But this persistence also has a horrifying potency, despite its barrenness, since, in contrast to Locke's difficulty in evading the ultimate deathliness of memory, memory here has a kind of excessive life: the 'spot' which had been indifferent to you before you inhabited it, 'clings to you & with memories of things which in your experience of them gave no such promise, revenges your desertion'. The damned spot will not go out.[9]

Shelley's expression of his feelings on being far from Marlow, and, implicitly, far from Peacock, forms also, therefore, a crucial set of reflections on the internally divided status of life. Above all, of course, it is a curse *of life* that what has been left behind continues to have an effect on us, despite its being, paradoxically, 'stript of life'. Shelley's absence from Marlow is a particular instance of the fact that, as he would come to write a year later in 'On Life', '[w]e live on, and in living we lose the apprehension of life'. His lament to Peacock reads very much as an anticipatory expansion of this statement in its suggestion that we feel compelled to do certain things on the basis, however, of increasingly imperfect knowledge. The statement that 'a *certain degree* of society [is] *almost* a necessity of life' – albeit one which, because Peacock will not be joining the Shelley party in Italy, cannot presently be fulfilled, thus leaving life *almost* necessarily indigent – and the fact that one quits a place because one is 'persuaded by some necessity [...] to leave it' – where the compulsion to leave the once indifferent spot may in fact be no compulsion at all but rather persuasion – are united in their hesitancy regarding what is and is not necessary to and in life. The pressure of living on, like that of moving on, is a necessity we feel, but do not in fact know, to be such, and one, moreover, that in its turn frustrates the fulfilment of other necessities of life.

In his letter to Peacock, Shelley speaks of how he 'often revisit[s] Marlow in thought'. This revisiting sounds like the 'repeated Exercise of the Senses, or Reflection on those kind of Objects' recommended by Locke for the refreshing of memory, but, as we have seen, Shelley is in fact much more bothered by the vengefulness, and hence the uncanny, paradoxical life of memory than by its atrophy. Were he able to revisit Marlow in fact rather than in thought, both of these concerns would presumably be dispelled, since uncanny memory would be replaced with once again living experience. There are reasons, however, for Shelley to doubt whether that would indeed be the case. In the summer prior to his leaving England for Italy, Shelley scrawled the following lines after or possibly during solitary visits to Virginia Water and Egham, both of which are in the vicinity of Bishopsgate, where he had lived with Mary two years earlier, and, slightly further away, Bracknell, where he had lived with Harriet and the Boinvilles earlier again:[10]

I visit thee but thou art sadly changed
Thy former home is now made desolate
It has become the path of homeless winds
The moon and stars and sun find entrance there
For their tired beams where once this busy heart
From many beatings, and in many thoughts
After its wanderings found a brief years [ ]
And I am changed, and many things are changed
The Earth the Forests and the Sky remain
These things remain
And unforgiving memories linger there
Which heap forth sorrow

(*Poems* I, p. 572)

Shelley's pencilled draft of these lines is barely decipherable, and it is, moreover, bifurcated after the line given here as 'After its wanderings found a brief years [ ]' by a drawing in ink of an apparently rather mythical landscape, featuring large, craggy mountains in the background and a sailing boat, quite heavily drawn, on a lake in the foreground (*BSM* XVII, 126/135).[11] There is another, more lightly sketched boat, immediately below and abutting the final line, despite the fact that plenty of space remains on the page underneath where the lines come to a halt. The imaginary topography of the large sketch interrupting the lines is as far as possible from being an illustration of either the house that the poem apparently addresses or the environs in which Shelley probably composed the lines (even if we allow ourselves to imagine that the lake at Virginia Water has been transported from semi-rural Surrey to a sublime landscape of the mind). The fabulous scene and, in particular, the depiction of two boats, whose sails signal their reliance on the 'homeless winds' and thereby also declare their own potentially infinite itinerancy, all mean that the lines are inscribed and imaginatively positioned in a setting that far exceeds that of the house explicitly being addressed in them. In addition, a page after these lines, Shelley drafted what seems to be an advertisement for a house exchange: 'Wanted to purchase by exchange for an equivalent secured on a large property in England, a villa in the neighbourhood of Naples' (*Poems* I, p. 517). The fact that the house offered for exchange is 'secured on a large property in England' harbours a certain irony: no matter how well 'secured' in legal terms property may be, established, reliable sanctuary in a particular dwelling remains an elusive ideal.

And yet, despite the evident imaginative straining beyond the scene of the 'former home' itself, that particular dwelling still exercises an unshakeable power over the poet: 'unforgiving memories linger there / Which heap forth sorrow'. Shelley's letter to Peacock suggests that such vengeful, lingering memories are a function of removal from a once, but now ineluctably no longer, indifferent spot – memories, he suggests there, that might be dispelled, were one able to revisit in fact a place that one can only revisit in thought. Here, on the contrary, a visit to the site of past life brings no such relief. Whereas the memories that remain are unforgiving and sorrowful, the lines cannot quite recall the benefit that the house conferred, only managing, at most, to gesture toward its sometime status as a shelter for the poet, where he 'found a brief years [ ]'. Admittedly, it is difficult to piece together lines 10–12, but the manuscript does appear to justify a reading of the memories as, at least, 'unforgiving', whereas the completion of the phrase 'a brief years [ ]' is altogether unreadable. The benefit the house conferred, that is, has been effaced – an effacement all the more poignantly realised since the alliterative recall of 'For their tired beams' and 'From many beatings' in 'found a brief years [ ]' serves to undermine the opposition between the house and the world from which it bestows a welcome refuge by forging a connection between the characterisation of the sanctuary the house offered, the condition into which it has fallen and what is provided relief from.

The effacement of the borders between the house and the rest of the universe, such that the house could no longer provide any refuge from either (explicitly) the natural or (implicitly) the social worlds, is a central concern of the lines. 'It has become the path of homeless winds / The moon and stars and sun find entrance there / For their tired beams': what was once a fixed abode has become a 'path' – a path, what is more, that leads nowhere in particular at all, since it is the path of 'homeless winds'. Likewise, the moon and stars and sun find 'entrance', but, crucially, no rest, for their 'tired beams', a phrase which, of course, might bring to mind the 'beams' of the house's decayed structure through which the light now ironically shines. What the house had represented was a pause from change ('many things are changed'), which is itself, as Shelley emphasises in his more famous sonnets 'To Wordsworth' and 'Mutability', implacable ('The Earth the Forests and the Sky remain / These things remain'). But now, since he is 'changed', the poet's 'wanderings' are resumed. Like the unceasing journeys through the heavens of sun, moon and stars, these wanderings are inevitably wearying, a point reinforced by the 'many beatings' of 'this busy heart', which are at once the vital functioning of this organ and the frequently repeated violent mortifications of the poet's emotional core. The collapse of the distinction between the literal and metaphorical, or, indeed, the anatomical and the emotional, in the 'many beatings' of the heart is thus an instance of a central insight of Shelley's into the nature of life. It is not simply (as here) that Shelley identifies life with suffering – the beating of the heart as inevitably concomitant with its battery – but, moreover, that the emotional (and intellectual and political) quality of life cannot be reduced in order to leave a basic vital essence or biological function that may meaningfully be thought of as 'life'.

The mist of familiarity

Life is, then, suffering, or pleasure, or frustration, or fulfilment; it is those states that, according to an account which Shelley would refuse, are held to be additional to life in its fundamental functioning. But to insist on the inevitable inseparability of life and its qualities is not, however, to hold that any and all of life's characteristics are good, nor, crucially, is it to suggest that life and its qualities understood in this way can never be substantially diminished. As we have begun to see in this chapter (in both the letter to Peacock and in 'I visit thee but thou art sadly changed'), the living of life frequently entails, for Shelley, its qualitative weakening. And it is precisely because life is, for him, ineluctably qualitative that its progressive reduction to an attenuated rump entails significant damage to life as it might be.

Shelley's characterisation of the effects of habit is a characterisation of diminished life. But that diminution has, so to speak, a dreadful life of its own. This is not unconnected to the simple fact that the more of life one has in the mere chronological sense, the more habit takes its hold, for in 'On Life', Shelley contends that '[a]s men grow up [...] they become mechanical and habitual agents. Their feelings and their reasonings are the combined result of a multitude of entangled thoughts, of a series of what are called impressions, blunted by reiteration' (*SPP*, pp. 507–8). '[H]abit stuns our senses', but it does so insidiously over time.[12] Significantly, Shelley's way of describing this process of anaesthetisation emphasises its abiding, though paradoxically deadened, life. So men thus mechanised are still 'agents', even though, under the sway of habit, agency is stripped of any meaning it might have and their 'feelings and reasonings' arise from a rankly fecund thicket of 'entangled thoughts'. One powerful reason why life is so vulnerable to this self-destructive attenuation is that, in its undiminished form, it is overwhelming. The domestication of life through habit brings it, as it were, down to earth and makes it liveable – where 'liveable' means lived in accordance with the everyday demands, comings and goings of the grown-up world. The sense that, in living, human beings become unaccustomed to life is, of course, a significant one in a number of places in Shelley's work, as, for instance, in the opening paragraph of 'On Life':

> Life, and the world, or whatever we call that which we are and feel, is an astonishing thing. The mist of familiarity obscures from us the wonder of our being. We are struck with admiration at some of its transient modifications; but it is itself the great miracle. What are the changes of empires, the wreck of dynasties with the opinions which supported them; what is the birth and extinction of religions and of political systems to life? What are the revolutions of the globe which we inhabit, and the operations of the elements of which it is composed, compared with life? What is the universe of stars and suns of which this inhabited earth is one and their motions and their destiny compared with life. Life, the great miracle, we admire not, because it is so miraculous. It is well that we are thus shielded by the familiarity of what is at once so certain and so unfathomable from an astonishment which would otherwise absorb and overawe the functions of that which is its object. (*SPP*, p. 505)

This is a critically important statement, which provokes a number of demanding questions, and we will have to return to it later. For the moment, I want to emphasise the apparent suggestion, with which it concludes, that we ought to be thankful that 'familiarity' distracts us from life, 'the great miracle'. The general tenor of this argument is anticipated by Montaigne's statement that 'usage hides the true aspect of things from us', a claim that he illustrates with a quotation from Lucretius: 'There is nothing which at first seems so great or so wondrous which we do not all gradually wonder at less and less.'[13] Indeed, Godwin, in an important section near the end of his *Political Justice* to which the opening of 'On Life' has a number of close affinities, likewise designates this 'true aspect of things' as 'wonder':

> We desire to stretch out our hand, and it is stretched out. We perform a thousand operations of the same species every day, and their familiarity annihilates the wonder. They are not in themselves less wonderful than any of those modifications we are least accustomed to conceive.[14]

Godwin goes on to focus particularly on the fate of 'the aged', for whom 'life delights no more', since its charm has faded in becoming familiar.[15]

Like Godwin's implicit recognition (which he echoes verbally) that 'those modifications we are least accustomed to conceive' are still wonderful, Shelley nonetheless concedes that we are not, in our habitual state, wholly strangers to powerful sensations: we are 'struck with admiration' at the 'transient modifications' of life. Yet this is nothing in comparison to the dangerously overpowering 'astonishment' we would feel were we fully to realise the miraculous nature of life itself. The sentence in which it is announced that '[i]t is well' that we are thus oblivious is remarkably involuted and requires careful untangling. (This, incidentally, is not a criticism of the articulation of Shelley's thinking: the involution of the argument at this point is quite fitting, since, as we learn later in the essay, the results of 'familiarity' are 'the overgrowth of ages', 'entangled thoughts' [*SPP*, pp. 507, 508].) First, 'what is at once so certain and so unfathomable' has itself become familiar, such that, we must infer, familiarity is not an obscuring patina somehow applied to life from without. The familiarising of life is produced by, and is part of, it. Were familiarity not produced, life would lose its functions – by which Shelley might be taken to mean the kinds of activity that produce the changes of empires, and so on, that he speaks of above – in astonishment at it, and thus be reduced, in fact, to one, perpetual non-activity: admiration at itself.

We might be tempted to agree, then, that the familiarising of life, and thus the distraction from its miraculous status, is necessary and beneficial to its living. But it is impossible not to discern in the concluding sentence to the opening paragraph of 'On Life' a hint of irony, or, indeed, a slight sneer at the commonsensical, worldly-wise renunciation of astonishment at life, with its consolatory bromide to the effect that all is for the best in the best of all possible worlds.

I want to return, in Chapter 4, to the implications of Shelley's repeated descriptions of the life obscured by custom as 'the great miracle' and as 'miraculous'. Here, however, it is necessary to grasp somewhat more fully the nuances of Shelley's understanding of the familiarity he seems both to be thankful for and to scorn. In attempting to come to terms with the effects of familiarisation on life, Shelley is responding to a central aspect of Hume's epistemology, as Kenneth Neill Cameron, for instance, recognised.[16] Significantly for Shelley's account of life and its 'functions', Hume famously describes 'custom' as 'the great guide of human life. It is that principle alone which renders our experience useful to us, and makes us expect, for the future, a similar train of events with those which have appeared in the past.'[17] Like Shelley's 'familiarity', which is its descendant, Hume's 'custom' is an expedient rendering experience 'useful', or, as Shelley might have put it, functional. Just before he declares the usefulness of custom, Hume sketches a scenario in order to show how useless experiences are until they become habitual:

> Suppose a person, though endowed with the strongest faculties of reason and reflection, to be brought on a sudden into this world; he would, indeed, immediately observe a continual succession of objects, and one event following another; but he would not be able to discover anything farther. He would not, at first, by any reasoning, be able to reach the idea of cause and effect; since the particular powers, by which all natural operations are performed, never appear to the senses; nor is it reasonable to conclude, merely because one event, in one instance, precedes another, that therefore the one is the cause, the other the effect. Their conjunction may be arbitrary and casual. There may be no reason to infer the existence of one from the appearance of the other. And in a word, such a person, without more experience, could never employ his conjecture or reasoning concerning any matter of fact, or be assured of anything beyond what was immediately present to his memory and senses.[18]

It is clear from this argument that it is experience itself (or, to be precise, '*more* experience') that makes experience useful. Custom is neither more nor less than repetition. The niggling doubts attendant on any attempt to employ mere reason in the drawing of inferences – 'Their conjunction *may be* arbitrary and casual. There *may be* no reason' – lead to the in fact inescapable conclusion that, without the benefit of further experience, the man 'brought on a sudden into this world' would be lost. Hume, incidentally, plays a bitingly adroit joke when he remarks that the conjunction of events may be 'casual', rather than causal. Hume is tempting the reader to think, perhaps, that the whole edifice of dogmatic metaphysical error is traceable to the misplacing of a letter, but, moreover, when 'causal' becomes 'casual' the sequence of events that we merely assume to be necessarily established has been reversed, just as Hume insists is entirely possible in the case of causes and effects, were it not for custom alone.[19]

The example of the individual 'brought on a sudden into this world' is a central one in the early pages of the *Enquiry*. His first appearance comes shortly before the passage I have just examined, in a phase of the argument where Hume is keen (as he often is) to question the assumption that human beings are born competent players of billiards. The point of this scenario is to characterise custom as, in fact, a kind of name for the absence of substantial knowledge about the operation of cause and effect:

> We fancy, that were we brought on a sudden into this world, we could at first have inferred that one Billiard-ball would communicate motion to another upon impulse; and that we needed not to have waited for the event, in order to pronounce with certainty concerning it. Such is the influence of custom, that, where it is strongest, it not only covers our natural ignorance, but even conceals itself, and seems not to take place, merely because it is found in the highest degree.[20]

Despite, as we have seen, the importance that Hume will go on to ascribe to custom in rendering our experience 'useful' to us, there is certainly something a little insidious about its operation here. Custom 'covers our natural ignorance' and, what is more, conceals itself in the process. We are, therefore, ignorant to begin with, and then ignorant that we are ignorant thanks to the power of the 'influence' of custom. Hume suggests that philosophers, who 'give themselves airs of superior wisdom and sufficiency', should be suitably chastened and that we ought 'to be modest in our pretensions'.[21] In that case, 'we may make a kind of merit of our very ignorance'.[22]

This scepticism concerning our habitual experience is intensified in Shelley's 'On Life'. Like Hume, Shelley, in a central statement for his thinking, holds to an apparently modest, yet also radical vocation for philosophy:

> Philosophy, impatient as it may be to build, has much work yet remaining as pioneer for the overgrowth of ages. It makes one step towards this

> object however; it destroys error, and the roots of error. It leaves, what is too often the duty of the reformer in political and ethical questions to leave, a vacancy. It reduces the mind to that freedom in which it would have acted, but for the misuse of words and signs, the instruments of its own creation. – By signs, I would be understood in a wide sense, including what is properly meant by that term, and what I peculiarly mean. In this latter sense almost all familiar objects are signs, standing not for themselves but for others, in their capacity of suggesting one thought which shall lead to a train of thoughts. – Our whole life is thus an education of error. (*SPP*, p. 507)

How are we to read the equivocal concluding statement of this paragraph? 'Our whole life is thus an education of error' may be taken to mean that our entire life needs must be dedicated to the progressive eradication of the plethora of fallacious conjecture into which we fall throughout our life; this, admittedly, is the interpretation suggested by the passage's emphasis on philosophy's task as pioneer. But whereas this reading takes 'an education of error' to denote a schooling *out of* error – in the sense that ignorance, uncouthness, and so on, may be educated and thus improved upon – the phrase may also be taken to suggest that our whole life educates us *in* error, and that, therefore, to live on is to be ever more deeply sunk in fallacy. Indeed, this is likewise supported by the fact that what philosophy must battle is 'the overgrowth of ages', and thus '[o]ur whole life' is the individual human span, as well as the 'human life' Hume speaks of as being guided.

The question of how to read the concluding statement of the above paragraph from 'On Life' is an important one, because it bears on the relation of Shelley's thinking to Hume's account of custom as 'the great guide of human life', which, up until this point, I have been rather implying is closely followed by Shelley. But in saying that '[o]ur whole life is thus an education of error' might at least partially mean that our life is the accretion of error, it is implied that life is not so much guided by custom or familiarity – the archetypal products of a 'whole life', entirely lacking to the individual, in Hume's phrase, 'brought on a sudden into this world' – but rather led astray. Shelley does learn from Hume that custom obscures our natural ignorance, and, in fact, he entertains, however sardonically maybe, the suggestion that such ignorance need be no bad thing if it allows life to function. Yet, in the end, he subtly, but nonetheless decisively, diverges from Hume in taking the familiar course of life ('our whole life') to be erroneous. This point comes out more clearly if we recognise the contrast between Shelley's regret at the 'misuse of words and signs' and

Hume's major concession to custom that it is the only principle 'which renders our experience useful'. In fact, very shortly after making this assertion, Hume states, somewhat contrary to his sense that custom gives us no real knowledge of the operation of cause and effect, that '[w]ithout the influence of custom, we should be entirely ignorant of every matter of fact beyond what is immediately present to the memory and senses'.[23] Even though Hume wishes to make our reliance on custom and, significantly, the ignorance it covers over fully known, he nevertheless casts its operation as ultimately benign; Shelley, contrastingly, is more deeply worried by its power to frustrate the 'freedom' in which the mind would have acted were it not for its influence.

The politics of custom

As is perhaps too infrequently recalled, 'On Life' developed out of the drafting of Shelley's 'A Philosophical View of Reform', and this important essay's focus on politics is certainly traceable in its associated fragment. To begin with, the opening paragraph's listing of 'changes of empires, the wreck of dynasties with the opinions which supported them; [...] the birth and the extinction of religions and political systems' among the 'transient modifications' of life clearly signals the underlying political concerns of the essay. (Indeed, even the 'revolutions of the globe which we inhabit', listed after these obviously political phenomena, are potentially suggested by 'the wreck of dynasties' and so hint at political uprisings, even as they clearly denote the planet's rotations.) And, further on in the essay, in the paragraph that I have just been discussing, the comparison of philosophy with the 'reformer in political and ethical questions' is in no way adventitious, not least since 'philosophical' and 'reform' are the keywords of the title of the essay out of which this fragment grew. Thinking about custom necessarily involves, for Shelley, addressing questions concerning the genesis and functioning of human institutions, for, as Michael Henry Scrivener has argued in an important discussion of Shelley's reception of Godwin's anarchism, law in particular is only 'a set of opinions on what is proper social behavior' – a set of opinions, however, that come through habituation to have the force, precisely, of law.[24] As with the operation of custom in the determination of cause and effect, there is thus ultimately 'no reasoning with the law', Scrivener claims, because it is not based on a principle of reason but rather on the established opinions of a particular class to which the rest of society has become habituated.[25]

Indeed, where Shelley somewhat wistfully regrets the deflection of the mind from the exercise of its original freedom by instruments of its own creation, the political import of his concern with familiarisation's impact on life comes fully into view. One of Shelley's most significant attempts to depict the beneficial effects of freedom from custom is his early story, 'The Assassins: A Fragment of a Romance'. This fragment's account of the Assassins' freedom from the limitations of custom is especially significant because it draws a direct connection between that freedom and apprehension. Early in the fragment, Shelley describes the conduct and manners of what is still, at this point, this 'little congregation of Christians':

> Acknowledging no laws but those of God they modelled their conduct towards their fellow men by the conclusions of their individual judgment on the practical application of these laws. And it was apparent from the simplicity and severity of their manners that this contempt for human institutions had produced among them a character far superior in singleness and sincere self apprehension to the slavery of pagan customs and the gross delusions of antiquated superstition [...] They esteemed the human understanding to be the paramount rule of human conduct, they maintained that the obscurest religious truth required for its complete elucidation no more than the strenuous application of the energies of the mind. (*Prose*, p. 124)

The mental muscularity of the Assassins is seen in their 'character far superior in singleness and sincere self apprehension to the slavery of pagan customs and the gross delusions of antiquated superstition'. Self-apprehension, in its association with 'singleness', would appear to entail a kind of intellectual confidence and self-possession. At the same time, since in 'living on we lose the apprehension of life', self-apprehension involves an acute sense of the life of the self, undistorted by the flummeries of human institutions which have taken over the administration, so to speak, of that life. This is, of course, to be distinguished from selfishness, for self-apprehension is central to the regulation of 'their conduct towards their fellow men', but, rather, apprehension here, as elsewhere in Shelley's work, is a key term by which he invokes an undimmed state, that is a feature at once of sense and understanding and thus indistinguishably ethical, intellectual and aesthetic.

The slavery of custom and its relation to the characteristic experience of the Assassins is addressed again, toward the end of the first of the fragment's short chapters, where the character of 'apprehension' is more fully developed. Shelley has been describing the 'valley of

Bethzatanai' where the Assassins live, and the 'strange scenes of chaotic confusion and harrowing sublimity surrounding and shutting in the vale [which] added to the delights of its secure and voluptuous tranquillity' (*Prose*, p. 128).

> The immediate effect of such a scene suddenly presented to the contemplation of mortal eyes is seldom the subject of authentic record. The coldest slave of custom cannot fail to recollect some few moments in which the breath of spring or the crowding clouds of sunset with the pale moon shining through their fleecy skirts, or the song of some lonely bird perched on the only tree of an unfrequented heath, has awakened the touch of nature. And they were Arabians who entered the valley of Bethzatanai, men who idolized nature and the God of nature, to whom love and lofty thoughts and the apprehensions of an uncorrupted spirit were sustenance and life. (*Prose*, p. 128)

Shelley opens this description, the language of which matches the valley's voluptuousness, with a complaint that there are few 'authentic records' of natural scenery – such as, presumably, we are to imagine this is. A major barrier to the authenticity of records of '[t]he immediate effect of such a scene' is that they are 'suddenly presented to the contemplation of mortal eyes'. The effect most frequently eludes 'authentic record' because deliberative 'contemplation' is subject to the limitations of 'mortal eyes', which cannot quite capture the effect in its immediacy and suddenness. Mortal eyes, of course, are not all-seeing, are situated in time and are thus condemned to view experience as fleeting. Nevertheless, even 'the coldest slave of custom cannot fail to recollect' moments in which the 'immediate effect' of nature is in fact discernible. This recollection – like the fact that, in response to the 'delights' of the valley, '[n]o spectator could have refused to believe that some spirit of great intelligence and power had hallowed these wild and beautiful solitudes to a deep and solemn mystery' (*Prose*, p. 128) – is, as Cian Duffy has emphasised in an insightful reading of this passage, involuntary.[26] It is perhaps fitting, then, that authenticity as a record of the kind of scene that Shelley evokes is nowhere explicitly claimed in and for this passage but is instead intimated by a responsive sumptuousness of articulation: in the phrases 'the *crowding clouds* of sunset' and even 'some *lonely bird perched* on the *only* tree of an unfrequented heath' the designations of natural objects are sonically inflected in their adjectival qualifications, thus testifying to the effect of nature's touch as being an awakening to apparently 'aesthetic' qualities in fact inherent to it – an awakening out of the habituated and abstract view of nature as what is just inertly there.[27]

Crucially, therefore, custom has not altogether closed down the potential for the kinds of experience by which Shelley characterises the Assassins. Admittedly, he concludes the opening chapter of 'The Assassins' with the admission that 'the enthusiasm of overwhelming transport' typical of the Assassins has declined, commenting that '[t]he necessity of daily occupation and the ordinariness of that human life, the burthen of which it is the destiny of every human being to bear, had smothered, not extinguished, that divine and eternal fire' (*Prose*, p. 129). But 'that human life', in so far as it is indigent in the experience characteristic of the Assassins, is indigent, in fact, in life. The passage in which Shelley describes the awakening touch of nature identifies 'the apprehensions of an uncorrupted spirit' with 'sustenance and life'. This goes far beyond the mere convention of describing particularly cherished experiences or relations as 'sustenance and life' (my work is my life, my marriage is my life) at the same time as unearthing the truth in that convention. Especially once we recall that, for the Assassins, 'the apprehensions of an uncorrupted spirit' are also 'self apprehension', it is possible to see how significant it is that those apprehensions both belong to an uncorrupted spirit but are also of that uncorrupted spirit. It is striking that Shelley's usage of 'apprehensions' here appears in a genitive phrase remarkably akin to 'the apprehension of life' of 'On Life': the apprehension lost in living on is both life's apprehension and apprehension that realises its own life. As Shelley puts it just a few sentences later in 'The Assassins', '[t]o live, to breathe, to move, was itself a sensation of immeasurable transport' (*Prose*, p. 129).

The opposition between custom and apprehension in 'The Assassins' is such that custom can never come entirely to dominate apprehension. It is central to the expression of Shelley's social hope in that early work that 'that human life' led by most people shelters at least the possibility that the apprehension of life may be recovered in it. It is not possible for 'the coldest slave of custom' to decide to exercise, so to speak, his or her apprehension, which is one reason why recollection of the touch of nature is, in his or her case at least, involuntary. But despite this intimation that custom's triumph can never be entirely complete, what is nonetheless emphasised throughout Shelley's work is the power of custom radically to shape human life into a form not recognisable as the kind of fully living life experienced by the inhabitants of the valley of Bethzatanai. In particular, the life fostered by custom is the living on of what has gone dead and thus of what is even unavailable to sense, as this exchange between Prometheus and one of his tormentors from the first act of *Prometheus Unbound* makes clear:

Fury
Blood thou canst see, and fire; and canst hear groans;
Worse things unheard, unseen, remain behind.

Prometheus
Worse?

Fury
In each human heart terror survives
The ravin it has gorged: the loftiest fear
All that they would disdain to think were true:
Hypocrisy and custom make their minds
The fanes of many a worship, now outworn.
(*Poems* II, p. 514; Act I; ll. 616–21)

The effect of habituation ('Hypocrisy and custom'), and thus what it enables to 'survive', is really neither a feeling nor a thought. Terror and fear are not properly feelings if they are 'unheard, unseen'; but nor is fear, in particular, a thought if it is directed toward what 'the loftiest […] would disdain to think were true'. Custom thus empties the mind, leaving it vacant for the oddly plural 'many a worship', each of which is as creditable as the other, devoid as they all are of sensible or cognitive content. The survival of terror is the survival of what has ceased to live.

It is instructive that, in the above lines, the narcotic effect of custom afflicts even 'the loftiest'. Exactly who is meant by this designation is not quite clear. On the one hand, the Fury may mean those occupying the highest slopes of the social hierarchy; on the other hand, he may, in his malevolent desire to discourage Prometheus in his rebellion, mean those, like Prometheus, who in their refusal to submit to hierarchical control elevate themselves above unjust configurations of society. Elsewhere in Shelley's work it is certainly clear that power hardly insulates those occupying the pinnacles of society from the effects of custom. Stanza XXIV of the fourth canto of *Laon and Cythna*, for instance, is keen to emphasise how few escape custom's sway:

— the Queen of Slaves,
The hoodwinked Angel of the blind and dead,
Custom, with iron mace points to the graves
Where her own standard desolately waves
Over the dust of Prophets and of Kings.
Many yet stand in her array — "she paves
Her path with human hearts," and o'er it flings
The wildering gloom of her immeasurable wings.
(*Poems* II, p. 131; canto fourth,
stanza XXIV, ll. 1622–9)

It is worth, first, noting the peculiar, morbid life that clings to custom's victims. Although she points to the graves in which lie the dust of those that she has vanquished, the portrayal of her minions as 'the blind and dead' hints, in fact, that they are not quite fully dead, since, if they were, it would be superfluous to describe them as 'blind'. Their blindness and deadness are characteristics of the life they lead as subjects of custom.

Custom's power to subjugate is, of course, the focus of the above stanza. The description of custom as 'Queen of Slaves' (which Shelley had already used in his draft poem, 'Otho', which I will touch on in a moment) is taken from Montaigne's essay 'On Habit', in which Montaigne cites a fragment of Pindar's. Montaigne writes that 'the impression I have is that there is nothing that custom may not do and cannot do; and Pindar rightly calls her (so I have been told) the Queen and Empress of the World.'[28] Montaigne, indeed, discusses the 'imperial sway' of custom extensively, although, ultimately, he counsels quietism in the light of the obstacles faced by any attempt to alter the established order of things. Shelley's revision (or misremembering) of the precise characterisation of custom in Montaigne is, then, revealing. Though the original description of custom (or law: Pindar's term is *nomos*) in Pindar as 'king of all things, mortal and immortal' (*Poems* I, p. 568, n.18) and Montaigne's slight revision of this maxim both make use of the metaphor of kingship, Shelley's further revision, making custom not simply king (or queen) of the world, but rather of 'Slaves', lays considerably greater emphasis on the political implications of custom's sway.

But it is also significant to note that custom is herself subject to her own dejecting wiles. Triumphant over 'Prophets and [...] Kings' as she is, her triumph is hardly celebratory, but rather 'her own standard desolately waves', itself apparently overshadowed by the 'wildering gloom' that she casts. Moreover, she is described as 'The hoodwinked Angel of the blind and dead'. The Longman editors gloss 'hoodwinked' usefully enough as '[b]oth "blindfolded" and "deceived"' (*Poems* II, p. 131, note to l. 1623) going on to suggest that Shelley is here recalling the characterisation of the goddess Ruin from book 19 of the *Iliad*, where she is said to blind and deceive men. Yet, were the transfer of Ruin's characteristic activities to Custom as straightforward here as this account might suggest, she ought surely to be described, in fact, as hoodwinking, rather than as hoodwinked. Empress as she is, custom is subject to her own tyranny.

What I might tentatively call the recoil of subjection intimated here is, of course, a perversion of the self-mastery that Shelley holds to be essential to 'Man, who man would be' in his 'Sonnet: Political Greatness' of

1821 (*Poems* III, p. 624; l. 10). The victim of custom is incapable of 'being himself alone' (*Poems* III, p. 625; l. 14), since he is the slave of custom, of course, but custom likewise is simply a mechanical operation, and thus its personification as empress can only ever be partial, since it is devoid of autonomy.[29] Humanity's self-submission to the tyranny of custom is central to Shelley's sketch of a poem entitled 'Otho' of 1817. I suggested above that the mention of 'the loftiest' by the Fury tormenting Prometheus might designate either those at the top of a hierarchical society or, contrastingly, those who (attempt to) elevate themselves above an unjustly configured hierarchy altogether. In *Laon and Cythna*, Shelley casts the former as subject to custom's sway; in what is likely to be the third stanza of the projected poem on Otho, he characterises those who hope for a transformation in human affairs, distinguishing them from those who are too weak to hope. In these lines, custom is again associated with recursive subjection, here taking advantage of those who cannot resist it:

> Those whom nor power, nor lying faith, nor toil,
> Nor custom – queen of many slaves – makes blind
> Have ever grieved that man should be the spoil
> Of his own weakness, and with earnest mind
> Fed hopes of his redemption – these recur
> Chastened by doubtful victory now, and find
> Foundations in this foulest age, that stir
> Me whom they cheer to be their minister. –
> (*Poems* I, p. 568; ll. 17–24)

This stanza picks up where the end of the first chapter of 'The Assassins' had left off, namely, with the hope for redemption that is inextinguishable despite circumstances not conducive to its cultivation – circumstances which, in fact, are the more radically inauspicious, since what is characterised as the mere 'daily occupation and the ordinariness' of human life in 'The Assassins' is here more fully epitomised by power, lying faith, toil and, of course, custom. The lines stage, as it were, a conflict between the kind of self-mastery lauded in 'Sonnet: Political Greatness' and the self-sacrifice of man to 'his own weakness', which here, as throughout the poems I have been discussing in this section, takes the form of, above all, custom.

The examples from *Laon and Cythna*, 'Sonnet: Political Greatness' and 'Otho' each outline Shelley's sense that fundamental to human emancipation from the sway of mere custom is self-determination. The reason that custom is seen to be so invidious, of course, is that it robs agents of their agency, replacing it with a set of rote behaviours and thoughts. It might seem, from this emphasis on republican independence, that Shelley's ire is chiefly directed at human beings who will not free themselves. Aside from the fact that this would perhaps be understandable in an age when republican insurrection seemed still to open onto a liveable near future, Shelley's idea of self-government is, in fact, complemented by a much more extensive account of the precise character of the effects of oppression than I have perhaps suggested so far. It is to this account that we now turn in the following chapter, where, in particular, I argue that tyrannical oppression is chiefly characterised for Shelley not by the power to inflict death but rather by the power to exploit life.

CHAPTER THREE

Mere wheels of work

In his book on Wordsworth's often implicit understanding of the social and economic conditions of emergent capitalism, David Simpson differentiates the destitute figures – 'the ghosts' – frequently encountered in Wordsworth's poetry from the characters met with in Gothic fiction that they might otherwise be taken to resemble:

> The ghosts are images of human alienation: of persons from persons, of children from parents, of workers from products circulating as commodities for the profit of others. They instance the virtuality that affects everyone's experience of a death-in-life enforced by specific historical conditions. As such these ghosts threaten the sunny common sense of the new man far more than anything enshrined in the genre of the Gothic, because they are resolutely part of everyday life: you can meet them on the road.[1]

The discharged soldiers, itinerant labourers, leech-gatherers and vagrants that populate Wordsworth's work are not, in fact, visitors from a shadowy supernatural realm but are rather the human detritus of a society and economy hardly constituted for their benefit. 'For such unfortunates', comments Simpson, 'the desire for home is only fully resolved in death, and being alive is a constant experience of transit and displacement.'[2]

In 'To Wordsworth', a poem which Eric Lindstrom has called 'an epitaph for a man still alive', Shelley mourned the passing of Wordsworth's status as the 'Poet of Nature' who 'wept to know / That things depart which never may return' (*Poems* I, p. 455; ll. 1–2).[3] Wordsworth's response to what Simpson calls the 'constant experience of transit and displacement', suffered by those condemned to depart without prospect of return, had been a stoic resolution, in which 'In honoured poverty thy voice did weave / Songs consecrate to truth and liberty' (ll. 11–12) – a resolution that yielded, according to Shelley, to mere acceptance of the authority of 'the State and Church of England', to, in Shelley's eyes, institutional examples of forces urging submission to a life of compelled servitude for the many.[4]

We saw at the conclusion of the last chapter how Shelley repeatedly imagines 'custom', the account of which in Hume fundamentally informs his discussion of familiarity in 'On Life', as the 'Queen of Slaves'. This chapter examines Shelley's attempt to depict what Simpson calls the 'experience of a death-in-life enforced by specific historical conditions'. In it, I argue that, for Shelley, life becomes such an experience when it is tyrannically appropriated by and made instrumental to the wishes of the few, and thus I borrow and develop Simpson's insight into Wordsworth's work, according to which the marginal, houseless and unfed figures of his poetry are the avatars, so to speak, of a society 'under the sway of commodity form and commodity time'.[5] It might be objected, of course, that Simpson's discrimination of Wordsworthian unfortunates from Gothic characters will not work when it comes to Shelley. After all, Shelley betrays a straightforward enthusiasm for the Gothic, especially in his early novels and poetry, of a kind not detectable in Wordsworth's more properly mundane fascination with the outcasts of society. True as this may be, this chapter nevertheless shows that Shelley's work, including much of his juvenilia, traces in its depiction of a host of unfortunates a set of concerns with the effects of commerce and the tyrannical oppression with which, for him, commerce is ineluctably allied.[6] In particular, Shelley doubts whether life is really life at all unless it is lived under specific conditions of, chiefly, liberty.

In establishing these claims, I investigate four main concerns in this chapter. Crucial to Shelley's view of tyranny, which Michael Henry Scrivener generally sees as identifying tyranny with 'hierarchical domination, the external determination of existence by a tyrannical idea ("God," "law," "nation") or by any variety of tyrants inhabiting the economic, religious, political, judicial, sexual, or social realms', is the supposition that tyrants are not solely or even chiefly characterised by their power to inflict death but as well or instead by their appropriation and exploitation of the lives of others.[7] For Shelley, the life of the labourer whose work is the basis of commerce is tantamount to the non-life of a slave. Indeed, I place Shelley's denunciation of monarchical and commercial exploitation in the context of discussions of slavery, not because I want to discuss Shelley's relation to campaigns for the abolition of the slave trade and slavery tout court but instead because of what thinking about slavery reveals concerning the exploitation of living individuals more broadly. (The Wordsworth of *The Excursion*, incidentally, had become in the Shelleys' eyes 'a slave', because of his submission to an unjust and merciless orthodoxy, and no longer 'a rock-built refuge stood / Above the blind and battling multitude'

[*Poems* I, p. 455; ll. 9–10].)[8] In particular, I discuss, first, whether for William Godwin slaves can be thought of as really human or really living, before, second, examining the consequence for a worker of being alive in a capitalist economy as it is envisaged in Marx's thought. These connected discussions help us to see the effects of the sale of human life on that life itself as they are imagined in a tradition of thinking to which Shelley belongs. Of course, the objection may be made to the connection I intimate between Godwin's account of slaves and Marx's of workers that there is in fact a considerable difference to be made between slaves and workers, however much the latter may be insufficiently rewarded for their toils. Shelley, certainly, thought of slavery as specifically abhorrent, lauding its abolition, along with greater equality between the sexes, in modern Europe as 'an improvement the most decisive in the regulation of human society' ('A Discourse on the Manners of the Ancients', *Works*, vol. VII, p. 227);[9] nevertheless, he was capable of seeing slaves, soldiers and industrial workers as alike afflicted in, for example, a passage of *Queen Mab*, canto V, that I discuss below. Whether driven to the sale of life 'by force or famine' (*Queen Mab*, *Poems* I, p. 314; canto V, l. 72) makes, it seems, little difference in a society so constituted that 'All objects of our life, even life itself' are up for sale (l. 181).[10]

For Marx, the fact that workers are at least minimally living is unfortunate for them; beginning with this suggestion, I examine how for the wandering Jew, in Shelley's presentation of him, life itself is punishment. Finally, I turn to Shelley's understanding of the conditions of properly living – conditions that are left unfulfilled for a range of the figures that haunt his poetry. Lucretius emphasises in his account of nourishment in the first book of *De rerum natura* that to the sustenance of all living things, certain things must necessarily be added, since, as John Mason Good's translation has it,

> matter thus appropriate, or e'en space
> For growth mature, form not the whole requir'd.
> The timely shower from heav'n must add benign
> Its influence too, ere yet the teeming earth
> Emit her joyous produce[.][11]

Lucretius's emphasis on the necessary conditions for life has recently been extended, for instance, in Judith Butler's claim that life is 'the condition of being conditioned' and that, therefore, '[t]here is no life without the conditions of life that variably sustain life'.[12] The conditions of life are, for Shelley, more than merely nutritive, however. While his poetry evinces an acute recognition both of the need for food, shelter and the like, and of these as essential to the realisation of freedom itself, he also emphatically insists that necessary conditions of properly living life include liberty, peace and justice.

The sale of human life

'The Voyage. A Fragment … Devonshire – August 1812' is, for the most part, 'disjointed' and 'diffuse', as the Longman editors say (*Poems* I, p. 247; headnote). But the poem does attempt to draw some conclusions from its rather disparate plot, and, in doing so, the final lines represent one of Shelley's earliest attacks on the injustice visited on the likes of the poem's main character by 'some bloated Lord / Some priestly pilferer, or some Snake of Law' (*Poems* I, p. 257; ll. 284–5):

> They have appropriated human life
> And human happiness, but these weigh nought
> In the nice-balanced Politician's scale,
> Who finds that murder is expedient
> And that vile means can answer glorious ends.
> Wide nature has outstretched her fertile Earth
> In commonage to all – but they have torn
> Her dearest offspring from her bleeding breast,
> Have disunited Liberty and life,
> Severed all right from duty, and confused
> Virtue with selfishness. – The grass-green hills,
> The fertile valleys and the limpid streams,
> The beach on the seashore, the sea itself,
> The very snow-clad mountain peaks, whose height
> Forbids all human footstep, the ravines
> Where cataracts have roared ere Monarchs were,
> Nature, fair Earth, and Heaven's untainted air
> Are all apportioned out …
>
> (*Poems* I, pp. 256–7; ll. 267–84)

This reflection comes after the poem has concluded with a 'sleek and pampered townsman' (*Poems* I, p. 256; l. 263) bluntly breaking the news of the deaths of his wife and all but one of his children to the poem's central figure. Like Hunt's Ariadne, abandoned by Theseus (another ruthless operator) and thus 'Bequeathed to death, while yet a living thing; / Bequeathed to death through every sharp distress, / Homeless, and fatherless, and husbandless',[13] the central figure of 'The Voyage', comparably destitute of family and home, is also a bequest to death in the specific sense not that he is dead, or even condemned to death, but in the sense that his life has become deathly. He is, as Hunt's description of Ariadne appositely has it, a 'living *thing*'.[14]

The reflection itself condemns the glory-seeking politician who finds all too easily that 'murder is expedient'.[15] But despite this emphasis on the death of the protagonist's family and the willingness of politicians to view murder as just another means to an end, the reflection in fact focuses as much on the power of 'Monarchs' et al. over life as well as over death. The appropriation of 'human life / And human happiness' does not entail the sheer annihilation of life in death but rather its radical perversion into unliveable life. It is especially notable that while the appropriation of human happiness does entail the transformation of happiness into misery – a transformation that this poem and much of Shelley's political poetry depicts – the consequence of the appropriation of human life is not such a straightforward reversal. Appropriated lives are hardly liveable, but they nevertheless are still lives, not as yet fully transformed into their opposite, death. Needless to say, this is no consolation for those leading an appropriable and tradable life.

Like human life, the beneficence of nature has also been perverted in 'The Voyage' according to a niggardly Malthusian logic.[16] In a poem that Shelley thought of as akin to his own *Queen Mab*, responding to Piers' rhetorically questioning observation (itself a response to the hard-bitten emphasis on 'the blasting breath of want') that 'the birds [...] yet find their simple food / Scattered abundantly', Southey's Wat Tyler remarks that

> No fancied boundaries of mine and thine
> Restrain their wanderings: Nature gives enough
> For all; but Man, with arrogant selfishness,
> Proud of his heaps, hoards up superfluous stores
> Robb'd from his weaker fellows, starves the poor,
> Or gives to pity what he owes to justice![17]

In Shelley's 'The Voyage', the poem's verbal echoes satirically perform the perversion of nature being lamented. That nature is, at the end of the passage quoted above, 'apportioned out', for instance, develops with remorseless logic the fact that, we are told at its beginning, 'human life' has been 'appropriated'; and similarly, where nature had '*out*stretched her fertile Earth', the possessive forces of tyranny now 'apportion *out*' even 'the snow-clad mountain peaks', both confining nature and distributing it partially, where nature itself had been unconfined and impartial in its bounty. The second of these echoes (between 'outstretched' and 'apportioned out') marks, therefore, a crucial difference between the action of nature and the action of tyranny. Whereas the former is abundantly diffuse, bequeathing its benefits '[i]n commonage to all', the latter is calculatingly discriminating and divisive, predicating this divisiveness on the fundamental disuniting of life and liberty. Writing eight years later, Shelley would return to his condemnation of Malthusian apportioning, in an appeal to liberty '[t]o judge, with solemn truth, life's ill-apportioned lot' ('Ode to Liberty', *Poems* III, p. 417; l. 263).[18] The reunification of life and liberty is essential, for Shelley, to life being liveable. In this regard, he might be seen to differ from the moment in the first canto of *Childe Harold's Pilgrimage*, where Byron says of 'the sons of Spain' that 'Fond of a land which gave them nought but life, / Pride points the path that leads to Liberty.'[19] The difference between Shelley and Byron here is subtle, but, I think, real. Despite the registering of a dissatisfaction with their country on the part of the sons of Spain – it has given them 'nought but life' – nevertheless, life here comes first, only to be followed, eventually, by liberty; Shelley, instead, emphasises that life and liberty, as it were, come together, only to be illicitly sundered.

Shelley's insistence on the necessary unity of liberty and life is central to his theories of both, and we will need to return to this insistence below. But I want for the moment to examine more fully his understanding of the appropriation of human life and, in order to do this, to examine canto III of *Queen Mab*, in which Shelley offers a critique of what Timothy Morton has aptly called the 'dyspeptic king', before turning to canto V's excoriations on commerce.[20]

Having called Ianthe's spirit out of her body, Queen Mab (the 'Fairy') shows her a range of scenes representative of human life, both as it is and might be. Many of these scenes serve to illustrate the Fairy's claim that 'Once peace and freedom blessed / The cultivated plain: But wealth, that curse of man, / Blighted the bud of its prosperity' (*Poems* I, p. 287; canto II, ll. 202–5). Wealth is a curse not just to those who do not have it but to those who do as well.[21] Canto III draws the attention of Ianthe's spirit to 'The King, the wearer of a gilded chain / That binds his soul to abjectness', a point reinforced by the pathetic juxtaposition of the courtiers' flattery with the monarch's status as 'slave / Even to the basest appetites' (*Poems* I, pp. 290–1; canto III, ll. 30–3). As we saw at the end of the last chapter, even those apparently inured to the worst ravages of society, those who wield power, are, in fact, subject to the effects of custom; here, similarly, even those who enslave others are themselves characterised as slaves. What is worse, of course, is that this regal, aristocratic slave is not just enslaved himself but also depends on the enslavement of others to maintain him in his obeisance to base appetites. In a Popean image of puffed-up littleness, courtiers are condemned for maintaining their own meretriciously ornamented lives by draining the lives of others:

> Those gilded flies
> That, basking in the sunshine of a court,
> Fatten on its corruption! – what are they?
> – The drones of the community; they feed
> On the mechanic's labour: the starved hind
> For them compels the stubborn glebe to yield
> Its unshared harvests; and yon squalid form,
> Leaner than fleshless misery, that wastes
> A sunless life in the unwholesome mine,
> Drags out in labour a protracted death,
> To glut their grandeur; many faint with toil,
> That few may know the cares and woe of sloth.
> (*Poems* I, pp. 293–4; canto III, ll. 106–16)[22]

The Fairy seems to change her mind about what it is precisely that fattens the 'gilded flies' of court: is it the court's own corruption or the mechanic's labour? In any case, it is certainly the latter on which she focuses, and it is reasonable to suggest that the court is corrupt in her view because of its illegitimate appropriation of the labour of the many. Cut off not just from the corrupting and false sun of the court but also from the source of life in nature – 'the unfailing sun / Sheds light and life', the Fairy remarks slightly later (*Poems* I, p. 297; canto III, ll. 193–4) – 'a sunless life' is living death, a life entirely consumed in labour not for its own renewal but for the gluttony of another.

While some might be tempted to view the denunciations of courtly excess in canto III as an attack on a kind of Heliogabalian profligacy very much (whatever the Prince Regent could be accused of in 1812) a thing of the past, canto V extends Shelley's critique, couched in closely similar terms, to a much more recognisably current phenomenon: commerce.[23] In the considerations of commerce in his correspondence with Elizabeth Hitchener, for example, it is clearly crucial to Shelley to examine commerce's relation to aristocracy and thus to establish the comparative merits and demerits of allegedly modern and superseded social systems. Initially, his concern is to distinguish his rejection of commerce from a high Tory disdain for new money and hence to make sure that aristocracy is the target of equal opprobrium. Thus, concluding a stern condemnation of the luxurious indulgence evident among London's elite, he remarks that 'All monopolies are bad', amplifying this judgement with the following clarification:

> I do not however when condemning commercial aggrandizement think it in the least necessary to panegerize hereditary accumulation – Both are flagrant encroachments on liberty, neither can be used as an antidote for the poison of the other […] Take the best aristocrat – He monopolizes a large house, gold dishes, glittering dresses, his very servants are decked in magnificence – how does one monopoly differ from another, that of the mean Duke from that of the mean pacer between the pillars of the exchange. (10 August 1811, *Letters* I, p. 132)

Two months later, however, it is commerce that comes in for especial scorn – while, of course, never leaving the viciousness of aristocracy in doubt: 'Vile as aristocracy is', he writes from York, 'commerce, purse-proud ignorance & illiterateness is more contemptible' (16 October 1811, *Letters* I, p. 151).[24] Crucially, the leaders of commercial society, as well as its more obvious victims, are viewed not just as being stupid (as in the later letter) but also (as in the earlier letter) as barely living components of a large, confining machinery: the man of commerce is 'the mean pacer between the pillars of the exchange'.[25]

It is toward the end of the attack on commerce in *Queen Mab*, canto V, that Shelley has often been taken to allude to Adam Smith's widely influential economic treatise in the lines, 'The harmony and happiness of man / Yields to the wealth of nations' (*Poems* I, p. 314; ll. 79–80), which, of course, further the sense that what renders man's social and individual life liveable ('harmony and happiness') has been ceded to the self-propelling machinery of national accumulation. Whether the allusion is to Smith (of whom Shelley showed some knowledge) or, as the Longman editors suggest, Volney's *Ruins* (of which he showed much more), the gluttonous monarchy of canto III can easily be extended to the more current and apparently rational false gods set up by commerce.[26] Indeed, the similarity both in the imagery and argument of the two critiques is striking:

> Commerce! beneath whose poison-breathing shade
> No solitary virtue dares to spring,
> But poverty and wealth with equal hand
> Scatter their withering curses, and unfold
> The doors of premature and violent death
> To pining famine and full-fed disease,
> To all that shares the lot of human life,
> Which, poisoned body and soul, scarce drags the chain
> That lengthens as it goes and clanks behind.
> (*Poems* I, pp. 312–13; canto V, ll. 44–52)

The image from canto III (l. 115) of life dragged on is repeated here, and it is an image to which Shelley would return in the Maniac's speech to Julian and Maddalo, where the chain is explicitly compared to life itself: '"Month after month," he cried, "to bear this load / And as a jade urged by the whip and goad / To drag life on, which like a heavy chain / Lengthens behind with many a link of pain"' (*Poems* II, p. 679; ll. 300–3). The emphasis in both 'Julian and Maddalo' and the lines quoted above on the lengthening of the chain behind the figure dragging it (the image is perhaps of a coiled chain progressively uncoiled and thus lengthened as it is dragged) suggests that this is a life entirely without prospect. Whatever appears prospective is illusory because the consequence of continuing to drag the chain onward is that the burden is increased rather than diminished. Life is an accumulated encumbrance. As Shelley makes clear, anticipatory emotions are redundant in the perpetual circulations of commerce, whose operatives he describes as

> Hardened to hope, insensible to fear,
> Scarce living pulleys of a dead machine,
> Mere wheels of work and articles of trade,
> That grace the proud and noisy pomp of wealth!
> (*Queen Mab*, *Poems* I, p. 314; canto V, ll. 75–8)

This image, of course, casts the workings of commerce itself as mechanical, as well as holding in the background the recognition that modern commerce relies on real machines. More significantly, the 'slaves' forced 'to perform / A task of cold and brutal drudgery' (ll. 73–4) are both producers ('wheels of work') and products ('articles of trade'). Their activity is doubly inanimate in that it is itself mechanical and reproduces them as machine parts.

They do not repine

In *Queen Mab*'s critiques of tyrannical exploitation, oppressor and oppressed grimly shadow one another. This is not only because, in the sense developed by G. W. F. Hegel in his much-discussed master–slave dialectic, tyrant and worker are mutually dependent.[27] More specifically for Shelley, the oppressor's gluttonous life is as impermanent and insubstantial as that of the worker is morbid and relentless. The worker's life is a bad eternity – he or she 'Drags out in labour a protracted death' – and, as such, he or she actually attains all-too-completely the evil twin of 'the fame / Which the vain-glorious of the earth / Seek to eternize' (*Poems* I, p. 295; canto III, ll. 138–40). Shelley, of course, is frequently scornful of regal monumentalisation, contrasting in 'The Monarch's Funeral: An Anticipation', for instance, the pretensions to lapidary immortality of the insane but living George III with the celebration in verse of the martyred Irish nationalist, Robert Emmet. Emmet will 'ever live in lays', while 'a coffined Monarch' will merely 'lay' (*Poems* I, p. 146; ll. 25, 34).[28]

But it is the real misfortune of slaves to be reduced in life, rather than in death, to the condition of stony persistence. This is William Godwin's riposte to those opposing the abolition of the slave trade on the presumption that slaves do not seem, at least, too much to mind being slaves, and, indeed, appear quite to like it:

> Are they contented? I am not contented for them. I see in them beings of certain capacities, equal to certain pursuits and enjoyments. It is of no consequence in the question that they do not see this, that they do not know their own interests and happiness. They do not repine? Neither does a stone repine. That which you mention as an alleviation [that is, that 'they are not conscious of the evils against which you exclaim'] finishes in my conception the portrait of their calamity. Abridged as they are of independence and enjoyment, they have neither the apprehension nor the spirit of men. I cannot bear to see human nature thus degraded. It is my duty, if I can, to make them a thousand times happier than they are, or have any conception of being.[29]

This foregoes two easier lines of attack against the pro-slavery lobby in order to turn its attention to the fundamentals of the debate. Godwin, that is, might either just have flatly contradicted the claim of those in favour of the status quo – slaves do complain of their condition – or have given quite obvious grounds as to why they do not – slaves are too terrified of the consequences should they voice their complaints, or there is no means for them to communicate such complaints, or both. These are no doubt sound enough arguments, but Godwin focuses instead on the basic crime of slavery: that it erodes the humanity of its victims. Of course, it is central to Godwin's argument that slaves are as much human beings as anyone in a happier condition: they have 'certain capacities' and are 'equal to certain pursuits and enjoyments', although Godwin's vagueness about what these might be quite eloquently intimates their systematic denial such that even slaves themselves might not be expected to know the pursuits or enjoyments to which they are truly, in a resonant term for this debate, 'equal'.

It is perhaps worth admitting that the view that individuals' desires are expressions of their own personalities, and that they know what is best for them, helps caution against the impositions of paternalism, however well intentioned. Such caution is behind the oft (and justly) felt need to avoid portraying slaves as mere victims while at the same time acknowledging the dehumanising effect of slavery on them.[30] Yet there is also a danger in prioritising such caution, as Godwin's argument here makes apparent. The assumption that uncomplaining individuals should be taken at their word – or lack of word – often acts as cover for a pernicious socio-economic arrangement because its basic assumptions are that society functions equally well for each of its members and that there is only so much (basically incidental and short-lived) damage that can be done to any human being's humanity. Godwin, however, questions such a view, especially as it is deployed by advocates of slavery to deflect attention away from the grossness of slavery's injustice. It is not because of a condescending view of slaves but, paradoxically, because of the clarity of his insight into the enormity of the offence of slavery that Godwin's view can seem patrician. Conversely, the pretence that slaves are like other human beings – if they were unhappy, they would say so – helps to condemn them to a condition in which they are not like other human beings. Godwin is strikingly emphatic on the point that the humanity of slaves is damaged by slavery: the condition to which slaves are reduced in not repining is the condition of inanimate materiality; in being denied independence and enjoyment, 'they have neither the apprehension nor the spirit of men.'

It is important not to demur from the consequences of Godwin's argument. Slaves are not, for Godwin, human beings in any acceptable sense, and thus his is an unusual argument to find on the pro-abolition side, since abolitionists of various stamps expended most of their energies attempting to establish the humanity of slaves.[31] What Godwin's remarks recognise is the profound vulnerability of humanity. In making human beings wholly subservient to the will of other human beings, slavery has real consequences for the humanity of slaves. This point is emphasised in Orlando Patterson's influential *Slavery as Social Death*, in which Patterson draws on a range of examples (not just on slavery in the Americas and Caribbean) to offer an account of the meaning of slavery in slave-holding societies. The slave, he remarks, 'was the ultimate human tool', a view given theoretical elaboration by, for instance, Aristotle.[32] The status of slaves as instruments was predicated upon what Patterson influentially described as 'social death': the denial of any social life to the slave in his or her own right.[33] Patterson offers Henri Wallon's account of slavery in ancient Greece – the practice of which in that society was, for Shelley, along with the suppression of women, a serious stain on its otherwise considerable honour – as illustration of this fundamental point:

> The slave was a dominated thing, an animated instrument, a body with natural movements, but without its own reason, an existence entirely absorbed in another. The proprietor of this thing, the mover of this instrument, the soul and the reason of this body, the source of this life, was the master. The master was everything for him: his father and his god, which is to say, his authority and his duty ... Thus, god, fatherland, existence, are all, for the slave, identified with the same being; there was nothing which made for the social person, nothing which made for the moral person, that was not the same as his personality and his individuality.[34]

'Religion', Patterson goes on to note, 'explains how it is possible to relate to the dead who still live. It says little about how ordinary people should relate to the living who are dead.'[35] Something of the difficulty involved in accounting coherently for the specific condition of the slave is discernible in Wallon's account of ancient Greek slavery. On the one hand, the slave is utterly dependent on the master for his or her social life. In his or her own right, as Patterson argues, he or she is socially dead. On the other hand, it is the natural life of the slave that the master exploits. In that sense, the slave's life is crucial to the use the master makes of him or her: he or she is, after all, 'an animated instrument'. Slaves live, but not, so to speak, from themselves (their functions are entirely directed by their masters) nor for themselves (the results of their living activity are wholly appropriated by another). The Fairy is being quite literal in *Queen Mab*, canto III, when she states that power '[m]akes slaves of men, and, of the human frame, / A mechanized automaton' (*Poems* I, p. 296; ll. 179–80).[36]

The problem with this kind of account, of course, is that machines do not suffer, whereas slaves do – or, if they apparently do not, that is really only evidence of another, invidious kind of suffering (which is Godwin's point above). Their transformation into instruments is socially but not naturally effected because they remain '*animated* instruments', and animation and instrumentality are painfully mismatched. An aspect of this mismatch is, in fact, well brought out in Shelley's description of soldiers as slaves in 'A Philosophical View of Reform':

> From the moment that a man is a soldier, he becomes a slave. He is taught obedience; his will is no longer, which is the most sacred prerogative of man, guided by his own judgement. He is taught to despise human life and human suffering; this is the universal distinction of slaves. He is more degraded than a murderer; he is like the bloody knife which has stabbed and feels not: a murderer we may abhor and despise; a soldier is by profession, beyond abhorrence and below contempt. (*Works*, VII, p. 41)

The soldier-as-slave feels nothing in response to the murders he is ordered to commit – and yet he does feel: he 'despise[s] human life and human suffering'. Of course, the life and suffering which he despises, Shelley implies, includes his own, and thus is his life doubly annulled, so to speak, since it is rendered both instrumental and the object of self-hatred. In the case of the slave, then, 'something is living that is other than life'.[37]

Life as punishment

This remainder of life which is not entirely exhausted in labour, or, in the soldier's case, in the specific labour of killing, is expended instead in feeling, specifically, in 'misery, and fear, and care' (*Queen Mab*, *Poems* I, p.315, canto V, l. 114). *Queen Mab*, to be sure, is hardly consistent on the question of the characteristic emotional experience of unfree labourers: on the one hand, they are 'insensible' to fear, etc., whereas, on the other, their lives are identified with precisely such emotions. The point to emphasise is that the life that remains to them is only suffering; they live, but they are not alive.

Karl Marx – a figure, as is often noted, who deeply admired Shelley – grasped the misfortune of being, in particular, a *living* tool and commodity in his early *Economic and Philosophical Manuscripts*. Taking Adam Smith to task for having stated in *The Wealth of Nations* that, on the one hand, the entire product of the worker's labour belongs to him or her, while, on the other, noting that the worker receives only the bare minimum of the result of his or her labours, Marx describes this bare minimum, in a manner strongly reminiscent of Godwin's account of the obliterated humanity of the slave, as 'just enough for [the worker] to exist not as a human being but as a worker and for him to propagate not humanity but the slave class of the workers'.[38] The problem for the worker is that his transformation into a mere tool is never quite complete: 'But the *worker*', Marx states, 'has the misfortune to be a *living* capital, and hence a capital *with needs*, which forfeits its interest and hence its existence every moment it is not working. As capital, the *value* of the worker rises or falls in accordance with supply and demand, and even in a physical sense his *existence*, his *life*, was and is treated as a supply of a *commodity*, like any other commodity.'[39]

Marx's word for the fact that the worker is alive – 'misfortune' – puts it mildly. As Patterson shows, slavery was frequently deployed as punishment for capital offences or was the fate of prisoners taken in battle.[40] Life rather than death as punishment for crime is the concern of Shelley's representation of the wandering Jew in a number of his poems, especially in his early 'The Wandering Jew; or, The Victim of the Eternal Avenger'. Geoffrey Hartman once described the wandering Jew as 'that strange figure revived in the Romantic period'.[41] Hartman's remark is an insightfully equivocal quip. Given that the wandering Jew cannot die, reviving him is superfluous, in that it is neither required nor wanted. On the other hand, he is precisely in need of what he scorned – of, that is, the revivification offered by Christ – because the life to which he has been condemned is the very exemplification of the living death to which the life offered by Christ is a radical alternative. Despite the contrast of his freedom to roam over the earth with the slave's brutal confinement, the life of the wandering Jew is in fact a version of the life of the slave: it is lived entirely in submission to a tyrannical will. That life itself might just be drudgery is, of course, an abiding concern of Shelley's whole career and the focus of his last, great poem 'The Triumph of Life'. That poem is anticipated in a pithily sceptical fragment of 1819, which also shows that the view of life elaborated in 'The Wandering Jew' as submission to 'the Eternal Avenger' runs like a thread through even the slightest examples of Shelley's work:

> Why would you overlive your life again?
> Ever press onward onward in the train
> Of the great Conqueror—till ye climb
> (*Poems* III, p. 233)

As the editors note, this is a homage to Adam's soliloquy after the fall in *Paradise Lost*: 'Why do I overlive, / Why am I mocked with death, and lengthened out / To deathless pain?'[42] But Shelley, in fact, doubles the intensity of Adam's despair in his version of Adam's question: 'Why would you overlive your life *again*?' Adam asks why he is still alive, but Shelley's line questions rather the desire to repeat life, as it were, from the start, and, in doing so, suggests that any living whatever is already too much, a suggestion which Emily R. Wilson has argued is central to the Western tragic tradition.[43] The second line's 'onward onward', in its barren reiteration, even as it insists on forward momentum, reinforces this idea that life is an onerous superfluity.

The portrayal of life as at once inert and onwardly propelled is a feature of his poetry to which Shelley returns throughout his career. Paolo, the wandering Jew figure in that eponymously titled poem, bewails how he hears '[t]he spirits of the tombless dead' taunt him with the declaration that 'Ever shall thy fated soul / In life's protracted torments roll' (*Poems* I, p. 67; ll. 854, 860–1). Moreover, while key to Paolo's punishment is being doomed to wander the earth, he nevertheless is fated 'to stand, / A monument to the Eternal's ire' (*Poems* I, p. 65; ll. 796–7). It might be tempting to dismiss this as inconsistent characterisation in this poem of Shelley's youth, but to do so would be to miss a crucial aspect of the way Shelley portrays oppressed life throughout his career – as compelled and yet as motionless. Narrating the immediate aftermath of his mockery of Christ on the Via Dolorosa, Paolo complains how neither death nor forgiveness would come, and 'The self-inflicted torturing pangs / Of conscience lent their scorpion fangs, / Still life prolonging, after life was fled' (*Poems* I, p. 60; ll. 635–7). The suggestion of a pun on 'still' – both remaining and motionless – evokes Shelley's portrayal of the wandering Jew as, indeed, wandering and, at the same time, as a 'monument'.[44] With the appearance of life, his life is yet not living; it is still life, *nature morte.*

Life lived in vassalage to an avenging conqueror is at once devoid of organising direction and subject to insistent compulsion. The poem in which Shelley most insistently records the disorganised compulsion of vanquished lives comes at the opposite end of his career from the early 'The Wandering Jew'. At the beginning of 'The Triumph of Life', the narrator, who 'sate beside a public way', tells how

> a great stream
> Of people there was hurrying to and fro
> Numerous as gnats upon the evening gleam,
>
> All hastening onward, yet none seemed to know
> Whither he went, or whence he came, or why
> He made one of the multitude, yet so
>
> Was borne amid the crowd as through the sky
> One of the million leaves of summer's bier.—
> (*SPP*, p. 485; ll. 44–51)

The movement of the chariot of 'Life' is repeatedly characterised as rolling in the early part of the poem, a mode of motion that draws attention both to its onward direction and to the repetitive circulation of its wheels. And this onward, yet returning action is explicitly extended in the lines above to the chariot's prisoners. The direction in which the people described here are travelling is at once compulsively uniform and chaotically discordant. On the one hand, they constitute 'a great stream'; on the other, they hurry 'to and fro'; then again, they are '[a]ll hastening onward'. Later in the poem, they are 'Raging around' the chariot (l. 111), and, furthermore, the poem's verbal music is infected with this kind of onward propulsion and return, as when, for example, the word 'rolled' is itself rolled into the phrase 'grown *old*' in the description of a particular group harnessed to the triumphal carriage: 'for where'er // The chariot rolled a captive multitude / Was driven; all those who had grown old in power / Or misery' (ll. 118–21).

In fact, this fascination with the rolling of the chariot and the rolling of its minions into its entourage links the opening section of the narration of the poet's vision with the poem's first forty lines that form its introduction. The final line of the introduction, of course, is 'And then a Vision on my brain was rolled' (l. 40), a fact that has already been brilliantly intimated in the syllabic unrolling of the line 'When a strange trance over my fancy grew', with its development from 'strange' to 'trance' to 'fancy' (l. 29). Apart from the rolling of the vision on the poet's brain, much rolls around him in this opening section. The physical position of the poet, that is, in relation both to his immediate surroundings and the cosmic diurnal cycle focuses on his pivotal position. With limbs stretched out, rather like Leonardo's Vitruvian man, the heavens above him and the sea at his feet, the night departs 'before' him as the morning emerges 'behind' (ll. 26, 27). This way of picturing the poet's position in relation to the diurnal cycle – which contrasts with the standard image of debased utopianism, that of the day rising before the viewer – emphasises the onward rolling of the universe and the fact that the day, following the night, will also roll away (ll. 24–9).

The poem's switches of direction are not owing to mere indecisiveness but rather are crucial to its registration of the peculiarly organised chaos of the great stream itself. In particular, the taut irony of motion without progress is evoked in the play here on the meanings of 'on' – a play that has been well documented, if not 'exhausted', in Derrida's catalogue of the different possibilities for understanding 'the "on" of living on'.[45] The people are like gnats 'upon the evening gleam', where 'upon' specifies their location, however ethereal that, in this case, may be; but at the same time they hasten 'onward', compelled forwards and thus perpetually off the spot that they occupy at any moment. This play on 'on' is central to the shape of what was once Rousseau's account of his inclusion in the great stream:

'But all like bubbles on an eddying flood
Fell into the same track at last and were

'Borne onward.—I among the multitude
Was swept; me sweetest flowers delayed not long,
Me not the shadow nor the solitude,

> 'Me not the falling stream's Lethean song,
> Me, not the phantom of that early form
> Which moved upon its motion,—'
> (*SPP*, pp. 497; 458–65)

The passage is propelled from 'on' to 'onward' to 'upon', but that propulsion is also heard in 'among', an apparently different positional term, and the rhyme of 'long' and 'song' that it anticipates, or into whose track, rather, it falls at last. While perpetually condemned to a position 'on' or 'upon' something else, such a position is at the same time never secure in 'The Triumph of Life' since whatever or whoever rests for a moment is the next moment moved on.

Conditioned life

It is worth pausing briefly to draw out some of the key features of the portrayal of oppressed or punitive life in Shelley's work that I have been investigating. Two in particular are worth emphasising. First, indigent life of the kind lived by slaves, famished workers, and the wandering Jew, is paradoxically superfluous. Life of this kind is overlife. Second, life in its attenuated state is radically bereft.

There has been considerable interest in the constitutive vulnerability of human life in certain strands of political and ethical theory – especially those that have attempted to account for the large-scale bureaucratised oppression witnessed during the twentieth century (and today). Taking their lead from Michel Foucault's sense that, at just the moment at which 'death was ceasing to torment life so directly [...] the fact of living [...] passed into knowledge's field of control and power's sphere of intervention', such accounts emphasise, as one of Foucault's prominent followers, Giorgio Agamben, has put it, that 'life and death are not properly scientific concepts but rather political concepts, which as such acquire a political meaning precisely only through a decision'.[46] Thus does the sphere of what has come to be called 'biopolitics' emerge. The subjects of such biopolitical interventions are thus, in their very life, constitutively vulnerable, and moreover, those decisions frequently render specific lives unliveable in Shelley's view. Shelley's perception of the twinned exploitation and nullification of life on the part of the 'Snake of Law', which results in what *Queen Mab* evocatively calls 'sunless life', is perhaps most comparable to the account of the vulnerability, or precariousness of life, developed in part out of an engagement with Agamben and in part in response to recent instances of state violence, by Judith Butler. Butler claims that the radical vulnerability of the life of oppressed people is owing not to 'the withdrawal or absence of law [...] but the very effects of illegitimate legal coercion itself, or the exercise of state power freed from the constraints of all law'.[47] Butler's contention is that life is always characterised by certain dependencies: 'there is no life without the need for shelter and food, no life without dependency on wider networks of sociality and labor, no life that transcends injurability and mortality'.[48] It might be added to such an account that there is no living life without the satisfaction of these needs and the sheltering, rather than exposure, of life in its injurability.

For Butler as for Shelley, therefore, precarious life is subject to identifiable social and political formations, such as, in terms recognisable from the works of Shelley we have been discussing, tyranny and commerce. As the considerable quantity of reflection on these questions at least prima facie demonstrates, the administration and exploitation of life in its precariousness is of central concern to contemporary political theory. But as Agamben's derivation from Aristotle of the distinction between *zoē* and *bios*, for instance, suggests, the relation between merely living and living in a particular manner – in the manner, say, of a human being – was a key concern in antiquity as well.[49] Plato's *Protagoras*, for example, which Shelley is more than likely to have read even if he nowhere explicitly mentions the dialogue, is one of the chief ancient sources for the myth of Prometheus.[50] Charged by the gods with suitably equipping mortal beings prior to their emergence on earth, Epimetheus took upon himself the distribution of the different aptitudes among the various creatures, leaving the inspection of his work to his brother Prometheus. Lacking his brother's defining characteristic of foresight, Epimetheus dispersed all the means of survival – hard feet for walking on the ground, fur for keeping warm, teeth and claws for self-defence, etc. – before remembering (too late) man. It was left to Prometheus, therefore, to procure means for man's survival, which he did by stealing for him 'the mechanical arts of Hephaestus and Athene, and fire with them'.

It is for this crime that Prometheus is punished by being 'bound to the Precipice' on 'A Ravine of Icy Rocks in the Indian Caucasus', as the opening scene description of *Prometheus Unbound* has it (*Poems* II, p. 477). Any book on Shelley must return (hopefully not like the eagle to the Titan's liver) to the seemingly inexhaustible *Prometheus Unbound*: in Chapter 5, for example, I wish in particular to re-examine its verbal dissolutions as an example of Shelley's poetic instantiation of the interanimation of self and other. But for the time being I want to stress Shelley's emphasis on the contrast between what we might call precarious life and liveable life.

Admittedly, the crime for which Shelley's Prometheus is punished is his cursing of Jupiter rather than the theft of fire. Nevertheless, the curse is part of his rejection of Jupiter's tyrannical sway and bespeaks his advocacy of the 'living thing[s]' (*Poems* II, p. 495; Act I, l. 305) to whom he wishes no pain. Furthermore, part of his penalty is the denial to him of 'flowers and fruits and happy sounds / And love, though fleeting', which are the comforts that 'All else who live and suffer' take from the Earth (*Poems* II, p. 488; Act I, ll. 187–9); and once he is redeemed, he may experience again 'all / That tempers or improves man's life, now free' (*Poems* II, p. 588; Act III, scene 3, ll. 47–8). That 'now free' hints at the value Prometheus places on freedom in making life liveable.

Contrastingly, of course, the cost of the disunity of life and liberty is the cessation of life as life. During the choric opening of *Hellas* – a poem, of course, explicitly dedicated to the celebration of a particular struggle for liberation (Preface to *Hellas*, *SPP*, p. 430) – the chorus divides into two for the following exchange:

SEMICHORUS I.
Life may change, but it may fly not;
Hope may vanish, but can die not;
Truth be veiled but still it burneth;
Love repulsed,—but it returneth!

SEMICHORUS II.
Yet were Life a charnel where
Hope lay coffined with despair;
Yet were Truth a sacred lie,
Love were Lust—

SEMICHORUS I.
If Liberty
Lent not Life its soul of light,
Hope its iris of delight,
Truth its prophet's robe to wear,
Love its power to give and bear.
(*SPP*, p. 434; ll. 34–45)

After this exchange, the Chorus reunites – a reunification that is significant, of course, given the exchange of assertion and qualification between the two semichoruses here. This exchange is not driven by disagreement, and yet nor does Semichorus I simply accept the correction of Semichorus II; rather, the qualification of the timeless assertions about life, hope, truth and love is precisely shared between the two semichoruses, Semichorus II's decisively intervening 'Yet' notwithstanding. This mutual interchange is, in fact, discernible at a much more minute level as well, in the lineaments of the statement of what it takes for life not to be a mere 'charnel'. Life would be such 'If Liberty / Lent not Life its soul of light'. This way of putting the relation between life and liberty refuses the process of extorted production and gluttonous consumption of the kind condemned in *Queen Mab*. Liberty, it is important to recognise, *lends* life its soul of light. Furthermore, the referential ambivalence of 'its' here suggests that while the 'soul of light' comes from liberty, so to speak, it might now also belong to life. What is being lent to life is now no less life's soul of light than it is liberty's. This suggestion is unfolded in the line itself, in its development from 'Liberty' through 'Life' to 'light'. Life may not be life without liberty, but, at the same time, it is only in this passage to and through life that liberty comes to light. Without this imaginative interchange of liberty, life and light, life is but a charnel, or, as Shelley wrote in 'On Love', without 'this want or power' – without, that is, 'that powerful attraction towards all that we conceive or fear or hope beyond ourselves when we find within our own thoughts the chasm of an insufficient void' – 'man becomes the living sepulchre of himself, and what yet survives is the mere husk of what he once was' (*SPP*, pp. 503–4). The definition of love as a 'want or power' is revealing, of course, because it shows that love is not exclusively definable as either a lack or a capacity. It lies both within and outside the self, and without it, in the retreat of man into himself, all that is found is emptiness. Liberty and life are alike dependent on imaginative extension beyond the self of the kind enacted in the extension of these terms beyond themselves in the line from *Hellas* above.[51]

Human life is, therefore, not self-animating, so to speak, but interanimated by liberty and by communion with others. Parasitic exploitation of the kind condemned in poems from *Queen Mab* to 'The Triumph of Life' is a grotesque travesty of this interanimation. I want to develop this sense of interanimation, especially to show its fundamental role in Shelley's poetic theory and practice, and so we will return to it later. I wish now, though, to begin the turn to Shelley's poetic theory and practice in the following chapter by examining his philosophy of artworks. This follows significantly on from the discussion here, because Shelley initially appears to view artworks similarly to how he views slaves: as once-living material, first deadened, and then reinvested with life by its creators and receivers.

CHAPTER FOUR

Happier forms

In the introduction to his lectures on aesthetics, Hegel dedicates an important section to considering 'the work of art in relation to the external phenomena of nature'.[1] He is trying to specify the character of artworks as products of human activity, and the distinction of artworks from natural products is an especially important aspect of this attempt. Hegel remarks:

> Here the ordinary way of looking at things took easily to the notion that the human art-product ranked below the product of nature; for the work of art has no feeling in itself and is not through and through enlivened, but, regarded as an external object, is dead; but we are accustomed to value the living higher than the dead. That the work of art has no life and movement in itself is readily granted. What is alive within nature is, within and without, an organism purposefully elaborated into its tiniest parts, while the work of art attains the appearance of life only on its surface; inside it is ordinary stone, or wood and canvas, or, as in poetry, a representation expressed in speech and letters.[2]

Hegel goes on to state that 'external existence' – 'the appearance of life' on the artwork's surface – is not, however, what makes art, art.[3] Instead, he emphasises the contrast, rather than any potential (and potentially illusory) similarity, between natural products and human works of art: the latter have received 'the baptism of the spirit' and they thus stand 'higher than any natural product which has not made this journey through the spirit'.[4] Giving the example of a painted landscape and the natural scene it depicts, Hegel claims – in defiance of Platonic suspicions of the untrustworthiness of mimesis – that the painting attains a higher standing because 'everything spiritual is better than any product of nature.'[5] In case this sounds a little dogmatic, he elaborates slightly, returning in particular to the questions of the differing lives of natural products and works of art. The latter, it is now argued, are superior, because, whereas individual things in nature are merely transient, 'the work of art persists, even if it is not mere permanence which constitutes its genuine pre-eminence over natural reality, but its having made spiritual inspiration conspicuous'.[6]

It is worth specifying a little more fully the difficulties that emerge from Hegel's attempt to articulate the relation of artworks to natural products. Hegel gives three examples of the kinds of material out of which works of art might be made. The function of this exemplification is to make it obvious that the life of artworks does not extend throughout their different material constitutions, as does, say, the life of a tree or the life of a blackbird. Artworks only look as if they are alive on the surface, but inside they are just dead.

If we ponder these examples, however, the deadness of the material involved comes to seem rather less straightforward than Hegel perhaps imagined. J. M. Bernstein has posed some cogent questions about the above passage from the *Aesthetics*, which he finds 'presumptuous, ominous, and ambiguous'.[7] It is presumptuous to claim, argues Bernstein, that the animation of the work of art is entirely the work of the spirit responsible for forming matter into art, and that, therefore, 'art's sensuous immediacy' can in no way be credited with the artwork's animation.[8] Connected to this is Bernstein's feeling of deep unease at the implications of Hegel's juxtaposition of animating spirit and dead nature. It seems that, for Hegel, 'it is a condition for nature to become a pure vehicle of mindedness that it be dead' and that spirit therefore relies for its authority on 'the slaughter of nature'.[9] What is especially unsettling here is the convergence, so to speak, of nature's metaphorical and literal death in the passage: nature has no authority over spirit (it is metaphorically dead), and, at the same time, it is actually dead, in order that spirit take all the limelight. But it cannot be quite the case (this is the ambiguity) that spirit is entirely to thank for art's animation, for art is spirit manifesting itself: 'medium-bound sensuousness must play a role in how spirit manifests itself in art [...] but since sensuousness in art is provided by dead nature, then dead nature must play a role in art's animation'.[10]

Like Bernstein, Shelley would have found Hegel's passage deeply suggestive in its presumptuousness, ominousness and ambiguity. The constitutive difficulty or ambivalence involved in seeing art's animation as reliant on the baptism of otherwise dead material by 'spirit', recognised by Shelley in some of his most important poems as well as some of his most tellingly inscrutable fragments, is the central focus of this chapter. This chapter therefore instantiates a shift in the focus of this book, from Shelley's epistemological and social-political concerns (examined in Chapters 1 to 3) to his poetics. Yet it is important to recognise that, in particular, it builds implicitly on the discussion of slavery in the preceding chapter: the artist's animation of material which is first deadened is disturbingly similar to the tyrant's deadening of the slave and subsequent bestowal of life on him or her merely through tyrannical fiat. Therefore, questions of artistic agency understood as the animation of matter, and thus also the relation of art to the nature off which it lives, are the twin focuses of this chapter.

We may start this investigation by posing additional questions of Hegel's attempt to account for the animation of art to those already posed by Bernstein – questions that are essential to Shelley. First, is each of the raw materials of art, so to speak, cited by Hegel dead matter in the same way? Is stone dead, as wood is dead, as a representation expressed in sounds and letters is dead? If not, might they all, in fact, be thought to have their own distinct lives instead? Stone seems the most unpromising in terms of its potential life, and Hegel's assumption that it is dead, at least, appears safe. Indeed, Shelley sometimes seems, in his 'Notes on Sculpture', to consider the material of sculpture as an impediment to art: commenting on a figure of Sleep, for example, he states that 'The hardness of the stone does not permit the arriving at any great expression' (*Works*, VI p. 330); but, on the other hand, in an early letter to Elizabeth Hitchener, he envisaged a 'stony power' alongside the 'vegetative power' of vegetables and the soul of man, which respectively 'constitute the essence of men, stones &c, as much make it to be what it is' (11 June 1811, *Letters* I, p. 101). Shelley is questioning Hitchener's adherence to a relatively orthodox belief in God here, although he is willing to go so far as to acknowledge God as 'the *existing power of existence*' (Shelley's emphasis). This letter radically throws into question the deadness of stones in their supposed contrast to the aliveness of vegetables, the greater aliveness of men and the ultimate aliveness of God. On the contrary, each of these entities, for want of a better word, is characterised by its own distinct 'power'. In this context, stone is hardly as dead as Hegel would assume.

Knottier still is the problem of wood. There are much clearer prima facie grounds for thinking that wood is not simply inanimate, since the trees from which it is harvested are living. It is a fact of the English language (and the French) that it fails to distinguish between living and dead wood, in the way that German may speak of *Wald* or *Holz*, as Horkheimer and Adorno, in a significant passage toward the end of *Dialectic of Enlightenment*, outline:

> Those who extolled the body above all else, the gymnasts and scouts, always had the closest affinity with killing, just as the lovers of nature are close to the hunter […] They measure others, without realizing it, with the gaze of

> the coffin makers. They betray themselves when they speak the result: they call men tall, short, fat or heavy. They are interested in illness and at mealtimes already watch for the death of those who eat with them, and their interest is only thinly rationalized by concern for their health. Language keeps pace with them. It has transformed a walk into motion and a meal into calories, rather as a living wood is just wood in everyday English and French [*ähnlich wie der lebendige Wald in der englischen und französischen Alltagssprache Holz heißt*]. Society with its death statistics reduces life to a chemical process.[11]

Horkheimer and Adorno's point is hardly a kind of linguistically founded patriotism – their book is not especially keen to propose the German-speaking lands as a refuge for life in the face of bureaucratic mortification. Rather, the failure to distinguish between living and dead wood is one instance of a much broader tendency to reduce life to what can be weighed and measured. The choice before the artist wishing to work with wood, then, is not a salutary one. Either connive in the reduction of life to a mere chemical process – chopping down a tree just curtails the process of photosynthesis and that is all the 'life' of a tree may mean – or else rely for your materials on, in Bernstein's resonant phrase, the 'slaughter' of an emphatically living organism.

But perhaps yet more unsettling is Hegel's suggestion that 'a representation expressed in speech and letters' is the mere dead interior of a work of art. The juxtaposition of dead letter and living spirit draws, of course, on a biblical precedent, but this juxtaposition is made to seem insecure – however tenable or not it may be on its own terms – when Hegel also assigns 'a representation [*Vorstellung*]' and 'speech' to dead materiality. Later in Hegel's *Aesthetics*, this ambiguity is more fully addressed. There is, Hegel recognises, a hint of paradox in suggesting that 'the proper external object in the case of poetry' is 'the *inner* imagination and intuition itself', and thus '*spiritual* forms [...] take the place of perceptibility and provide the material to be given shape, just as marble, bronze, colour, and musical notes were the material earlier on'.[12] This distinction of poetry from sculpture, architecture, painting and music, on the grounds that its particular element is that of 'ideas', has the consequence that its relation to sense is somewhat ambivalent:

> For [...] poetry, like music, contains that principle of the self-apprehension of the inner life as inner, which architecture, sculpture, and painting lack; while, on the other hand, in the very field of inner ideas, perceptions, and feelings it broadens out into an objective world which does not altogether lose the determinate character of sculpture and painting.[13]

This unexpected benefit – that poetry still has something of the 'determinate character' of the, so to speak, more material arts – is recast only a few sentences later, however, as being not quite determinate enough to satisfy sense: 'poetry is incapable of reaching the definiteness of sense-perception'.[14]

Rather than offering an interpretation of Hegel's theory of poetry, I have wanted in these introductory remarks to draw out a number of difficulties concerning the examination of poetry's relation to its material constitution – difficulties which are at the centre of Hegel's extended consideration of the nature of poetry as distinct from the other arts. These questions are likewise fundamental to Shelley's conception of the life of poetry and, especially, of the vulnerability and dependency of that life. Like Hegel, Shelley wishes seriously to think through the relationship between the more than merely apparent life of art and the habitually valued (and therefore, because *merely* habitually valued, unvalued) life of nature. For Shelley, neither wood nor sounds and letters are categorised straightforwardly as dead matter, awaiting recuperative animation by spirit. The agency of reanimation, and its dependency on what it would reanimate, is a critical question for him. It is not often the case, in Shelley's work, that spirit is wholly to thank for the bestowal of life on otherwise dead materials, for those materials themselves are never altogether dead. The second half of this chapter examines these claims, turning to Shelley's treatment of wood and words as both material and living in two poems that deal with what I want (non-trivially) to call arboreal suspended animation: 'With a Guitar. To Jane' and the 'Ode to the West Wind'. What I hope to show is that Shelley's verse repeatedly returns to the kind of sensuous thingliness discussed by Bernstein as a condition of animation; he is a poet for whom matter, with which spirit is interwoven, is already fecundating.

The non-existent universe

We have been thinking so far about the implicit need for art, as Bernstein resonantly puts it, to slaughter nature as a condition of its (art's) animation. Putting things this way, of course, assumes that nature is in some way alive before the animating agency of the artist (perversely) slaughters it in preparation for its baptism. But is it the case that nature just confronts the artist (or anyone) as living? This is a significant question for Shelley, which he addresses in the second paragraph of 'On Life', where he imagines our response were the universe and everything in it to be imagined afresh:

> If any artist (I do not say had executed) but had merely conceived in his mind the system of the sun and stars and planets, they not existing, and had painted to us in words or upon canvas, the spectacle afforded by the nightly cope of Heaven and illustrated it by the wisdom of astronomy, great would be our admiration. Or had he imagined the scenery of this earth, the mountains, the seas and the rivers, and the grass and the flowers and the variety of the forms and masses of the leaves of the woods and the colours which attend the setting and the rising sun, and the hues of the atmosphere, turbid or serene, these things not before existing, truly we should have been astonished and it would have been more than a vain boast to have said of such a man, 'Non merita nome di creatore, sennon Iddio ed il Poeta.' But now these things are looked on with little wonder and to be conscious of them with intense delight is esteemed to be the distinguishing mark of character of a refined and extraordinary person. The multitude of those men care not for them. It is thus with Life – that which includes all. (*SPP*, pp. 505–6)

It is easy enough to be drawn in by the inflationary rhetoric of the passage's depiction of the artist's imaginative power, only for that paean to art to end in bathos. We would, Shelley twice cautions, only be amazed at what the artist imagines were the things that he conceives 'not existing'. But, of course, they do exist: there are stars and planets and leaves and flowers; the sun does rise and set; the colours of the atmosphere do change. It is, therefore, a vain boast after all to declare that the poet deserves the name of creator.

There are reasons, though, to resist this apparently logical deflation. This first paragraph of this playfully written fragment is sceptical of the starkness of the distinction between natural and human processes, at least in so far as such a stark division would ground the conclusion that the world just does already exist, no matter how human beings interact with it. Listing some of the 'transient modifications' of life with which we are struck, Shelley asks:

> What are changes of empires, the wreck of dynasties with the opinions which supported them; what is the birth and the extinction of religions and of political systems to life? What are the revolutions of the globe which we inhabit, and the operations of the elements of which it is composed, compared with life? (*SPP*, p. 505)

Life itself is obscured because we expend all our attention on its epiphenomena, thus ignoring 'the great miracle' itself. Note too that human and cosmic processes are imagined in the same terms, such that there is a slippage between political and cosmic revolution.[15] Whether 'the revolutions of the globe which we inhabit' refers to 'the extinction of religions and political systems' or to 'the operations of the elements of which it is composed' is left tautly undecided, and thus no clear distinction is drawn between the machinations of human affairs and the workings of the cosmos. Both, moreover, are mere distractions when compared to life; neither is more or less transient than the other.

In addition, the existence of the sun and stars and planets which the artist is cast as imagining is not as secure as might at first be assumed. It is worth observing that the regular recurrence of the 'nightly cope', and of the setting and rising sun, means that these things are prone to merely habitual noticing and thus to a loss of wonder in regarding them: the expectation that the sun will rise in the morning after it has set the previous night is, of course, the paradigmatic case of the operation of custom in Hume's account of cause and effect. And, as we saw in Chapter 2, one consequence of customary expectation is, for Shelley, the loss of the wonder that, in elaborating his theory of causality, Hume is implicitly happy to do without. For Hume, loss of wonder is the affordable price to be paid for useful cognition predicated on experientially established cause and effect. Another, more conducive presence behind the paragraph from 'On Life' under discussion is a passage it closely echoes from book II of *De rerum natura*, where, urging despite its disconcerting novelty the acceptance of the proposition that space is infinite in every direction, Lucretius asks his reader, as mental preparation for accepting that proposition, to imagine that

> The vault of heav'n cerulean, spangled thick
> With stars, and with th' effusive lustre chear'd
> Of sun, and moon refulgent—were, at once,
> This scene celestial o'er the race of man
> To burst abrupt—how would the nations start!
> What wonders, then, be trac'd! with what vast toil
> Would e'en the sage the prospect preconceive!
> Yet now, full sated with the scene sublime,
> Man scarce lifts up his listless eyes to heaven.[16]

Though it might seem that Shelley would concur with Hume's sacrifice of wonderment when he declares that '[i]t is well that we are thus shielded by the familiarity of what is at once so certain and so unfathomable from an astonishment which would otherwise absorb and overawe the functions of that which is its object' (*SPP*, p. 505), it is necessary to recall that those functions – the functions of life – are just the 'transient modifications', the 'changes of empire' and so on, that he lists at the beginning of the fragment, and the 'series of what are called impressions, blunted by reiteration'

(*SPP*, p. 508) that he names later. Most significantly, it is not merely that it would be pleasant, according to Shelley, to admire life once in a while, but that the loss of admiration for life through reiterated impression is, in fact, the loss of any real recognition of it at all. Admiration is not a mere additive to apprehension but rather essential to it, for, in Shelley's view, impoverished perception of life is impoverished life. Shelley's belief that 'nothing exists but as it is perceived' is fundamental here, of course, for if nothing exists except as it is perceived, and if life is in the usual course of things concealed behind a 'painted curtain' (*SPP*, p. 506), then life cannot be perceived. In that case, because it is not perceived, life does not exist.

It is perhaps worth stressing the degree to which the thought experiment of the artist imagining the world and everything in it, 'these things not before existing', is a rejection of the kind of pragmatic relegation of wonderment countenanced by Hume – a specific rejection that is at least hinted at in the descriptions of life as 'miraculous', which ostentatiously fly in the face of Hume's strictures on miracles by conceiving of life itself as a 'great miracle'.[17] We saw in Chapter 2 the importance to Hume's argument of the imagined figure of a man 'brought on a sudden into the world' – a figure anticipated, by the way, in Lucretius's imagination of the various features of the cosmos bursting abruptly before the nations, which Hume is perhaps recalling.[18] Hume deploys the figure of the man suddenly faced with everything in the universe in order to show that the idea of cause and effect is only the result of custom acquired through experience. For Hume, anyone 'brought on a sudden into the world' would be wholly at sea, not having at his disposal the customary means to organise his experience and establish for himself any useful knowledge. Shelley in 'On Life', however, considers whether the gain of useful knowledge is not also the loss of wonder. It is to further this consideration that he elaborates the scenario of the cosmically imaginative artist in 'On Life'. Since most people – the 'multitude of those men' – no longer wonder at anything at all, in conceiving of the world and everything in it, the achievement of the artist would be to bring everything suddenly and wonderfully before people once more. In this way, 'Poetry reproduces the universe.'[19] And, contrary to what seems to be Hume's sense that the man unaccustomed to the world would simply be prey to a chaotic welter of impressions that could not be said to cohere into 'experience', Shelley's 'A Defence of Poetry' suggests instead that poetry institutes a new order in place of the mechanical regulation established by habit, in a paragraph again making use of (and this time claiming to justify) the putative saying of Tasso:

> It makes us the inhabitants of a world to which the familiar world is a chaos [...] It creates anew the universe after it has been annihilated in our minds by the recurrence of impressions blunted by reiteration. It justifies that bold and true word of Tasso – *Non merita nome di creatore, se non Iddio ed il Poeta*. (*SPP*, p. 533)

The description of the artist's imagination, then, does not end in the bathos of the realisation that, since what he imagines does already exist, we have no reason actually to be astonished at anything that the artist may imagine. On the contrary, it becomes clear instead that those things have, under the sway of custom, indeed ceased to exist in an emphatic sense. Shelley develops Lucretius's request that we consider what it would be like to be confronted for the first time with the universe by inserting the artist in this scenario: it is the artist who throws before mortals everything in the world. While initially Shelley simply wants to envisage the artist conceiving of the universe in his mind, without executing it, he does go on to ask us to imagine that, subsequent to this conception, the artist 'had painted to us in words or upon canvas, the spectacle afforded by the nightly cope of Heaven'. It is not, it turns out, that *no* execution of the artist's conception takes place, and, moreover, the artistic execution in words or on canvas that does indeed take place would in a sense significant to Shelley be the execution of things that had ceased to exist before the artist's intervention. The great admiration and astonishment that Shelley describes is the admiration and astonishment we feel for art but which is habitually lacking in our feelings toward '[l]ife, and the world'. Furthermore, the extraordinary artifice of the passage itself – especially in its relatively expansive description of *what* the artist imagines, in addition simply to telling us *that* he or she imagines, and thus its adoption of the role of the artist that it evokes – itself seeks to elicit this admiration. In collapsing, that is, the distinction between the artist imagining and a *description* of the artist imagining – the distinction, put another way, between art and aesthetics – the passage thus attempts to perform the reintegration of delight and knowledge that the essay claims is essential to apprehension and thence to existence as such.

Forms more real

The account of the artist given and, crucially, performed in 'On Life' is thus poised between censuring Tasso's 'vain boast' that only God and the poet deserve the name of creator and proclaiming it. 'A Defence of Poetry' captures well the characteristic role of the poet when it states that he does not create a new universe but rather renovates one that has gone dead: '[i]t creates anew the universe after it has been annihilated in our minds by the recurrence of impressions blunted by reiteration' (*SPP*, p. 533). There is a subtle difference between creating the universe 'anew' and creating a new universe, on which Shelley's sense of the artist's role relies. The ageing of the universe is a consequence of the deadening of experience through the repetition of impressions.

The most important figure in Shelley's poetry who suffers under 'the curse which binds us to be subjected to the accident of surrounding impressions' (*SPP*, p. 533) is, of course, Prometheus. Poetry, Shelley declares in 'A Defence of Poetry', is capable of defeating that curse, and, in Act I of *Prometheus Unbound*, the Earth hopes that that declaration is true. Taking pity on her son's state, the Earth sends 'those subtle and fair spirits / Whose homes are the dim caves of human thought' to 'speak comfort' to him (*Poems* II, pp. 516–17; Act I, ll. 658–9, 663). The spirits are cave-dwellers – the 'caves', here, 'of human thought' – but that is not the only place where they are at home, for they also 'inhabit, as birds wing the wind, / Its world-surrounding ether' (ll. 660–1). There is something odd about this combination of dwellings. The image of the cave is one of seclusion and confinement, whereas 'world-surrounding ether' is, instead, encompassing and expansive. Being at home in a cave is quite different from the kind of peripatetic inhabitation of the ether, in accordance with which the spirits are compared to 'birds [that] wing the wind', a simile that in turn carries a faint but nonetheless significant suggestion that the birds not only inhabit the wind but that they moreover have some kind of effect on it. Above all, the two habitations of the spirits are actually connected: the world-surrounding ether and the caves are both metaphors for human thought. Human thought is both dark and recessive *and* expansively all-encompassing; the innermost recesses of human thought, therefore, are not ultimately confined – however dim in its furthest reaches, a cave, after all, must have an opening, no matter how minuscule.

The spirits, then, inhabit human thought, as it were, continuously, both in its darkest and its most ethereal reaches. But it is not just that they dwell in human thought wherever it is; they are also in some sense the products of it. The first, subtly punning hint of this is Ione's remark to Panthea as the spirits emerge that 'more come / Like fountain-vapours when the winds are dumb, / That climb up the ravine in scattered lines' (ll. 666–8). That the spirits are observed in 'scattered lines' should already alert us to the fact that they are at least comparable to poems, but this impression is strengthened when we realise, first, that they are 'scattered' like the ashes and sparks of 'Ode to the West Wind' (published, of course, in the same volume as *Prometheus Unbound*) and their relation to human thought is more generally suggested as well, perhaps, by the fact that they seek to master a ravine like that which is the focus of human thought's relation to nature in 'Mont Blanc'. The spirits, therefore, are not mere dramatis personae (however idealised) but instead mount the ravine like the 'human mind's imaginings' in 'Mont Blanc' and are distributed like the poet's 'words among mankind' in the great ode. The spirits, that is, are themselves poems.

The poetic nature of the spirits is likewise ingeniously developed throughout their appearance in Act I of the lyrical drama. Ione, for example, exclaims, 'And hark! is it the music of the pines? / Is it the lake? is it the waterfall?', to which Panthea responds, ''Tis something sadder, sweeter far than all' (ll. 669–71). 'Our sweetest songs are those that tell of saddest thought', declares 'To a Sky-Lark' (*Poems* III, p. 476; l. 90), and 'Julian and Maddalo' is similarly insistent on the origin of poetry in suffering. Panthea's response to her sister – that the sound Ione hears is 'sweeter far *than all*' – suggests moreover that the sounds associated with the spirits surpass natural sounds, especially since she is effectively correcting Ione's guesses that the sounds are of pines, or the lake, or the waterfall.

But, ultimately, thought is not as free from material sustenance as this might be taken to suggest. In order to bring this fully into view, we need to turn now to the famous song of the Fourth Spirit, which seems at once to disavow the poet's relation to nature and to insist upon it:

On a Poet's lips I slept
Dreaming like a love-adept
In the sound his breathing kept;
Nor seeks nor finds he mortal blisses,
But feeds on the aërial kisses
Of shapes that haunt thought's wildernesses.
He will watch from dawn to gloom
The lake-reflected sun illume
The yellow bees i' the ivy-bloom,
Nor heed nor see what things they be;
But from these create he can
Forms more real than living man,
Nurslings of immortality!—
One of these awakened me,
And I sped to succour thee.

(*Poems* III, pp. 520–21; Act I ll. 737–51)

Central to this song seems to be an avowal of the Poet's superiority to mere mortality. For instance, the Longman editors append to the lines setting forth the Poet's capacity to make 'Forms more real than living man' a comparison to Byron's 'The Dream' (1816): 'The mind can make / Substance, and people planets of its own / With beings brighter than have been, and give / A breath to forms which can outlive all flesh' (quoted in *Poems* II, p. 521). Byron's echo of Satan's boast that 'The mind is its own place, and in itself / Can make a Heav'n of Hell, a Hell of Heav'n' becomes in 'A Defence of Poetry' explicit quotation (*SPP*, p. 533).[20] Indeed, Shelley himself once counselled the listless Byron as follows:

> You say that you feel indifferent to the stimuli of life. But this is a good rather than an evil augury. Long after the *man* is dead, the immortal spirit may survive, and speak like one belonging to a higher world. But I shall talk bombast, when I mean only to tell a plain truth in plain words. (16 July 1821, *Letters* II, p. 309)

On one level, the Fourth Spirit's song is evidence of this tendency to view poets as supra-mortal, casting the Poet as bluntly dismissive of the offerings of mundane existence: 'Nor seeks nor finds he mortal blisses.' This dismissal of the earthly is held to be the basis of his poetic ability, as the central lines narrating the poet's observation of the bees and his subsequent creation of 'Forms more real than living man' 'from these' suggest. This kind of attitude to nature was, of course, central to Harold Bloom's reading, in *Shelley's Mythmaking*, of Shelley's opposition to what might be called, after Blake, vegetative nature. In a characteristically stirring rebuttal of (in 1959) still tenacious New Critical strictures on Shelley's alleged otherworldliness, Bloom commented that the Fourth Spirit presents a Poet loftily regardless of the bees – he neither heeds nor sees them, despite watching them all day long – and thus of nature as such. The Fourth Spirit, that is, presents a Poet 'who on principle will not keep his eye on the object, who denies objects of experience, who despises commonplace, ordinary, *natural* perception'.[21]

Stirring as this is, any mention of *Shelley's Mythmaking* is nowadays accompanied, at the very least, by the introduction of a handful of caveats – and this mention is no exception.[22] First, Bloom takes it for granted that it is the Poet, rather than the bees themselves, who neither heeds nor sees what the bees are. This assumption is partly owing to the fact that Bloom's reading is based on a now superseded text that seems especially to reinforce such a reading; in any case, if the Poet neither heeds nor sees the bees, why is he said to watch them as obsessively as he does? Why, that is, does he bother? Sharon Ruston's answer to this question results in a position the reverse of Bloom's. It is not at all that the Poet rejects natural perception; indeed, 'The yellow bees i' the ivy-bloom' are already, for Ruston, '[t]he scientific phenomena which occup[y] the poet's attention.'[23] But this does not seem to get the song quite right either, viewing it as a description of the Poet as naturalist and his poem as a write-up of observations. Moreover, what makes a phenomenon 'scientific', in this as in any case, requires fuller explanation than is given here.

We can gain some insight into how the Poet spends his days, and, in turn, how what he observes and does not quite observe, affects his poems if we return both to what the song of the Fourth Spirit actually says and, also, to how it sounds. First, the Poet does not exactly watch the bees themselves: 'He will watch from dawn to gloom / The lake-reflected sun illume / The yellow bees i' the ivy-bloom.' What he is watching is the illuming of the bees, not by the sun but by the sun's reflection in the water. As often in Shelley's work, the precise coordinates of perception are difficult to fix here, not because he struggles to pay attention to any one thing at once but because he wishes to give as precise as possible a sense of the various ways in which attention must be directed. So, for instance, the yellowness of the bees may here owe as much to the fact that they are bathed in the yellow light of the sun (and 'bathed' is the term hovering behind this description, given not only that things might very well be bathed in sunlight but, moreover, that the sunlight is first reflected in the lake, an element yet more literally conducive to bathing), as to the fact that they are themselves already yellow.

That would seem to mean, then, that the Poet need not be viewed as having taken any special notice of the bees at all, preferring instead to focus on the sun's illuming of them. Bloom would appear to be half right after all, not least because on this account the bees are already the passive recipients of the sun's illumination, just as out of them the Poet will create something yet higher. But if we attend to the poem – rather than visualise what it describes, or construct out of it some sort of thesis – and particularly attend to the operation of its sounds, something quite different emerges. The fact that the yellowness of the bees is at once borrowed from the light of the sun, which is itself reflected, and is their own colouring performs an intricate pattern of sharing on the song's thematic level, in which a thing's defining characteristics are at once also shared with or borrowed from something else, and this is a pattern echoed (which is, again, telling) in the operation of the poem's rhymes and assonances. The bees, even if they are not seen, are there, it would seem, in the poem after all, persistently making themselves heard in the sonic modulations of the following three lines: 'The yellow *bees* i' the ivy-bloom / Nor *heed* nor *see* what things they *be*; / But from *these* create he can.'[24] After the bees are named in the first line here, the second line is replete with echoes of their name before ending on the homonym 'be'. This terminal word is given extra emphasis both by heavy end-stopping and, especially, by the fact that it breaks from the preceding triplet only to find its echo in the song's concluding lines after an intervening triplet.[25] In the first of those three intervening lines, 'But from these create he can', the rhyme of 'these' with the earlier 'bees' might seem already to enact the transmutation that the spirit describes, yet it also suggests that that transmutation is as much a capacity of the sonic material of 'bees' as it is of the Poet's intellect to reconfigure nature into something altogether 'more real'.

The persistence in difference of 'bees' across these lines profoundly qualifies Bloom's suggestion that the Poet simply floats clear of (or, out of principle, turns his back on) the scene he surveys. But neither does it confirm Ruston's sense that the poem is significantly analogous with (or the result of) scientific investigation and its articulation. Specifically, the Spirit's declaration of the Poet's mere supersession of mortal things (such as bees) is qualified by the fact that the song is in a significant sense reliant on the modulation of the sonic material of 'bees'. This argument is not dependent on the assumption that the modulations of the song's 'bees' are onomatopoeic, although it does insist that the apparently exclusively intellectual contrivance of poetry relies on the symphonic articulation of mere syllables. The song is no song, at least in the central lines, without the music of 'bees'.[26] In fact, a comparable articulation and transmutation of the elements of the word 'Poet's' occurs in the rhyme words of the first three lines, 'slept', 'adept' and 'kept' – a transmutation, furthermore, already anticipated in the first line itself, 'On a poet's lips I slept', where the *p*, *t* and *s* of 'poet's' 'appear to play hide-and-seek before meeting again, repeated three times, in the rhyme'.[27] It is notable that this kind of instrumentation is effected on the words 'Poet's' and 'bees', since the relation of the Poet to the bees is crucial to the song's imagination of the mortality or immortality of the former's creations, juxtaposed with the ambivalently regarded (if not disregarded) bees. On the one hand, the word that names the Poet himself is subject to the same kind of alteration and transmutation as that to which the bees are subject; on the other hand, it is the mere material of both 'bees' and 'Poet' that make the music of the song.

It is the case, then, neither that the Poet is wholly oblivious to natural phenomena, however much he might sometimes wish to be, nor that his verse is simply a report of observations of phenomena that are always already 'scientific'. We will return to the contortions of what might provisionally be called source material when, in the concluding chapter, I examine the role of Lord Bacon in 'The Triumph of Life'. But I wish in the meantime to continue to focus on the way that the song of the Fourth Spirit tarries, so to speak, with mortality, explicit protestations notwithstanding. Indeed, the spirits in general are deeply interested in mortal welfare, as we learned when they introduced themselves in concert slightly earlier: 'From unremembered ages we / Gentle guides and guardians be / Of Heaven-oppressed mortality' (*Poems* III, pp. 517–18; ll. 672–4). Moreover, immortality is not an automatic benefit in *Prometheus Unbound*, just as it is not elsewhere in shelley's work. This is obvious here, of course, because the Spirits are not called upon in this instance to minister to 'Heaven-oppressed mortality' but instead to Heaven-oppressed immortality in the shape of Prometheus, whose suffering is exacerbated by its unending duration predicated upon his undying nature.

In contrast, despite disregard for 'mortal blisses' on the part of the Poet in the Fourth Spirit's song, the Poet is himself noticeably mortal. Before coming to the aid of Prometheus, the Spirit had been asleep on the Poet's lips and had dreamt 'In the sound his breathing kept'. Breathing is perhaps the archetypal sign not of any life, but of mortal life; at once the most physically intimate condition of living, it at the same time depends utterly on a surrounding and ever expanding atmosphere shared with others. The Poet's works are 'Nurslings of Immortality', a phrase which already suggests not that they are timeless, but that they are young, prone to grow and change. But moreover, these nurslings are identifiable with the sound that the Poet's own breathing kept, a sound that is then kept in turn – and therefore not 'kept' in any possessive sense – by recipients of the poem. This kind of interaction already obtained between the Poet and the enamoured Fourth Spirit, for the Spirit slept 'in' the sound of the Poet's breathing, so that the Spirit did not just notice the sound as an external datum presented to sense, but, on the contrary, was surrounded by it, in the way that the air surrounds the Poet before being taken in (and let out again) by his breathing. (The striking similarity, incidentally, of the depiction of breathing here to the conception of poetic tradition, 'which at once connects, animates and sustains the life of all', in 'A Defence of Poetry' [*SPP*, p. 522] is instructive.) The Poet's breathing thus sustains his own life and at the same time becomes the medium in which the Spirit subsists prior to waking. The pattern thus kept by the Poet's breathing is his poetry, dependent on and shaped by the mortal rhythms of his body.

Poetry's radical hybridity

The interanimation of poem and reader that I have just been discussing will be a central concern of Chapter 6. As it is imagined and enacted in the Fourth Spirit's song in Act I of *Prometheus Unbound*, this interanimation both grounds the claim of poetry to immortality in mortal, breathing bodies and, significantly, radically qualifies the poet's claim to an animating agency with regard to putatively dead matter. I want now to turn to this question of agency more fully by examining the dissolution of speech, and hence of its speakers, in Shelley's verse. Indeed, the dissolving power of speech and, particularly, singing is a central fascination of Shelley's poetry from, at least, 'To Constantia'. The transitions from the final line of that poem's first stanza, 'I am dissolved in these consuming extacies', to the first of its second, 'I have no life, Constantia, but in thee', show that dissolution does not involve consumption as annihilation, but rather the transmutation of one substance into another.[28] This is announced, of course, in the shift from the suggestion that the effect of Constantia's voice on its hearer is, to put it bluntly, lethal, to the admission that the hearer does have a life, albeit 'in' the singer.

Much more could be said about 'To Constantia', especially the significance of its sound patterning, but I want to focus here instead on the exchanges between Ione and Panthea in *Prometheus Unbound*. In an insightful essay that concludes with a meticulously sensitive reading of Panthea's speech near the beginning of Act II of *Prometheus Unbound* (*Poems* II, pp. 530–2; Act II, scene 2, ll. 56–108), John Wilkinson has argued that 'through following a poem (not just any poem), a reader can become involved in the evocation and enactment of a radical hybridity, pulling together ways of thinking about the world modernity has categorically but falsely separated'.[29] Wilkinson develops his sense of 'radical hybridity' to show how, in Shelley's work, 'the physical emerges through breaks and pulses and continuous circulation'.[30] The commonality of breathing fundamental to the song of the Fourth Spirit becomes – especially throughout the final act of *Prometheus Unbound* a strong emphasis on dissolution. This emphasis is neither nihilistic, nor symptomatic of the haziness with which Leavis charged Shelley, but rather a radical realisation of the interdependency of different lives on one another. Dissolution involves the transformation and preservation of one substance into and in another substance, to which it, as much as anything else, contributes. Various dissolutions are performed, for instance, in the following exchange between Panthea and, this time, Ione near the beginning of Act IV:

Ione

Listen too,
How every pause is filled with under-notes,
Clear, silver, icy, keen, awakening tones,
Which pierce the sense, and live within the soul,
As the sharp stars pierce winter's chrystal air
And gaze upon themselves within the sea.

Panthea

But see where, through two openings in the forest
Which hanging branches overcanopy,
And where two runnels of a rivulet,
Between the close moss, violet-inwoven,
Have made their path of melody — like sisters
Who part with sighs that they may meet in smiles,
Turning their dear disunion to an isle
Of lovely grief, a wood of sweet sad thoughts —
Two visions of strange radiance float upon
The ocean-like inchantment of strong sound
Which flows intenser, keener, deeper yet
Under the ground and through the windless air.
(*Poems* II, p. 623; Act IV, ll. 188–205)

Earlier, one of the furies had tormented Prometheus with the threat that they 'will dwell / Beside [the soul which burns within]' (*Poems* I, p. 506; Act I, 485–6); here, rather than withdrawing the invasiveness of this threat, it is suggested that the 'under-notes' and 'awakening tones' live yet more intimately 'within the soul'. In fact, this exchange is redolent of earlier episodes of the poem. The augmentation of Ione's 'keen', for instance, in Panthea's 'keener' reprises the development of 'keen' noted by Wilkinson in Panthea's earlier speech at the beginning of Act II. The effect of the repetition of 'keen' here is again to 'solicit a return', from the conclusion of Panthea's speech to the beginning of Ione's. Where Ione's 'keen' was a step in the progressive adjectival clarification of '*under*-notes' into 'awakening tones', the 'inchantment of strong sound' at the end of Panthea's speech returns, by way of 'keener' (again the penultimate term in an adjectival chain), '*Under* the ground'. From the beginning of Ione's speech to the end of Panthea's, the perspective has been raised from and returned to what lies underneath, while the different senses of sight and sound have, it seems, been variously prioritised.

Thus, in the above exchange between Ione and Panthea, the enchanting effect of language is not tantamount to the exertion of control over its hearer. Rather, to borrow Laura Wells Betz's account of an earlier passage in the poem, a model of enchantment-as-control is here 'countered by a model of spell-casting in which one singer's transfixing language produces not the silence or paralysis of the listener, but instead that person's song in response'.[31] And thus, moreover, the borders between self and world, in the exchange between Ione and Panthea, are fluid, as are the borders between Ione and Panthea themselves, and those between the otherwise disarticulated bodily senses. In particular, it might seem that Ione and Panthea emphasise different senses: Ione wishes Panthea to listen; Panthea wishes Ione to see. Ione's instruction, 'Listen too', is especially emphatic. This is not only owing to the fact that Panthea has already been describing a sonic phenomenon – 'the deep music of the rolling world' – but much rather because the instruction, 'Listen too', makes the ear listen out, so to speak, for what comes after the turn of the line, not least because the instruction 'Listen too', may well be heard as 'Listen to'. The pause of the comma and line ending is precisely filled with an 'under-note', which is the result both of anticipation and retrospective recognition.

The aural equivocation on 'Listen too', plays on the border between a general instruction – 'listen as well as look' – and a specific direction – 'listen to that'. This is a play, as it were, within one particular sensory operation (listening), but the divisions between the different senses themselves are also dissolved in and across these speeches. Not only does Panthea's attention quickly shift from the *sight* of the 'two runnels of a rivulet' to the 'Ocean-like inchantment of strong *sound*' coming from the now invisible because underground stream, but also her imperative 'But see' echoes the conclusion of Ione's speech in 'the sea'. Her instruction preserves and adapts her sister's speech through sound. The words that we see – such as 'sea' – have an undertone that dissolves the distinction between different speakers and, indeed, that between sight and sound.

This blending of senses, selves and world entails an opening up, as it were, of artistic agency to the materials on which, and different agents on whom, it would act. But, contrary to what a critical outlook prioritising a strong grasp on whatever lies within the poet's immediate purview would contend, such blending is not the sign of a weak sensibility. Shelley makes this clear in the following passage of 'On Life':

> Let us recollect our sensations as children. What a distinct and intense apprehension had we of the world and of ourselves. Many of the circumstances of social life were then important to us, which are now no longer so. But that is not the point of comparison on which I mean to insist. We less habitually distinguished all that we saw and felt from ourselves. They seemed as it were to constitute one mass. There are some persons who in this respect are always

> children. Those who are subject to the state called reverie feel as if their nature were dissolved into the surrounding universe, or as if the surrounding universe were absorbed into their being. They are conscious of no distinction. And these are states which precede or accompany or follow an unusually intense and vivid apprehension of life. As men grow up, this power commonly decays, and they become mechanical and habitual agents. Their feelings and reasonings are the combined result of a multitude of entangled thoughts, of a series of what are called impressions, blunted by reiteration. (*SPP*, p. 507)

Godwin, in *Political Justice*, had considered reverie to be a 'state of mind' in which 'there is nothing that perceptibly links [thoughts] together, where they totally elude the memory and instantly vanish'. Conceding that 'thoughts of reverie [...] perpetually take their turn with our more express and digested thoughts, even in the most active scenes of our life', he nevertheless casts as the epitome of, in Shelley's phrase, '[t]hose who are subject to the state called reverie', '[t]he indolent man [who] reclines for hours in the shade'.[32] It is important to recognise how different from Godwin's understanding of reverie Shelley's is. Whereas for Godwin, the 'indolent man' is awoken from reverie by intense sensation, such as 'acute pain, or uneasy expectation',[33] Shelley thinks that reverie instead characteristically precedes, accompanies, or follows 'an unusually intense and vivid apprehension of life'. And, although the declaration that those subject to the state of reverie 'are conscious of no distinction' might suggest that this state is not, in fact, particularly distinct, the state of indistinctness between self and world is described here as in fact being, on the contrary, distinctly and intensely felt. The state is distinct not only because it is unmistakable but also because its unusual occurrence contrasts with the common decay of the capacity for it. There is a radical distinction at work here between two types of indistinctness: the 'distinct and intense' feeling of indistinctness between self and world, on the one hand, and the simply indistinct mesh of entangled and reiterated thoughts and impressions on the other.[34] Likewise, just as the experience of indistinctness between self and world is not seen to suggest any diminution in strength of feeling (quite the opposite), so it does not lead to the indigence of the self more generally in relation to the world. Again, it is the habituated and mechanised self, which 'habitually distinguishe[s]' itself from the world, that is in fact lacking. Reverie – contrary to Godwin's conventional understanding of that term, and in accord with Rousseau's radically revisionary view of it – is, as Edward Duffy has claimed, for Shelley 'a way of knowing, untouched by either the neglect or the ridicule of the enlightened'.[35] Dissolution into the surrounding universe is perhaps surprisingly described as a 'power', and though the decay of this power is concomitant with the bestowal of agency '[a]s men grow up', that agency is scarcely worth the name because, far from denoting the exercise of potential, it is rather 'mechanical and habitual'. Dissolution of self into world or absorption of world into self, and not the demarcation of boundaries around a bastion of distinct selfhood, is the condition of the powers of the self. Wilkinson recognises this fundamental insight of Shelley's theory and, crucially, practice, when he remarks of *Prometheus Unbound* that what the sonic dissolutions of that poem enable is 'the simultaneous connection and disconnection which makes loving and thinking possible (among other things)'.[36] That '(among other things)', for all its parenthetical discretion, has a double meaning. On the one hand, Shelley's verse enables loving and thinking along with comparable activities equally taken for granted, but, moreover, the fecundating transformations of linguistic thingliness in his verse enables loving and thinking in a context that includes others alongside the agent of those activities. And that agent must realise that it too is as thingly as the things in the company of which it finds itself.

The lives of trees

I hope it is clear by now that although Shelley's work does often evince a tendency toward the rejection of mortality in favour of the immortal productions of poetry, his poetic practice and theory primarily emphasises the mortal, material life of poetry. I will conclude this book by returning to the mortal life of poetry by showing how it is related to what I want to call the interanimation of poem and reading in an account of a central section of 'The Triumph of Life'. Here, however, I wish further to develop the role of the interconnection between, broadly speaking, nature and art in Shelley's conception of poetic artifice and in his poetic practice itself.

The various settings in which Shelley composed his poetry were often cause for reflection by Shelley himself. Here, for instance, is the well-known description of where he wrote (most of) *Prometheus Unbound*:

> This Poem was chiefly written upon the mountainous ruins of the Baths of Caracalla, among the flowery glades, and thickets of odoriferous blossoming trees which are extended in ever winding labyrinths upon its immense platforms and dizzy arches suspended in the air. The bright blue sky of Rome, and the effect of the vigorous awakening of spring in that divinest climate, and the new life with which it drenches the spirits even to intoxication, were the inspiration of this drama. (*Poems* II, p. 473)

The rich profusion of images might be taken to suggest that inspiration is pictured, according to convention, metaphorically here. But then the line between the literal and metaphorical is especially blurred in the passage. On the one hand, this is just a description of a particular season ('spring') and the 'climate' of a particular place at that season; on the other hand, that season is concomitant with a 'vigorous awakening' and that climate is 'divinest'. Neither mere record of time and place of composition, nor idealisation of landscape without reference to real conditions, therefore, this account reanimates the dead metaphor of 'inspiration' and, thereby, subtly hints at the materiality of poetic composition. Like the odours of the blossoming trees, poetry's patterning of breath makes the otherwise simply assumed presence of air distinctly noticeable, thus restoring to admiration something to which we are deadened through mechanical repetition even though our lives depend on it.

Human artifice, then, can never merely float free of its material bases. But more than simply propounding a reductive materialism of art, Shelley's materialism instead evinces a complementary commitment to the artistically generative capacities of those things not traceable to human artifice. In relating how the poem was written among 'thickets of odoriferous blossoming trees which are extended in ever winding labyrinths upon its immense platforms and dizzy arches suspended in the air', furthermore, Shelley suspends the distinction between the relics of human civilisation and the prolific natural growth that has overtaken them. Indeed, the glades and thickets are shaped in such a way that it is no longer possible fully to distinguish between what is ruin and what is natural growth.[37] Thus, the blossoming trees form 'labyrinths' – Shelley is drawing, of course, on a myth of unfathomably intricate architectural artifice – and the syntax suggests that the 'dizzy arches suspended in the air' could be either the shapes made by the overgrowing trees, or the remains of the ruined building, or a combination of the two impossible now to disarticulate. The point to emphasise here is that it is just at the moment that he is describing the setting in which he contrived the poem that Shelley suspends in the air, so to speak, the distinction between culture and nature.

Of course, it is also the case that Shelley sometimes views the relation between culture and nature as oppositional, however much they may somehow be reconciled in the end. In order to investigate this aspect of Shelley's work, I want to turn now to his late lyric, 'With a Guitar. To Jane'. Summarising this poem, Judith Chernaik remarked that '[t]he natural world is conceived in terms of its sounds – many-voiced fountains, echoes, pattering rain; these merge naturally into the sounds of the guitar, which both echoes and interprets natural sound'.[38] Chernaik's statement that the guitar 'echoes *and interprets* natural sound' already intimates that the relation between guitar and tree may be other than the relationship of natural merging that she takes to be at work between the sounds of nature and the guitar. In a sensitive account, Jonathan Bate instead reads this poem as an acute problematisation of art's relation to the nature it lives off. On the one hand, Shelley's estimation that once the felled tree is hewn into the shape of the guitar, it lives 'in happier form again' is viewed as motivated by his Neoplatonism, Shelley's implication being 'that in its guitar-form the tree transcends its original particular Apennine hillside' in order to offer 'the idea or intellectual form of nature'.[39] However, the guitar is, Bate notes, described as a 'slave' and as an 'idol' 'wrought' from wood.[40] The attempted idealisation of nature, therefore, is betrayed at the outset by the violent working of recalcitrant material on which it depends – a violent working, moreover, that only succeeds in producing an unwilling vassal to the artist's will which is, at the same time, an impious affront to the sacredness of nature.[41] No matter how much we appreciate the guitar's music, its birth is violently destructive of nature.

'With a Guitar. To Jane' does seem to view art and nature in starkly oppositional terms. In particular, the idea that the mere dead wood of the guitar might actually be alive, or at least be capable of life, is initially treated with what seems to approach puritan scepticism. The guitar is 'this idol' (l. 43). Carved from material, the guitar has no life of its own. But although the guitar is designated an 'idol', and thus something which only has life imputed to it, the poem does not clearly maintain that such imputation is necessarily false. The possibility that the conferral of life upon the guitar, despite its deadness, might be legitimate is connected to the insistence from the beginning of the poem that Jane teach it. She is instructed, that is, to 'teach it all the harmony, / In which thou can'st, and only thou, / Make the delighted spirit glow' (ll. 4–6). The 'delighted spirit' is most prominently, at this stage, the spirit of the listener delighted by the harmony that Jane teaches the guitar. However, given that the guitar is also the beneficiary of this instruction, this 'delighted spirit' might also be that of the instrument itself. Even so, during the poem's early lines, were the guitar to have a spirit, it is one that still requires to be taught; knowledge, at least, must still be imputed to it. The guitar's spirit – even if it has one – is still empty in comparison to the thinking spirit that must teach it. A few lines later, the poem's speaker, Ariel, describes the guitar as 'this silent token', invoking the senses of 'token' as gift and, especially because this is a *silent* token, as cipher. That the guitar is a cipher, the in-itself-empty bearer of meaning imposed upon it from outside, confirms it, all suggestions to the contrary, as an idol.

Despite this conclusion with regard to the understanding of the guitar-as-idol in the opening lines of the poem, it has begun at least to emerge that while life may only be imputed to idols, this imputation is not, for Shelley, necessarily or wholly or always false. In another poem to Jane Williams, he again appears to allow that she might succeed in enlivening the guitar in some way. In the lyric first known as 'An Ariette for Music', and now simply entitled 'To Jane', the poet declares: 'So your voice most tender / To the strings without soul had then given / Its own' (*SPP*, p. 479; ll. 10–12). This account of Jane's enlivening of the strings already harbours the suggestion that they might be ensouled. Shelley exploits the ambivalence of 'its own' here: the soul is that of Jane's voice, of course, but it is possible to read these lines as suggesting that, in being given the soul of Jane's own voice, the strings are now accorded a soul of their own. As G. Rostrevor Hamilton put it some years ago in an impressively attentive discussion of Shelley's use of the word 'own', '[i]n a world of interchange nothing is exclusive or merely receptive, waiting upon a force from without'.[42] The strings may very well receive their soul from Jane's voice, but they do not *merely* receive it, as they would were they utterly soulless to begin with.

This sense that the life of the guitar is not simply bestowed upon it by the player who plays it, emerges more strongly during the course of 'With a Guitar. To Jane'. To begin with, of course, the guitar is already itself a work of art, rather than merely the instrument by which a work of art is to be made, since it is, after all, the product of the skill of an 'artist'. Though emphasising the guitar's fabrication may seem merely to refocus attention from the skill of the player onto the skill of the maker, it nevertheless slightly complicates our attempt to grasp where art supersedes, or emerges from nature (and the difference between art's supersession of or emergence from nature is precisely what is at issue here). Furthermore, the fact that the artist's purpose in making this idol was 'To echo all harmonious thought' (l. 44) more profoundly qualifies the guitar's position as the passive object of the imputation of life and thought. The reason the guitar was made in the first place is given again, slightly further on, in lines whose internal rhyme 'wrought' and 'taught' chimes with the earlier terminal rhyme 'wrought' and 'thought': 'The artist wrought this loved guitar, / And taught it justly to reply / To all who question skilfully / In language gentle as thine own' (ll. 58–61). The exhortation to Jane to teach the guitar harmony, with which the poem opens, is more fully explained – and, again, further qualified – here. At the beginning of the poem, the guitar is firmly under Jane's tutelage. It is, as Bate comments, a 'slave of music', and, given that Jane is to teach it harmony, she shares in music's mastery over the guitar. But we should be careful, even at the beginning of the poem, not to assume that slaves are spiritless or that they lack knowledge.[43] Ariel, Shelley's persona in this poem, is both a spirit and a slave. Moreover, the poem's concern with the association between previous life and knowledge evokes the Platonic doctrine of the pre-existence of the soul and, perhaps in particular, the *Meno*, in which Socrates experiments on a slave in order to show that knowledge is recollection.[44] The guitar is not simply the receptacle, then, of what it is taught. On the contrary, the artist that wrought it meant it 'to echo all harmonious thought' (l. 44), both in the sense that it responds to the thought of she who will play it, and also in the sense that it echoes the sounds that it has witnessed as a tree on the Apennine hillside. It can do this because in its life as a tree, the guitar had already learnt 'all harmonies' from those of the plains and skies to the airs of evening, and, furthermore, 'it knew / That seldom heard mysterious sound' (l. 75) which the world 'enkindles' as it 'floats through boundless day' (ll. 77–8). This knowledge is extraordinary in two specific ways. First, in knowing the sound that the world 'enkindles', the tree knows of something infinite. The world's course through the universe might initially seem to be subject to the kind of onward propulsion associated throughout Shelley's writing with the barrenness of 'living on': the world is 'driven on its diurnal round'. This 'diurnal round' is not, though, the world's onward march, but is instead a cyclical journey and thus, although floating 'through boundless day', the world is not merely adrift. Given that this journey is infinite, the music that it enkindles is also infinite. Second, this knowledge of the infinite is moreover extraordinary because the 'mysterious sound' is 'seldom heard' owing not to its rare occurrence but to the small number of those capable of hearing it. Significantly, this knowledge – the tree's knowledge – is capable of being reanimated in the guitar into which the tree was made. Should adequate questioning prompt the guitar to respond and to tell its knowledge, the result is not merely the impartation of information but the re-enactment or reliving of that knowledge. The tree was wrought so as 'To live in happier form again' (l. 56).

As discussed above, this line is pivotal for Bate, who sees it as implying the transmutation of the limited, particular, natural tree into a universal and intellectual work of art. It is in that way that the tree lives 'in happier form'. But why, then, is it said 'To live in happier form *again*'? Bate views the repetition implied here as redundant, an excessive and thereby destructive reduplication of what, frankly, would have been better left alone, for '[a]rt is an attempt to recover the very thing which has been destroyed so that art can be made'.[45] Such a reading, however, cannot fully account for why the guitar is a 'happier form': is it because it is happier than the timber from which it is made because it manages to recover something of its life as a tree, or is it happier than the tree was in the first place?

These alternatives, I suggest, are left acutely suspended. Reanimation is imagined not just as perpetuation of suspended life but as restoration and transformation at once. The supposition that what the poem is unembarrassed to cast as the tree's experiences are just the projected imaginings of the guitar's owner or player is explicitly refused, for the guitar will withhold or share them according to its questioner's skill:

> All this it knows, but will not tell
> To those who cannot question well
> The spirit that inhabits it:
> It talks according to the wit
> Of its companions, and no more
> Is heard than has been felt before
> By those who tempt it to betray
> These secrets of an elder day.—
> (*SPP*, pp. 478–9; ll. 79–86)

The secrets of 'an elder day' are the secrets that it learnt, as we have seen, as a tree 'On the wind-swept Apennine' (l. 48). What is required of the guitar's player is not for her to invest it with spirit but rather for her to coax out of it something lodged within it. And it is in the material of the guitar that its learning abides. We may, then, read Chernaik's statement that the sounds of nature 'merge naturally into the sounds of the guitar' quite literally. The sounds of the guitar do not somehow merely represent, or, worse, assist in the consolatory representation of, the sounds of nature, but rather the sounding of its wooden body is the sounding of a natural material. Moreover, it is notable that Shelley concludes his enumeration of the 'harmonies / Of the plains and of the skies' (ll. 65–6) by drawing attention to the sounds of processes that are directly necessary to the life of the tree: 'pattering rain and breathing dew / And airs of evening' (ll. 73–4). Without these, there would be no guitar.

This insistence on the intertwinement of the guitar's sounds with the sounds of sustaining nature is echoed, fittingly, in the sounding of the poem that accompanies the gift of the guitar to its intended player. The play of coaxing out something lodged within is performed in two lines that announce the entwinement of spirit and guitar both in (to borrow from Chernaik again) explicit interpretation and the echo of verbal material: 'The spirit that inhabits it: / It talks according to the wit'. The monosyllable 'it', which refers to the guitar (at whose centre, incidentally, it is lodged: gu*it*ar), is common to 'spir*it*' and 'inhab*its*'. At a number of places in the early books of *De rerum natura*, Lucretius illustrates his contention that the same 'fixt elementals' (*elementa*) may combine in different ways to constitute different things by drawing an analogy with his own verse:

> Thus, though the lines, these doctrines that recite,
> Flow from the same fixt elemental types,
> Yet line from line, in sense, in sound compar'd,
> Egregious differs. Re-arranged alone,
> Such the vast power by graphic types possest![46]

Good's translation deftly draws out the point of Lucretius's comparison between the letters that make up the words of his poem and the elements that make up all things by playing on 'elemental' and 'graphic' 'types'. Lucretius's play on the similarity and difference between 'versibus' and 'verbis' in the Latin performs his point, of course, and a few lines later he offers another, more virtuoso instance of this performance:

> See, then, as earlier sung, how much imports
> Th' arrangement, motion, magnitude, and form
> Of primal seeds combin'd: and how the same,
> Transpos'd but little, fuel quick convert
> To flame, bright blazing up the swarthy flue:
> As FLUE and FUEL, terms of different sound,
> Of different sense, their letters but transpos'd,
> Each into each converts with magic speed.[47]

Shelley takes this redeployment of the same elements in different contexts even further in 'With a Guitar. To Jane', for there the multiple intercalation of 'it' is emphasised by the pause and resumption of 'it: / It' across the line-break – a pause that seems to leave the spirit stubbornly lodged in the guitar, but followed by a resumption that coaxes it out. A comparable play occurs at the beginning of 'To Constantia', a poem closely related to 'With a Guitar. To Jane' in more ways than the merely biographical. There, in the poem's complex shift of focus from Constantia's voice hovering over the poem's speaker to the animating power in her fingers as they play a (here unspecified) musical instrument, the syllables *ing* and *in* echo out across the lines:

> Thy voice, slow rising like a Spirit, lingers
> O'ershadowing me with soft and lulling wings;
> The blood and life within thy snowy fingers
> Teach witchcraft to the instrumental strings.
>
> (*SPP*, p. 108; ll. 1–4)

It is surely no accident that the play on *ing* and *in* sonically evokes what Constantia does: s*ing*. It thus enacts the lingering of Constantia's singing voice in the poem's tribute to it, but also interweaves the blood and life 'within' Constantia's fingers as she plucks the 'instrumental strings'. Likewise, in the lines from 'With a Guitar. To Jane', the similar resonance of 'it' inextricably weaves together spirit and guitar. Although the explicit emphasis is on the spirit's inhabitation of the guitar, the transmutation of 'it' in these lines conversely suggests that it, the guitar, as much inhabits the spirit. While the guitar's telling is explicitly viewed as the response of its spirit to skilled questioning, that it is the body of the guitar, made of wood from which it takes even its 'highest holiest tone' (l. 89), upon which that telling relies refuses a separation of the guitar's spirit and knowledge from its body and sound. That knowledge is nowhere spelled out in the poem, and will nowhere be spelled out in response to skilful questioning, but, instead, the movement of its eliciting is prefigured in the movement of the most mundane of the poem's syllables.

Here, oh hear!

It is worth, perhaps, attempting to summarise the argument I have just been making. The lodging of 'it' in the lines from 'With a Guitar. To Jane' enacts the entwinement of spirit and guitar, the lodging of one in the other. In addition, its transposition across these lines performs the coaxing that the recipient of the guitar, who is also the recipient of the poem and thus its initial reader, is to perform. But more than this, it is vital that the involvement of guitar and spirit is most fully articulated not in discursive argument (informed, say, by Shelley's alleged Cartesianism or Neoplatonism or blend of the two) but rather in its sounding landscape. We may not be in the sounding landscape of the 'wind-swept Apennine', but the poem's transmutable sonic materials are far removed from the supersession of the sounds of nature by and in art.

I want, having offered this reading, to turn in concluding this chapter to Shelley's 'Ode to the West Wind'. As in 'With a Guitar. To Jane', the fecundity of mere matter – of, in particular, the lifeless remains of trees – is pivotal to the imagination of the relation between animating agent, natural material, and artistic work in the 'Ode to the West Wind'. In one of the finest accounts of the 'Ode', Garrett Stewart gives a hearing to the poet's desire, expressed in the lines 'Be thou, Spirit fierce, / My spirit! Be thou me, impetuous one!', to identify himself with the wind. I quote at length, in view of the intricacy of Stewart's account:

> [T]he wind's spiritualized velocity impels identification, impels fusion – so the speaker dreams. It is an impetus that, once scripted as the quatrasyllabic 'impetuous', introduces – by way of phonetic rebus – the pronoun 'you.' That encrypted pronoun is placed, and suddenly played, against the first person authorial plural of 'us', though still in the objective case. It thus takes part in a swift but no less emphatic positing of subject and object that – given the spondaic precedent of 'Be thou me' – blends into the phonemically lent splendour of *impet/you/us/one*. Such is a desideratum – difference subsumed to unity, lack transcended – written only in the chord progressions of a natural harmony, not traced anywhere upon the legible face of things, whether of nature or of poem. Indeed, it is produced only by what the next tercet reflexively highlights as 'the incantation of this verse' (l. 65) – to be heard and not seen.[48]

The announcement of the desideratum for difference subsumed to unity in the incantation of 'impetuous one' is, furthermore, a sonic consummation of the 'autumnal tone' that the wind will take from both forest and poet, and the 'tumult' of its 'mighty harmonies', whose echo of each other is taken up and modified in turn in 'impetuous'. Crucially, the impudence of this impetuousness inverts the Victorian wisdom that children should be seen and not heard, for it is 'heard and not seen'. Indeed, it is not even possible to know where to look for it: as Stewart points out, as soon as 'you' is 'placed' it is 'suddenly played' and the desideratum that its encrypting announces is 'not traced anywhere upon the legible face of things' even as it is heard in the audible sound of things.

The contrast between the poet's desire and his (anticipated?) fate in the lines 'Oh! lift me as a wave, a leaf, a cloud! / I fall upon the thorns of life! I bleed!' (*Poems* III, p. 210; ll. 53–4) emphasises the opposition between rooted 'thorns of life', and the volatile energies of animation. That the latter can neither be placed nor tracked but is everywhere discerned is vital to the energy of the poem's sound. In fact, this is announced in the exclamation that concludes the first stanza: 'Wild Spirit, which art moving every where; / Destroyer and Preserver; hear, O hear!' (*Poems* III, p. 206; ll. 13 and 14). In the initial 'hear, O hear!' we are liable to register – that is, to hear – the homonym 'here' in 'hear'. From the other way round, so to speak, Richard Lovelace deploys the same homonymic pun to moving effect in his at once wounded and angry lyric 'Orpheus to Beasts' in his collection *Lucasta* of 1649. Lovelace evokes Orpheus's misery by contrasting the proximity of the site of Eurydice's death – 'Here, here, oh here Eurydice, / Here was she slain;' – to the absence of the 'music of her face' – an absence which is only the more deeply felt in view of the paucity of lyric compensation: 'You'd drop a tear, / Seeing more harmony / In her bright eye, / Than now you hear.'[49] The pathos of the opening line lies in the hope echoing through it that Eurydice may 'hear, hear, oh hear' Orpheus, or even that we may hear her, when, in fact, it is indicating the spot where she was silenced forever.

The tragic rootedness of Lovelace's Orpheus to the spot where his lover died is in profound contrast to Shelley's playing off of 'hear' in rhyme, at the end of the first stanza of the 'Ode', against 'every where'. Since the 'Wild Spirit' is 'moving every where', it is conceivable, indeed necessary, that it will at some point move 'here'. But that location, like 'every where', is not within sight: 'here' is only heard, and thus, as Stewart emphasises, the wind's presence 'here' is only performed in the sound of words. The 'here' of the 'Ode' is nowhere to the eye and everywhere to the ear.[50]

This complication of location is reflected in a concomitant complication of what we are to understand by the poem's impetuousness. First, the course of this impetuousness, as it circles between the poet and the wind, is not finally to be determined, for it does not move in a straight line. As is well known, 'Ode to the West Wind' comprises five stanzas, each in turn comprising twelve lines, or four interlocking units, of terza rima, followed by a concluding couplet. This, of course, makes the form of the stanza of the 'Ode' comparable to that of the sonnet, and the entry on 'terza rima sonnet' in the *New Princeton Encyclopedia of Poetry and Poetics* takes Shelley's ode as its chief example. It dissents from the view that the stanzas that make up 'Ode to the West Wind' are similar to the sonnets of Spenser because 'the Spenserian sonnet allows little room for the forward momentum of [terza rima]; and its final couplet does not function as a refrain or invocation as those in Shelley's cycle do'.[51] On the one hand, the 'terza rima sonnet', of which the 'Ode' is taken to be an example, is to be distinguished from the Spenserian sonnet because it has greater forward momentum. On the other hand, its closing couplet, unlike that of the Spenserian sonnet, is a refrain or invocation; indeed, Shelley's poem is itself a 'cycle'. Thus, the form of 'Ode to the West Wind' is to be distinguished from Spenser both because it moves forward more decisively *and* because it circles back on itself more forcefully.

Second, further to the refusal of impetus to be limited to merely forward drive, enacted in the poem's circling motion, the energies of the 'Ode' also at once converge and disperse, as, for instance, in the following five lines, from the poem's last two tercets:

Drive my dead thoughts over the universe
Like withered leaves to quicken a new birth!
And, by the incantation of this verse,

Scatter, as from an unextinguished hearth
Ashes and sparks, my words among mankind!
(*Poems* III, pp. 211–12; ll. 63–7)

In the drafts for 'Ode to the West Wind', Shelley strove to find the correct placement for 'Scatter'. First, '~~Among~~ / ~~Then, like the scattered beams~~' was rejected, but scattering returns in the following redraft:

~~Like~~ ashes from an unextinguished hearth
~~Scatter them~~
Mingled with sparks; scatter [a]mong <mankind>[52]

In the version I quoted above, fore-stressed and separated both from the conjunction introducing it and from its object, 'Scatter' finally gathers unto itself the incantatory power invoked for 'this verse'. Yet the convergence of this power here, in 'Scatter', is the result of the impetuous movement of 'this verse', of its interposition of conditional clause and simile, of the rupture and propulsion effected in and across a tercet break. It is a convergence dependent upon a dispersal, which, moreover, asks for dispersal in its turn, for, that is to say, the scattering of the poet's words 'among mankind'. The concentrated specificity and indeterminate openness of that instruction captures (if that, in this context, can be the right word) the life of verse performed by this poem, a life that can be pinned to no spot but is everywhere felt.

In the final chapter, I investigate further this at once specific and indeterminate aspect of verse by exploring what I want to call the interanimation of poem and reader, but, before that, I address fully what has been implicit in this chapter: the consequences of Shelley's claims for the power of the sound of words.

CHAPTER FIVE

Sounds of air

The last chapter showed that the materials of art are not, for Shelley, merely inert prior to their animation by the artist. On the contrary, those materials are already, for him, living. Yet such a view is held, on some accounts, to be frankly irrational and hence superstitious. This chapter examines Shelley's response to those accounts. In particular, it shows that central to his poetics is a defence of the sounds of poetry against supposedly rationalist critiques in which they are held to be merely decorative, or otherwise nugatory. Such critiques, moreover, are only 'supposedly rationalist' because, for Shelley, they diminish not just the putative enchantments of poetry's sonic texture, but also reason itself. The sound of poetry is central to Shelley's attempt to think past, as it were, the habitual blunting of perception that is a consequence of the insistence on the part of 'reasoners and mechanists' (*SPP*, p. 528) that anything not capable of being rendered wholly and lucidly explicit is either recalcitrant, dead material, or mischievous and antiquated superstition, or, what is most often held to be the case, both. Shelley's poetic theory and practice insist instead that poetry's sonic texture is resistant to reason's demands that meaning be always explicit, without, on the other hand, descending into mere irrationalism. It is in verse's sonic materiality that, for Shelley, its life and its capacity of reanimation inheres.

This chapter has three sections, each of which is concerned with the claim – theoretically explicit or practically implicit – that poetry is living, and, in particular, with the defence of that claim against rationalist attempts to mortify poetry. The first section establishes what is at stake in this defence by tracing a crucial piece of Shelley's critical vocabulary to Theseus's attempt toward the end of Shakespeare's *A Midsummer Night's Dream* to expose poetry as akin to lunacy. Poetry is lunatic in particular because of its willingness to see what is not alive as living, and, for Theseus, reason must involve the exorcism of poetry's false animism.

Theseus's speech is significant in this chapter not because of its remarkable purchase amongst English Romantic writers, to whom it was, despite itself, a celebration of the imagination.[1] I focus instead on showing that Shelley's deployment of the terms 'apprehension' and 'comprehension' has a significant anticipation in Theseus's attempt to pose the latter – as rational – against the former – as the specific vice of the lunatic, the lover and the poet.[2] Crucially, this attempt is shown to miscarry: Theseus cannot oppose reason to poetic madness in quite the way he would wish because he ultimately cannot decide which of 'apprehension' or 'comprehension' is, on reason's own terms, the more reliable.

Having shown that Shelley takes up the association of poetry with apprehension, albeit in a much more nuanced version than Theseus's, I go on to argue that Peacock's critique of poetry in 'The Four Ages of Poetry' fails because Shelley is able to show that Peacock's particular investment in a reason opposed to poetry is itself superstitious. I turn in the concluding section to 'The Witch of Atlas' and the 'flux of sound into superseding sound' of, again, *Prometheus Unbound* in order to show that the sonic material of poetry is itself efficacious and not – as Theseus and Peacock would contend – inert.[3] The sound of verse opens possibilities just at the moment where paraphrasable content closes them by mourning their annihilation.

Apprehension and the poet

According to one account of the relation between poetry and reason, then, poetry madly insists on seeing life where it is not, whereas the very aim of reason is to exorcise the spirits with which, to the unenlightened, the world teems. Unlike the rational observer – the kind of observer that Theseus is when dispassionately (if indulgently) hearing of the excesses of the quartet of lovers at the heart of *A Midsummer Night's Dream* – the poet cannot coolly fix his attention on anything: 'The poet's eye in a fine frenzy rolling, / Doth glance from heaven to earth, from earth to heaven' (V.i.12–13). The promiscuous wandering of his eye between worlds hardly prevents him either from seeing life in every object on which his glance does happen, however fleetingly, to fall – the poet is always ready to suppose bushes bears – or, worse still, from creating the illusion of existence for airy nothings.

Of course, it does involve a degree of misprision to take Theseus as offering an account of poetic imagination to which a poet might wish to subscribe. But the reason why Theseus has nonetheless so often been received as an advocate for poetry is not just the willingness of poets flightily to ignore argumentative context. To begin with, as Paul A. Olson once noted, Theseus does make 'some implicit distinctions between the poet and his mad colleagues', since only lunatics and lovers are wholly outside of the purview of reason, and thus 'poets, however much they are possessed by a *furor poesis*, may deal in imaginings apprehensible in more rational terms'.[4] One powerful reason for thinking this (though not the one adduced by Olson) is that where Theseus does seem to attempt to oppose reason to poetry, his reasoning is itself flawed, and the problems with his argument are clearest in his manipulation of the terms 'apprehension' and 'comprehension'. According to Theseus, lovers and madmen, to whom poets will shortly be added, 'have such seething brains, / Such shaping fantasies, that apprehend / More than cool reason ever comprehends' (V. I. 4-6). We saw in the introduction that the philological record shows that the meaning of 'apprehension', as it migrated into English from Latin, was volatile; it is necessary briefly to re-clarify Shakespeare's understanding of 'apprehension' here before showing how Theseus fails to control its multiple senses. In particular, for Theseus, comprehension is straightforwardly rational, and apprehension is, as it were, more than rational – an excess that Theseus deplores as illegitimate. Yet, as I outlined in the introduction, the specific understanding of apprehension prevalent at the time that Shakespeare was writing – apprehension as, that is, an at once intellectual and sensible capacity – suggests that Theseus is here going to find it difficult dogmatically to oppose apprehension, of which he is suspicious, to comprehension, which he lauds. There is already a hint of inconsistency in Theseus's initial juxtaposition of cool reason and exceeding apprehension at lines 5–6 of his speech. The brains of lovers and madmen seethe, surging up and at least threatening to overflow; contrastingly, their fantasies – the very things with which their brains are moiling – are in fact not portrayed chiefly as formless but, on the contrary, as giving form, as 'shaping'. Theseus contrasts apprehension and comprehension again, a few lines further on, and here they are opposed in a rather different way to his initial opposition between excessive apprehension and coolly rational comprehension. If, he says, imagination 'would but apprehend some joy / It comprehends some bringer of that joy' (ll. 19–20). Whereas at the beginning of the speech, apprehension strays beyond the bounds of whatever is comprehended, here it is comprehension that goes beyond what is apprehended. Theseus's description of lovers and madmen as possessing at once 'seething brains' and 'shaping fantasies' already suggests, contrary to his intention, that going on to depict the imaginations of poets as simply overflowing formal bounds would be difficult, and here it is comprehension that exceeds apprehension, not the other way around. To be sure, Theseus may very well think that the joy that is apprehended is illusory, but that does not prevent comprehension – which was directly associated with the rigours of reason earlier – from exceeding apprehension. The dogmatic oppositions that Theseus wishes to establish prove impossible, in fact, for him to keep in place.

The Romantic reception of this speech saw it, as noted above, as extolling imagination, which, despite itself, it is. One of Theseus's criticisms of the poet is that his eye is undisciplined, but elsewhere in *A Midsummer Night's Dream* it is precisely with the frustration of the eye's capacities that the ear comes to apprehensive life, so, for example, 'Dark night, that from the eye his function takes, / The ear more quick of apprehension makes', where 'quick' is, of course, both fast and living (III.ii.178–9). Poetry might, therefore, be characteristically apprehensive not just because, in that its particular medium is sonic, it is capable of giving to 'airy nothing / A local habitation and a name' but also because it 'pays the hearing double recompense' (III.ii.181): its nothings are 'airy' since it is in musical airs that they are given shape.

As I established in the introduction, Shelley, like Shakespeare, conceives of 'apprehension' as both intimately sensory and, at the same time, exceeding beyond the calculations of ratiocination. The affectivity of apprehension is central, for instance, to Ianthe's recognition of her transformation near the opening of *Queen Mab*, and the proximity of the following description, in which the Fairy Queen calls Ianthe's soul out of its body, to Theseus's speech is notable:

> She knew her glorious change,
> And felt in apprehension uncontrolled
> New raptures opening round:
> Each day-dream of her mortal life,
> Each frenzied vision of the slumbers
> That closed each well-spent day,
> Seemed now to meet reality.
> (*Poems* I, p. 277; canto I, ll. 192–8)

Despite having been removed from her body, Ianthe still feels.[5] Like the poet's rolling eye, her visions are 'frenzied', and these visions, which occur at the margins of her waking 'mortal life', are newly realised in her 'glorious change'. Now, in her changed state, it becomes clear that the dreams 'That *closed* each well-spent day' do not merely mark a hiatus in waking life but rather they in turn open out onto a whole new field of possible experience: she 'felt in apprehension uncontrolled / New raptures *opening* round'. Similarly, Ianthe's 'glorious change' involves a revolution, so to speak, in the direction of her life. Whereas the body, 'for a time the unwilling sport / Of circumstance and passion, *struggles on*' (*Poems* I, p. 275; canto I, ll. 152-3 [my emphasis]), the soul is not impelled onward but instead feels new raptures *round* it. Ianthe's new experience relies on a greater involvement of experience with what it experiences than is habitual. That the word 'raptures' can describe both the kind of feelings that Ianthe is having and what is going on around her suggests a confluence between soul and reality of the kind explored in the previous chapter's discussion of dissolution. Such a confluence is further suggested by the possibility of two interpretations of these lines. The word 'uncontrolled' can qualify either 'apprehension' or '[n]ew raptures', or, indeed, both, and it is the placement of 'uncontrolled' at the line's end which enables this ambivalence. This word is thus both controlled – deftly placed as the terminal word of its line – and uncontrolled – its semantic sense is precisely rendered equivocal by that positioning.

The result of Ianthe's uncontrolled apprehension is remarkably close to Theseus's account of poetic bodying forth: her frenzied visions, which, in mortal life, are but visions, now appear to become real. The freedom of apprehension that she newly enjoys is a poetic faculty in the sense that Theseus unintentionally develops, because her new apprehensions 'meet reality', are made real in a way that her daydreams and frenzied slumbers presumably had not been before.

This identification of apprehension as a poetic faculty emerges still more clearly just where Shelley is questioning the turn taken by one of the most important poetic careers to the development of his own vocation as poet. One of the few compliments paid to Wordsworth-Peter that is more than merely backhanded in *Peter Bell the Third* praises the way his 'apprehension clear, intense, / Of his mind's work, had made alive / The things it wrought on; I believe / Wakening a sort of thought in sense' (*Poems* III, p. 116; part fourth, ll. 308–11). Wordsworth-Peter may have had 'as much imagination / As a pint-pot' (p. 115; ll. 298–9) (an especially caustic putdown from the teetotal Shelley, perhaps), but his apprehension, at least, is praiseworthy.[6] Apprehension is exclusively the property of neither sense nor thought, and it is clear but also intense, thus refusing the kind of distinction upon which Theseus insists between cool reason and poetic frenzy. Concomitantly, although things are 'wrought on' by the mind, they are nevertheless not wholly inert if their being 'made alive' might be thought of not precisely as the animation of dead matter but rather as akin to the '[w]akening a sort of thought in sense'. This phrase closely echoes stanza XXXIX of the first canto of *Laon and Cythna*, where the Woman is explaining the particular character of her knowledge of 'the dark tale of history' (*Poems* II, p. 83; canto I, stanza XXXVIII, l. 460) and narrates how '"When first the living blood through all these veins / Kindled a thought in sense, great France sprang forth"' (XXXIX, ll. 469–70). It is significant both that thought is not superadded to sense as a kind of external patina but is rather 'Kindled' 'in' it, and that what is ultimately responsible for that kindling is not, say, the soul or spirit, but 'the living blood'. Likewise, in *Peter Bell the Third*, apprehension, in awakening what is slumbering in mortal life, thus suspends the disabling distinctions between mere sense and the thought by which it is to be rationalised.

This understanding of apprehension as both enlivening and, in this specific regard, characteristically poetic is central to Shelley's most concerted criticism of rationalism's opposition to poetry in 'A Defence of Poetry'. As I sketched in the introduction, for instance, the relation of vitality and apprehension is fundamental to the famous description of the language of poets as 'vitally metaphorical; that is, it marks the before unapprehended relations of things, and perpetuates their apprehension' (*SPP*, p. 512). The meaning of 'vitally metaphorical' is submitted to quite rigorous specification here, which is indicated by Shelley's unusually delimiting 'that is': the language of poets is 'metaphorical' because it marks relations (that is clear enough from standard definitions of metaphor), and it is 'vitally' so because it apprehends what was not previously apprehended. Bringing to apprehension, so implies this explanation of how the language of poets is vital, is bringing to life, and perpetuating in apprehension, like the prolongation of the pleasures of play attempted by the child (*SPP*, p. 511), is perpetuation in life of what would otherwise die away.

The capacity for apprehension is, then, fundamental to the understanding of what it is to be a poet in 'A Defence of Poetry'. As Shelley puts it, 'to be a poet is to apprehend the true and the beautiful' (*SPP*, p. 517). Although he also says that poetry 'acts in a divine and unapprehended manner, beyond and above consciousness', this does not mean that it is itself unapprehending, for, returning to the question of poetry's particular mode of action a little further on, in order to defend it from the charge of immorality by showing that poetry's action is not the same as that of '[e]thical science', Shelley remarks that '[p]oetry acts in another and diviner manner. It awakens and enlarges the mind itself by rendering it the receptacle of a thousand unapprehended combinations of thought' (*SPP*, p. 517). This echo of the description of the language of poets as 'vitally metaphorical' does not say that the combinations of thought that poetry makes possible are unapprehended but rather that the mind, without poetry, lacks the capacity for them. It is not, therefore, that apprehension is merely to be identified with consciousness – as the statement that poetry acts in an 'unapprehended manner, beyond and above consciousness' might be taken to suggest – but rather that consciousness is diminished when it shrinks from apprehension. It is this diminution of consciousness when severed from apprehension – or, to put this another way, of reason when sundered from poetry – to which I now wish to turn.

Peacock's prudent omissions

Over-investment in consciousness divested of its relation to apprehension, in the way advanced by Theseus, is an error in the opponents of poetry that Shelley seeks to expose as superstitious. This entails that his defence of poetry takes a particular form. It is not, that is, that Shelley simply wishes, irrationalistically, to defend mere delusion. In his 'To Percy Shelley: On the Degrading Notions of Deity', Leigh Hunt, after all, praises Shelley as the enemy of pernicious fallacies which are themselves described in a manner very similar to that of Theseus: the deluded bigots to whom Shelley is opposed are

> Wise as the clown, who plodding home at night
> In autumn, turns at call of fancied elf,
> And sees upon the fog, with ghastly feeling,
> A giant shadow in its imminent might,
> Which his own lanthorn throws up from himself.
> (*Poetical Works*, p. 242; ll. 10–14)

But nor is it that Shelley wishes to show, *pace* poetry's detractors, that poetry is in fact perfectly rational on their terms, even if they have failed to see this. Much rather, the aim of his defence of poetry is to demonstrate that the understanding of reason evinced by poetry's opponents is in itself insufficient.

We can begin to see the consequences of this if we look at one of the relatively rare moments in which Shelley explicitly addresses his antagonist in 'A Defence of Poetry', namely, Peacock. Having just indulged in a digression concerning the origin and development of drama, Shelley notes in particular a telling omission in Peacock's account of the alleged poverty of contemporary verse:

> The Author of the Four Ages of Poetry has prudently omitted to dispute on the effect of the Drama upon life and manners. For, if I know the knight by

> the device of his shield, I have only to inscribe Philoctetes or Agamemnon or Othello upon mine to put to flight the giant sophisms which have enchanted him, as the mirror of intolerable light, though on the arm of the weakest of the Paladins, could blind and scatter whole armies of necromancers and pagans. (*SPP*, p. 519)

It would perhaps be prudent to read this passage's references to enchantment and necromancy as characteristic of the playful mockery typical of a dispute between friends. But prudence – that rational quality most fundamental to the political economy that Peacock wished to advance – is precisely what is called into question here. The prudence that Peacock is taken to evince is itself, in fact, in the service of a sort of disabling mystification. Peacock has 'prudently *omitted*' to include a discussion of drama, and thus his dexterous avoidance of this particular matter (which contrasts starkly, for example, with Milton's 'bold neglect of a direct moral purpose' [*SPP*, p. 527]) is in the service not of clarity but, in fact, of obfuscation.[7] (It is also worth noting, by the way, that Shelley's discussion of drama is, conversely, a digression – a refusal to abide by the rules of rationality that demand the unidirectional pursuance of a single line of argument.) In general, the prudential treatment of the allegedly extravagant claims of poetry in 'The Four Ages of Poetry' is, Shelley shows, actually in the service of the kind of enchantment that entails unreflecting acceptance of a raft of professionalised and pre-approved wisdom. This is what Shelley, evoking the travesties peddled by Socrates' mercantile opponents, aptly calls 'giant sophisms', and which in Act III of *Prometheus Unbound* the Spirit of the Hour magnificently condemns as 'reasoned wrong glozed on by ignorance' (*Poems* II, p. 608; Act III, scene 4, l. 167).

But if Peacock's prudent opposition to the superstitious nature of poetry is itself superstitious, how are the sophisms into which he falls to be dispelled? Shelley's suspicion of Peacock's rationalised political economy, in its unilateral dissociation from poetry, does not entail a straightforward restoration of every superstition that the supposedly all new intellectual disciplines set out to dethrone; obviously, were that the case, his description of Peacock as 'enchanted' would have no force. Dispelling sophisms is still necessary, even – or especially – if self-proclaimed disenchanters can be shown in fact to be under their spell. For Shelley, it would seem not that more rigorous prudence is required for this task, but rather, more enchantment – where enchantment is understood not simply as myth but as already an attempt at enlightenment, and one, moreover, that operates with materials wrongly treated by figures like Peacock as merely dead and thus ripe for investment with meaning by thought. In particular, enchantment in this sense views the sounds of words not as empty material to be invested with meaning by reason but rather as already both material and meaningful.

We can begin to see what this means by looking in more detail at Shelley's imaginatively romanticised scene in which Peacock is a dark knight and he his adversary. The list from which Shelley will choose an inscription for his shield, 'Philoctetes or Agamemnon or Othello', is not just a list of plays but a set of potentially magically efficacious words. Admittedly, Shelley means to recall the manner in which those dramas, as he had put it slightly earlier in 'A Defence of Poetry', 'produce a common effect in the representation of the highest idealisms of passion and of power' (*SPP*, p. 518). And to be sure, the subject matter of each of these plays has much in common: each portrays the fall of a figure compromised by an all-too-human tragic flaw from the heights of martial heroism down to a position of virtual animality.[8] Thus are *Philoctetes* and *Agamemnon* and *Othello* connected, and thus do they produce the effect of which Shelley speaks. By inscribing these words on his shield, therefore, he means to bring to mind the admirable way that drama, wholly ignored by Peacock, has addressed moral, political and psychological questions of profound and abiding concern. After all, as he goes on to claim, '[t]he connexion of scenic exhibitions with the improvement or corruption of the manners of men, has been universally recognized' (*SPP*, p. 519).

But that is not all that Shelley hopes to conjure by emblazoning 'Philoctetes or Agamemnon or Othello' on his shield. What would be changed had he chosen to respond to Peacock by reminding him of the power of 'Philoctetes or Agamemnon or King Lear', thus replacing *Othello* with a play which Shelley, only slightly earlier in 'A Defence of Poetry', favourably compares with the *Agamemnon* and even ventures to suggest is 'the most perfect specimen of the dramatic art existing in the world' by virtue of its blending of 'universal, ideal and sublime' comedy with tragedy (*SPP*, p. 519)? *King Lear* is a different play from *Othello*, of course, concerned with different passions and powers, but if Shelley's intention was solely to call to mind the grand moral, political and psychological topics addressed in the history of drama, then perhaps mentioning 'the most perfect' instance he could think of would have been a useful tactic. But the passions and powers called to mind are not all that is changed in this replacement, for through the replacement of 'Othello' with 'King Lear' would be lost the precise quality of the evocation of 'Philoctetes or Agamemnon or Othello'. Although the concluding doubled dentals of 'Philoc*tetes*' and the multiply palindromic 'Aga-mem-non' would remain, the modulated echo of those features in the return upon itself of '*Othello*' would be gone, as would the 'o's of that word which at once mark its outer limits and themselves picture the circling movement of the word itself; the particular energy of this set of words, redoubled through its recursive recoil as it also rises to its climax, would, were *King Lear* to replace *Othello*, be dissipated.[9]

Shelley exposes Peacock's omission of a proper discussion of 'the effect of the Drama on life and manners' by alluding to the large philosophical questions with which he is keen to show that it does deal; but he aims also to criticise the prudence on which Peacock's argument relies by intimating that the words 'Philoctetes or Agamemnon or Othello' themselves have a power that is decried or simply ignored in Peacock's rejection of poetic enchantment. The particular quality of specific words is as important in Shelley's riposte to Peacock as the contents for which those words stand. In 'A Defence of Poetry', Shelley repeatedly claims that the sounds of words and the sonic rather than semantic connections between them are a fundamental part of poetry's influence and a fundamental part of what and how it knows. Words are neither mere labels for, nor mere decoration of, always already completed reasoning; rather the sounds of their letters and their combinations are fundamental to poetry's claim against Peacockian prudence. Against Peacock's denunciation of poetry, therefore, Shelley does not offer a *weak* defence of it – one that would aim to show that poetry was in fact capable itself of being a versified instance of the political economy with which Peacock wished to replace it. Rather, Shelley's defence is much stronger in that it aims to show first that Peacock's rationalism has not, in fact, extirpated the enchantment whose extirpation it essentially requires, and, moreover, that enchantment itself is not in the first place entirely vulnerable to the kinds of charge that Peacock makes against it. By eliminating what it takes to be the irrationalism of enchantment in the service of establishing itself as lucidly rational, Peacock's prudence in fact condemns itself to stupidity.[10] Extirpation of what is castigated as illusion often entails the banishment of truth as well.

In the course of her insightful critique of the lacunae that emerge in readings of Shelley as a predominantly sceptical poet, Laura Quinney remarks that 'Shelley waged a keen-minded and principled resistance to what he perceived as the inherent rhetorical advantage of skepticism and grimness [...] [He] was trying to subvert the equation of tragic affect and sublime style with literary power. Hence he defied the automatic authority of demystification.'[11] Even in those discussions of Shelley for which Quinney feels some sympathy, 'the intellectual strength of his poetry', she comments, 'is seen to flow from disillusionment – even in the case of the deconstructive analysis, where disillusionment may not belong to Shelley himself but is in any case required of us'.[12] Shelley was indeed keen to resist the sceptic always ready to paint the colours of poetry grey. Moreover, he saw the disavowal of enchantment as itself a kind of rhetorical strategy, as, that is, a version of enchantment. Quinney's description of Shelley's defiance of 'the automatic authority of demystification' is, then, especially apt because an '*automatic* authority' makes a blind function of the exercise of authority, which, in turn, relies not on living acknowledgement but on mechanical, and thus mystified, acquiescence.

Shelley's resistance to the 'automatic authority of demystification' should not, of course, be taken to suggest submission to the automatic authority of mystification. It is important to note that, despite his opposition to Peacock's attempt to replace poetry with political economy, Shelley's rejection of the latter, as Philip Connell has usefully established, is more qualified than has often been thought to be the case.[13] Shelley shares aspects, at least, of Peacock's regard for a number of central figures associated with the gradual, ongoing and also reversible emergence of humanity from injustice and superstition.[14] 'The exertions of Locke, Hume, Gibbon, Voltaire, Rousseau, and their disciples, in favour of oppressed and deluded humanity', acknowledges Shelley in 'A Defence of Poetry', 'are entitled to the gratitude of mankind' (*SPP*, p. 530). He goes on to attempt to specify the achievements that can be credited to these enlighteners: less nonsense talked over the past couple of centuries; fewer burned heretics; and the – albeit, as it would turn out, temporary – abolition of the Spanish Inquisition.

Worthwhile as the achievements of Locke et al. are, however, it is clear that Shelley views them as far from decisive in the process of human amelioration. In a note to the above list of enlighteners' names, he states that in putting these thinkers together he is following 'the classification adopted by the author of the Four Ages of Poetry', but he also tries to rescue one of them from the damnation by faint praise to which the rest remain condemned by remarking that 'Rousseau was essentially a poet. The others, even Voltaire, were mere reasoners' (*SPP*, p. 530, n. 2).[15] This opposition between poet and mere reasoner also importantly obtains, for Shelley, between Plato and Aristotle: in a discussion of Christianity in the notes to *Queen Mab*, he refers to 'the reveries of Plato and the reasonings of Aristotle' (*Poems* I, p. 397). Although he is drawing on a dismissive phrase from the Baron d'Holbach's *Système de la nature* (1770) here, his opposing of Plato and Aristotle in these terms is hardly to the detriment of the former, as another comparable opposition, this time from the preface to *Prometheus Unbound*, between Plato and Bacon (with whom Shelley would gladly go to Hell) and Malthus and Paley (with whom he would rather not go to Heaven), makes clear.[16] The opposition between poetry and 'mere' reason or 'reasonings' is fundamental not least because it allows Shelley to avoid the charge that his advocacy of poetic enchantment is opposed to reason as such. The precise focus of this opposition also enables him to argue that reason itself is damaged by its self-separation from what it would dismiss as poetic decoration. *Mere* reason is no more reason than what it seeks rationalistically to condemn.

It is necessary at this point, having explored Shelley's critique of the 'reason' mobilised by Peacock against poetic enchantment, to turn more fully to a fundamental if largely implicit aspect of that critique, namely, Shelley's understanding of language. This is a fundamental aspect of Shelley's critique because part of that critique concerns, as I summarised in the introduction, the question whether the assumption that meaning ought to be straightforwardly explicable is really tenable, and, moreover, whether the deletion or downgrading of certain aspects of language – such as its sound in particular – is a necessary tenet of rationality at all. The quite specific and highly developed character of Shelley's understanding of language has, of course, been a central focus in commentary on his work. Numerous commentators have paid attention in particular to Shelley's conception of language as agonistically poised between poetic and primarily denotative conceptions of it.[17] In particular, Shelley argues in 'A Defence of Poetry' that poetic language successfully perpetuates the apprehension of previously unremarked relations 'until the words which represent them, become through time signs for portions or classes of thoughts instead of pictures of integral thoughts; and then if no new poets should arise to create afresh the associations which have been thus disorganized, language will be dead to all the nobler purposes of human intercourse' (*SPP*, p. 512).[18] On the one hand, words are essentially inert, a set of labels whose sonic material is only ever entirely subservient to – because at best a secondary reinforcement or decoration of – semantic sense; on the other hand, such signs are a diminished version of what words are. The second of these views – the one that initially prevails, in fact, in Shelley's conjectured history – entails that the sound of a word is not rendered nugatory by the sense to which it conducts.

I want to return to some of the corollaries of this battle between rival conceptions of language in the following chapter, but here it is necessary to emphasise that Shelley is resistant to a view of language according to which the basic function of words is maximal explication. Words, for Shelley, are not just labels. In particular, precisely that aspect of a word which is thought to be subservient to its definition – its material constitution and, especially, its sound – is neither, in fact, to be rejected as irrelevant, nor, if not wholly rejected, consolingly accommodated as mere decoration. Crucially, the sounds of words are part of what Shelley envisages as the way that verse thinks:

> Sounds as well as thoughts have relations, both between each other and towards that which they represent, and a perception of the order of those relations has always been found connected with a perception of the order of the relations of thoughts. Hence the language of poets has ever affected a certain uniform and harmonious recurrence of sound, without which it were not poetry, and which is scarcely less indispensible to the communication of its influence, than the words themselves without reference to that peculiar order. (*SPP*, p. 514)

It is well to be reminded at this point of the embattled nature of language because of the slightly provisional nature in which this passage is articulated. To say that sounds have relations '*towards* that which they represent' is not to assert an established connection, once and for all, but is, rather, to evoke a tendency, a kind of perpetual relational transport. And to claim that 'a perception of the order of those relations has always been found connected with a perception of the order of the relations of thoughts' not only makes the latter perception conditional on the former, but to say as well that it 'has always been found' to be so hints that this connection, even if it is 'always' the case, is not anticipated or expected, but, rather, each time discovered or hit upon. This provisional, potentially missable quality of the relation among sounds and 'towards that which they represent' is perchance evident in the sound patterns of the passage itself, of which Michael O'Neill has acutely remarked that

> Shelley sandwiches 'found' between 'sounds' and 'sound' as if to verify his idea that the relations of sound are close to being the ground and foundation of the 'perception of the order of the relations of thought.' And the way 'recurrence' flowers out of the near-rhyme between 'connected' and 'affected' mimics a similar enactment of sound's relation with thoughts.[19]

These sandwichings and flowerings are indeed offered 'as if to verify' Shelley's argument about the centrality of sound to thought;[20] but sheltering in that 'as if' is also the acknowledgement that they are fragile, prone to be unnoticed, ignored or dismissed.[21] And unnoticed, ignored or dismissed along with them would therefore be something fundamental to thought itself.

The main concern of the claim about sounds from 'A Defence of Poetry' is, of course, with the relations subsisting between sounds, but it must follow from Shelley's argument there that if sounds are to recur, then there must be single instances of sound to recur, and hence, in turn, that words themselves must not only be considered with reference to the peculiar order of the recurrence of sound but also with reference to their own individual sounds. Apparently fleeting minutiae of verse are thus viewed by Shelley as capable of reanimation. It is important to emphasise this point because Shelley is keen to make it – albeit, admittedly, focusing variously on words or sentences or lines – at a number of places in his work. Elsewhere in 'A Defence of Poetry', for instance, he initiates a discussion of authors usually categorised as prose writers by claiming that

> [t]he parts of a composition may be poetical, without the composition as a whole being a poem. A single sentence may be considered as a whole though it be found in the midst of a series of unassimilated portions; a single word even may be a spark of inextinguishable thought. (*SPP*, p. 515)

Care needs to be taken if we are to grasp precisely what Shelley is saying here. We might, for example, readily assent to the claim that a sentence may have merit as a flourish of epigrammatic wit or as an isolated philosophical insight, despite being muffled by acres of mediocrity. But that fairly uncontroversial position is not quite the position that Shelley is advancing here, and this becomes clearer when he also claims that even a word 'may be a spark of inextinguishable thought', a claim that relies not only or indeed chiefly on how that word might be defined, but on what it is. It is in this light that we must understand the contention that in poetry 'a word, a trait in the representation of a scene or a passion, will touch the enchanted chord, and reanimate, in those who have ever experienced these emotions, the sleeping, the cold, the buried image of the past' (*SPP*, p. 532). The sentence or word, therefore, is poetic not necessarily, and certainly not exclusively, because it captures something in a way that might be straightforwardly communicable and thence explicable. On the contrary, the poetic quality of sentences and words is much more likely not to be straightforwardly translatable in such a way.

That Shelley's focus is not exclusively on the meaning but as well on the effects of the sounds of words is especially apparent in a supposed conversation between him and Byron, in which 'Byron' objects to the attempt of 'Shelley' to argue that the beauty of a line – in this case, 'How sweet the moonlight sleeps upon this bank' from *The Merchant of Venice* (V. I. 54) – relies on the 'sounds and syllables' of the line as much as on its metaphor.[22] It should be pointed out that, in one regard, this conversation may appear inconvenient for the argument I have just been making, because in it 'Shelley' asks (rhetorically), 'Is not a line, as well as your outspread heroics, or a tragedy, a whole, and only as a whole, beautiful in itself?'[23] It may be thought, that is, that I have been attempting to show – both here, theoretically, and practically, in the last chapter's discussion of 'Scatter' in 'Ode to the West Wind' – that he holds even single words in isolation to be poetic. Yet, it is in fact central to Shelley's valorisation of individual words that they are capable of initiating trains of thought, either as a 'spark of inextinguishable thought' or as the reanimation of the buried past. There is, significantly, a danger for language in this initiation of a train of subsequent associations, and we will return to this in the following chapter. But it is important to emphasise here that the point of the examples I have discussed so far and of the putative conversation 'Byron' is the importance Shelley ascribes to the sounds of words and their sonic interaction. In particular, 'Shelley' responds in the following way to the objection made by 'Byron' that the interactions of sounds and syllables are 'mechanical contrivances':

> I don't say that a poet must necessarily be conscious of all this, no more than a lady is conscious of every graceful movement. But I do say that they all depend upon reason, in which they live and move, and have their being; and that he who brings them out into the light of distinct consciousness, beside satisfying an instinctive desire of his own nature, will be more secure and more commanding. But what makes this metaphor beautiful? To represent the tranquillity of moonlight is the object of the line; and the sleep is beautiful, because it gives a more intense and living form of the same idea; the rythm [*sic*] beautifully falls in with this, and just lets the cadence of the emphasis dwell upon the sound and sense of the sweet word 'sleep;' and the alliteration assimilates the rest of the line into one harmonious symmetry. This line, therefore, is it not altogether a work of art?[24]

In a valuable essay on Shelley's conception of the language of poetry, Stuart Peterfreund has highlighted the way in which, in this conversation, 'Shelley' 'does seem to ascribe to sound a symbolic dimension much like that discussed by Socrates in the *Cratylus*'.[25] Peterfreund adduces the example of the comment by 'Shelley' on how 'the *l* in moonlight prepares one for the *l* in sleep, and glides gently into it', remarking that this description of the gliding of the *l*s is in tune with the line's description of a river bank: Shelley 'unpacks the mataphor [*sic*] latent in the notion of [l] as a "liquid," associating the sound with the motion of a body of liquid – a river'.[26] Peterfreund is certainly right to bring out this aspect of Shelley's understanding of the sounds of words, but, as he acknowledges, Shelley is also concerned with 'the affective dimension of phonological repetition and patterning', which we need quite clearly to distinguish here from its ascribed symbolic or metaphorical dimension, since it is crucial to the argument of 'Shelley' against 'Byron' to emphasise that there are 'many simultaneous operations' at work in any given line of verse and thus, here, operations in addition to those of metaphor.[27]

It is particularly salient, then, that the word 'sleep' gives 'a more intense and living form of the same idea', namely, the idea of the tranquillity of the moonlight. The effect of the sound of 'sleep' is not imitative of its sense in that it is not lulling, but, on the contrary, animating. Words, sentences and lines are poetic – or, as 'Shelley' has it here, are works of art – not primarily in so far as they accord with the requirements of distinct consciousness and hence accord with the requirement that any given word's significance may be rendered explicit through recourse to definition, or, similarly, to symbolic ascription, but rather in so far as they act with intensity. Moreover, words not only 'live and move, and *have* their being', but, in addition, 'sleep' in particular is praised because it '*gives* a more intense and living form of the same idea'. It is crucial to 'Shelley' here, therefore, that words both live and enliven, and that that enlivening capacity does not depend on conformity to established lexical expectations.

This non-conformity to the exact strictures of lexical meaning is not, however, the mark of unreason. In insisting on the dependence 'of all this' on 'reason, in which they live and move, and have their being', 'Shelley' differs subtly from the account of prosodic artifice given by Raymond D. Havens, who suggests that, rather than chance shaping poems a particular way, 'a much larger part is played by what is loosely termed the artist's instinct – that sense of fitness which we all possess, heightened and intensified until it becomes creative. This is a feeling', he goes on,

> often strong but not reasoned, an intuition – for example, that a certain passage is right but that another should be lighter or more vigorous [...] A good swimmer or motorist does not see an obstacle in his path, decide 'I must turn to the right to avoid that obstacle', and then direct his muscles to make the turn. He makes the turn automatically on seeing the obstacle.[28]

Havens' insistence that such unconscious articulation is 'not reasoned' and thus made 'automatically' is, despite its superficial similarity to the account of 'Shelley', crucially different from his sense of what is involved in the composition of a line of verse. Havens relies on an assumed opposition between instinct and intuition, on the one hand, and reason, on the other, according to which the former is mechanical, the latter, willed. Were that opposition accepted, 'Byron' would, despite the magisterially minute reading of the line from Shakespeare offered by 'Shelley', prevail: sounds and syllables would then be 'mechanical contrivances'. But such an opposition is in fact disabled, not by being collapsed, but rather by the alternative opposition between 'distinct consciousness' and 'reason' proposed by 'Shelley'. The latter, here, is thus not the faculty for making explicit, but, Shelley holds, is not the less reasonable for that.[29]

The supposed conversation between 'Shelley' and 'Byron' is thus important because it again emphasises the degree to which Shelley is prepared to question the disenchanting and sceptical rejection of the belief that poetry is efficacious, which here quite clearly means animating. As we have seen, Shelley thinks that *that* view, despite its own self-presentation, is not devoid of superstition. Although in his conversation with 'Byron' it is fundamental to 'Shelley' to attend to the individual line in an especially focused way, it is nevertheless worth recalling the context from which 'How sweet the moonlight sleeps upon this bank' is taken. In particular, Lorenzo, whose line it is, goes on to explain to Jessica that music has a particularly calming effect: on hearing 'any air of music touch their ears', a group of wild colts 'make a mutual stand, / Their savage eyes turn'd to a modest gaze, / By the sweet power of music' (*Merchant of Venice*, V.ii.76–9). It is for this reason, Lorenzo claims, that 'the poet / Did feign that Orpheus drew trees, stones, and floods, / Since nought so stockish, hard, and full of rage, / But music for the time doth change his nature' (ll. 79–82). These lines are deftly equivocal in their description of the poetic convention of Orpheus's powers. On the one hand, it is acknowledged that the poet's portrayal of Orpheus as enchanting inanimate objects is only 'feigned' – an acknowledgement that is maybe further hinted at in the fact that 'Orpheus drew trees, stones, and floods', not only in the sense that he commanded them but also, perhaps, in the sense that he portrayed ('drew') them in art. But, even if Orpheus's powers are conventionally imagined, that convention is nevertheless justified, 'Since nought so stockish, hard, and full of rage' is immune to the effects of music. The slight suspicion attaching to the standard depiction of Orpheus is then recalled in the recognition of the tenuousness of the power of music, for it is only 'for the time' that music changes the nature of brutes, but that power is nonetheless asserted. Thus, while it is acknowledged that the power of music is not established once and for all, the lines from *The Merchant of Venice* immediately following that instanced by 'Shelley' in opposition to the stockish opposition of 'Byron' emphasise that the effect of music is not to conduct to irrational frenzy but, rather, the opposite.

Sounds of air

It is necessary briefly to remind ourselves of some of the main features of this discussion so far. In particular, although reason claims the power of thinking for its exclusive property, Shelley insists that poetry, so to speak, inhabits reason, and that, moreover, once poetry is evicted from reason, reason itself becomes vacuous. And it is a key difference between the powers of insight that reason claims for itself and those of poetry that poetry is only provisionally, temporarily capable of illumination and is vulnerable to the force of abstraction.

The combination of what I might call the rational non-triviality of the sounds, in complex relation to the definitions, of words; a characterisation of Peacock's attack on poetry not as fulfilled rational disenchantment but rather as superstitious; and the recognition that poetry is ineluctably mortal, are fundamental to Shelley's assessment of one of his most important poetic and political forebears: Dante.[30] I will address the specific question of Shelley's attempts at terza rima in the following chapter, but here I want briefly to consider his accordance of the principal role in the liberation of Europe from papal tyranny to Dante, not chiefly, however, thanks to his principled argument but rather precisely thanks to the language in which his critique of Catholic corruption was articulated:

> Dante was the first religious reformer, and Luther surpassed him rather in the rudeness and acrimony, than in the boldness of his censures of papal usurpation. Dante was the first awakener of entranced Europe; he created a language in itself music and persuasion out of a chaos of inharmonious barbarisms [. . .] His very words are instinct with spirit; each is as a spark, a burning atom of inextinguishable thought; and many yet lie covered in the ashes of their birth, and pregnant with a lightning which has yet found no conductor. (*SPP*, p. 528)

Shelley is keen to point out that Dante's role as enlightener is not dependent on a disenchanted view of language – quite the opposite. Thus, Dante's awakening of Europe from its entrancement is not predicated on a brisk rejection, like Luther's, of what could easily be viewed as the core of priestly mystification: the view that specific words are spiritually efficacious and that, therefore, they have a living relation with what they name. There is certainly more than a hint, too, that Luther's 'rudeness and acrimony' is itself rather akin to the likewise mighty unmannerly 'papal usurpation' that he would criticise.[31] What is fundamental to this description of Dante is that his status as an awakener from superstition is bound up precisely with the fact that his language is neither the product nor expression of perfected disenchantment.

But also, even here, Dante's achievement is a vulnerable one, because not all of it has found appropriate recipients. Tillotoma Rajan, for example, has argued that 'Shelley's reading of *The Divine Comedy* proceeds on the principle that the work is to be found in unassimilated portions of the text, in revolutionary sparks that a later reader develops, often in opposition to what the major portion of the text seems to say.'[32] Rajan quotes Wilhelm von Humboldt's aperçu that '[l]anguage is not a work (*ergon*) but an activity (*energeia*)' as justification for this kind of necessarily interventionist reading.[33] For Rajan, therefore, his view of Dante is an important instance of Shelley's 'theory of poetry as a self-displacing energy, from which arises both the need for and the reconception of the supplement of reading'.[34] Thus, despite its vast potential ('each [word] is as a spark, a burning atom of inextinguishable thought'), Dante's poem is reliant on its conductors to realise, in every sense, that power. This sense lies behind the otherwise somewhat awkward conjunction of birth and pregnancy in the above passage. Conduction of the real power of his words involves both discovery of them in their immediately post-partum state, so to speak, and also, in fact, the bringing to birth for the first time of that with which they are pregnant. Thus, uncovering them from beneath 'the ashes of their birth' is not mere discovery but also renewal, and thus, as Jerrold E. Hogle has aptly stressed, '[f]or Shelley any figure or construction within an existing piece of writing, whether its author is alive or dead, is in transit from a previous use into the present one *and* from the present order into a future reinterpretation'.[35] This, of course, is consistent with the view established early in 'A Defence of Poetry' that poetry is in need of reanimation lest its words harden into mere terms and thus lose their connection with living, just as it has the capacity of reanimation itself.

One way of thinking about the description of Dante's language in 'A Defence of Poetry', then, is to view it as offering a radical revision of poetry's ageing process. The birth of poetic works (or poetic words) is not the initiation of their irreversible progress toward death but rather the beginning of their wait for a conductor who will, in fact, not just realise their birth but also that with which they are in turn pregnant. I want to turn now to a related but different – because apparently regretful – account of the relation between poetry and youth in 'The Witch of Atlas'. I wish to do this not just in order further to refine my account of Shelley's ideas about poetic (and, in particular, sonic) reanimation but in order to show how some of the claims I have been making for poetic sound, against the rationalizing insistence that language must be maximally explicating, might actually be borne out in verse. This is, of course, an especially apt poem in which to see these claims for poetry evinced, because, as Harold Bloom put it some years ago, '[p]oetry is a witch because, like magic, it competes with religion and philosophy as a discipline apprehending reality'.[36] What I want to focus on here, though, is the way in which poetry itself, as it were, acts in competition with semantic sense in 'The Witch of Atlas'.

In the poem's fourteenth stanza, Shelley describes the cavernous habitation of the poem's central figure, the witch:

> The deep recesses of her odorous dwelling
>   Were stored with magic treasures—sounds of air,
> Which had the power all spirits of compelling,
>   Folded in cells of chrystal silence there;
> Such as we hear in youth, and think the feeling
>   Will never die—yet ere we are aware,
> The feeling and the sound are fled and gone,
> And the regret they leave remains alone.
> (*Poems* III, p. 579; ll. 153–60)

There are significant echoes, of course, between these lines and characterisations of poetry elsewhere in Shelley's work. For instance, the 'cells of chrystal silence' here are anticipated in the wonderfully evocative lines toward the end of the prologue to *Alastor*: 'And Silence, too enamoured of that voice, / Locks its mute music in her rugged cell' (*Poems* I, p. 467; ll. 65–6). And the association of poetry with odour is, of course, a vital feature of the garden in which grows 'The Sensitive-Plant': 'The snow-drop and then the violet / Arose from the ground with warm rain wet / And their breath was mixed with fresh odour, sent / From the turf, like the voice and the instrument' (*Poems* III, p. 295; ll. 13–16). One of Shelley's finest modes is a fugitive observation, just beneath the level of distinct consciousness, and that is in evidence here in 'The Sensitive-Plant', where the definite snowdrop and violet are tentatively joined by a rose still merely in bud, so to speak, at the beginning of the second of the quoted lines in the word 'arose'. Shelley is especially fond of this pun: it is at work again in his description in *Adonais* of how 'Chatterton / Rose pale', where the image of Chatterton as a pale rose is fleetingly evoked, which I discussed in Chapter 1, and it is also, perhaps more clearly in evidence in his version of lines from Calderón's *El príncipe constante*, where he justifiably translates 'Ã florecer las rosas madrugaron' as 'The roses arose early to blossom' (*Poems* III, p. 67). (*Madrugar*, incidentally, means to rise early or to dawn, so 'arose' is both accurate and chimes felicitously with 'roses'.) In the above lines from 'The Sensitive-Plant', the hint of 'a rose' in 'arose' is perhaps a deft recognition on Shelley's part that roses bloom some time after violets, which, in turn, come after snowdrops: while those flowers have already displayed themselves, the rose is yet to bloom. But, more importantly, the fact that what might be seen or, in this context, smelt (that is, 'a rose') is in fact *heard* in 'arose' also attempts to enact a synaesthetic folding of scent, sight and sound together.[37] The concatenation of scent and sound in particular is apparent, furthermore, both here and in the lines from 'The Witch of Atlas' above, in the recollection of 'ode' in the words 'odour' and 'odorous'. Two senses despotically prevailed over by the visual, therefore, are championed.[38]

The most significant and frequently noted echo (by Bloom and others) of these lines from 'The Witch of Atlas', however, is the portrayal of poetry as a cave-inhabiting witch in 'Mont Blanc'. Apostrophising the Ravine of Arve in that poem, Shelley had imagined the ravine 'In the still cave of the which Poesy, / Seeking among the shadows that pass by, / Ghosts of all things that are, some shade like thee, / Some phantom, some faint image' (*Poems* I, p. 544; ll. 44–7). What is remarkable about these lines is their subtle but daring suspension of time. Unlike classical visits to the underworld in which a departed relative is encountered, here it is left undecided whether the 'form' of the ravine is a past version of it, a reflection of its current state, or an anticipation of what it will become. True, the shadows 'pass by', but the ghosts are of 'the things that *are*', not 'were'. Moreover, and especially given that the ravine is 'seeking' among shadows that 'pass by', the cave itself is 'still' – not primarily, perhaps, in the sense that there is no movement in it, but rather in the sense that it abides. Within the cavern of poetry in 'Mont Blanc', poetry pleats together the past – just as it seems to fade irrecoverably away into shadows, shades, phantoms and faint images – with the present and the future.

This subtle but daring suspension of time is likewise what occurs in the lines from 'The Witch of Atlas', but here, rather than on the level of syntax and lexis, the recoil of memory just as it seems to be vanishing is enacted in the sounds of words. The feeling and sound may be 'fled and gone', but this may not necessarily mean that they are dead and gone, not least because the phrase 'fled and gone' gently demurs from striking the note of decided finality in the more common phrase that it echoes.[39] But 'fled and gone' does not just summon an association – that is, the association with 'dead and gone' – in order to refuse it; it also establishes an association in the modulation effected in the transposition of the *f* and *l* of 'feeling' into 'fled'. It is, of course, these letters that 'fled' shares with 'feeling' that make the difference between 'fled' and 'dead'.[40] Even as it is fleeing, elements of feeling remain.

This kind of elusive and allusive modulation is also, incidentally, evident in the workings of rhyme within and between the stanzas surrounding the one I have been examining. Thus, for just one multiply ramifying instance, the *a* and *b* rhymes of stanza 12 – 'made', 'shade', 'betrayed' and 'beside', 'abide', 'wide', respectively – are closer to one another than labelling them *a* and *b* would suggest, not only in the repetition in each of the terminal *d*, but also in the modulation of the [eɪ] of 'made', etc., into the [aɪ] of 'beside'. Moreover, both of these sets of rhymes are likewise sonically related to the concluding couplet, 'dead' and 'footed', of the previous stanza, whilst 'wide' especially comes to resonate, both sonically and semantically, with the 'skies' and 'eyes' of the couplet at the end of this stanza. Shelley described in 'A Defence of Poetry' how the 'evanescent visitations of thought and feeling' arise and leave unpredictably but that 'in the desire and the regret they leave, there cannot but be pleasure, participating as it does in the nature of its object' (*SPP*, p. 532). This can be seen in the 'recurrence of sound' (*SPP*, p. 514) in the sonic modulations of 'The Witch of Atlas'. In particular, where in stanza 14 Shelley regrets the loss of the sounds that we hear in youth, the line which announces that regret performs in fact its own recollection of those 'Sounds of air': 'yet *ere* we *are* aw*are*'. Explicit description is here countered by sound. Shelley's distinction between 'distinct consciousness' and 'reason', from the conversation with 'Byron' discussed above, is in evidence again here in the suggestion of two modes of awareness. On the one hand, Shelley regrets the absence of the explicit awareness that would allow us maturely to recognise the waning of powers taken for granted in youth. Yet, contrary to this mode of awareness is another implicated in the sounds of words. Sounds of air have not fled but are there – can be felt there in 'ere we are aware'.

The pain of change, the change of pain

The sounded repetition of 'air' thus bears an important kinship with what Garrett Stewart has called the 'anti-puns' that he finds in *Adonais* – where in the line 'And cold hopes swarm like worms within our living clay', we may paradoxically hear of 'cold hopes warm' (*SPP*, p. 422; stanza XXXIX, l. 351) – and, vitally, in the description in 'Hymn to Intellectual Beauty' of how 'Love, Hope, and Self-esteem, like clouds depart / And come, for some uncertain moments lent.–' (*Poems* I, p. 529; ll. 37–8).[41] Stewart comments:

> Call it an interstitial anti-pun, or antiphone, or transegmental drift, but in any case the inner ear may well be made alert to the suggestion that it is ultimately 'for summons' ('for *some unc*ertain') that 'certain moments' are indeed briefly 'lent' to the craving spirit. In the flux of language itself, then, esemplastically transformed, we are to hear the invitation to another life, a life perhaps dedicated to the very words that have, in every sense, shaped its *calling*.[42]

What is crystallised in the 'interstitial anti-pun' on which Stewart focuses is the tautly paradoxical nature of the at once undeniable and fleeting visitations of intellectual beauty. That the 'summons' is announced in and through 'some uncertain moments' performs the evanescence of intellectual beauty's calling: the summons is only announced in 'moments lent', however certain, and thus only announced, as it were, under the breath. The intricacy with which the visitations of beauty to 'life's unquiet dream' must be effected is brought out again in the following lines: 'Man were immortal, and omnipotent, / Didst thou, unknown and awful as thou art, / Keep with thy glorious train firm state within his heart' (ll. 39–41). The condition for man's immortality and omnipotence, these lines declare, is that the spirit of beauty keep its 'glorious train' established within his heart, but were the train to be held in 'firm state' then it would cease to be a 'train'. Immortality and omnipotence may not be bestowed by beauty on man, though life and power may be. Similarly, in the regret for the lost experiences of youth in 'The Witch of Atlas', we are summoned to hear in esemplastically transformed language the recollection of a life that is not altogether lost. And, moreover, this transformation is not sonic reinforcement, merely, of something that is also or already semantically claimed; it is, rather, the opposite. The echo that the verse performs tells us something that the semantic signification certainly does not. It adds to our knowledge of the sounds of air – which could only otherwise be either nostalgically or disenchantedly described – by performing them.

This addition to our knowledge about something that is otherwise seen to have vanished is characteristic of the recursive patterning of Shelley's verse. Mark Kipperman, in *Beyond Enchantment*, describes how Shelley's poetry is preoccupied by the danger that the mind might become entangled in images of its own making without realising it. Kipperman comments on lines 49–59 of 'Mont Blanc' that the 'attempt at imagining the indeterminate' in these lines 'ends only in empty recursiveness'.[43] The passage Kipperman is discussing concludes thus: 'For the very spirit fails / Driven like a homeless cloud from steep to steep / That vanishes among the viewless gales!' (*Poems* I, p. 545; ll. 57–9). Kipperman's comment, that these lines contain the recognition of the spirit's entrapment in 'empty recursiveness', does not, in fact, quite discern their direction. The spirit is not recursive here: it nowhere turns back but is instead driven onward. Contrastingly, recursiveness in Shelley is rarely empty but is instead the attempt to reanimate what is otherwise hollowed out. Shelley's recursive poems are, to borrow Stanley Cavell's phrase, 'texts of recovery', not of regression.[44]

One aspect of Shelley's texts of recovery is, as I have argued in this chapter, his recovery of those aspects of language categorised in the polemics of *mere* reason either as irrelevant or as the shelters of superstition. It is nevertheless important to emphasise that this is not to say that he irrationally propounds a blanket advocacy of superstition. Of course, Shelley is a fierce critic of malevolent mystifications – he is clear that, as Laura Wells Betz has put it, 'tyranny is a form of negative enchantment' but often at precisely the same time as he aims to defend beneficently efficacious enchantment.[45] Thus, for example, in the early poem 'A Tale of Society as It Is: From Facts, 1811' the speaker comments that 'though I could not pour the useless prayer / Would weep upon the grave and leave a blessing there' (*Poems* I, p. 198; ll. 119–20).[46] Likewise, later, in *Prometheus Unbound*, Shelley would cast Jesus as having been betrayed by the afterlife of his words, which have 'outlived him' and had the effect of '[w]ithering up truth, peace, and pity' (*Poems* II, p. 510; Act I, ll. 548–9).[47] Again, however, *Prometheus Unbound* is far from simply condemning the efficaciousness of words; rather, 'the text serves as a container for spell-casting power that can counter-charm tyranny'.[48] One way of imagining what plenitudinous, rather than merely empty, recursiveness (to borrow Kipperman's term) might involve, even in the midst of apparent despair, comes at the end of Shelley's 'lyrical drama', to which we must again, in concluding this chapter, turn our attention. All those arrayed for the play's conclusion – including Ione, Panthea, the Earth, the Moon, and a variety of voices and spirits – exhort Demogorgon to 'Speak: thy strong words may never pass away' (*Poems* II, p. 647; Act IV, l. 553). Demogorgon responds by first announcing that 'Conquest is dragged captive through the deep' and that 'Love, from its awful throne of patient power [...] springs' (*Poems* II, pp. 647–8; Act IV, ll. 556–60). Despite these victories, however, the possibility is not entirely rejected that 'Destruction's strength' might break the bars to its pit. Should that happen, '[t]hese are the spells by which to reassume / An empire o'er the disentangled Doom':

> To suffer woes which Hope thinks infinite;
> To forgive wrongs darker than Death or Night;
>   To defy Power, which seems omnipotent;
> To love, and bear; to hope, till Hope creates
> From its own wreck the thing it contemplates;
>   Neither to change nor falter nor repent:
> This, like thy glory, Titan! is to be
> Good, great and joyous, beautiful and free;
> This is alone Life, Joy, Empire, and Victory.
> (*Poems* II, p. 648; Act IV, ll. 570–8)

This advice is more complex than it initially looks. First, the only thing that is actually what it appears to be is the darkness of the wrongs that are 'darker than Death or Night' – everything else only is *thought* or *seems* to be the case. But those wrongs, by virtue (or, so to speak, by vice) of being darker than the darkest things in human imagining, cannot readily be conceived of. Second, and most important, the character of hope is deeply non-straightforward here in the specific sense that hope must not or cannot, according to Demogorgon, just look forward. The Norton editors append to the most free-standing and unqualified of the 'spells' announced here – namely, 'To love, and bear' – a note suggesting that 'Demogorgon expresses these timeless admonitions in timeless infinitives' (*SPP*, p. 286, n.3); but the movement imagined in the instruction 'to hope, till Hope creates / From its own wreck the thing it contemplates' draws into question the temporality of this passage and certainly any view that would suggest that it has no temporality. After all, Demogorgon is describing a situation here in which the hand of eternity is 'infirm' (*Poems* II, p. 648; Act IV, l. 565). Demogorgon's hope recoils on itself because its characteristic effort is to recover what appears to it to be lost. The apparent moment of despair is potentially also the moment of renewal.

Indeed, *Prometheus Unbound*'s concluding effort of renewal is anticipated in Prometheus's opening speech at the start of Act I. Just as Prometheus complains that there is 'No change, no pause, no hope!' (*Poems* II, p. 479; Act I, l. 24), in a line that allies hope with change and pause, so the linguistic fabric of the speech performs both change and pause. Prometheus claims that he is visited by no 'sound of life', but in the very teeth of his complaint, the sonic involutions of his speech are the sound of a striving, enduring, but also temporary and vulnerable life.

There are many examples of this – such as the proliferation of transpositions in 'The crawling glaciers pierce me with the spears' (l. 31), where 'glacier*s pierce*' is both recalled and modulated in 'spears',[49] but where also, between 'glaciers' and 'pierce' themselves, the group -cier- is transformed into -ierc-, already enacting a preparatory modulation in the very enunciation of what itself comes to be differentially echoed. This line, concerned with the pain inflicted on Prometheus, performs change in the churning of its letters, and, moreover, Prometheus's speech repeatedly returns in sound to its central concerns of pain and change: 'reign and triumph' (l. 10); 'vain revenge' (l. 11); 'had I deigned to share the shame' (l. 18); and 'they disdained not such a prostrate slave. / Disdain? ah no, I pity thee' (ll. 52–3). But most crucial of all is the following transposition: 'Ah me, alas, pain, pain ever, forever! / No change, no pause, no hope! Yet I endure' (ll. 23–4). The complaint that there is no change confirms precisely Prometheus's predicament in 'pain ever, forever!' It would be possible to view the repetition of [eɪn] throughout this speech as a gravitation of the voice both toward the sound of 'pain' as well as the sound of pain in a barely articulate jabbering of 'ay! ay! ay!'. Furthermore, 'pain' thus comes to be sonically connected to what has caused it – the '*reign* and triumph' of Jupiter – and what offers a false prospect of escape from it – '*vain* revenge'. But at the same time, the resonance of [eɪn] throughout the speech, and especially its transposition from 'pain' to 'change', intimate the change of which Prometheus despairs. 'The effect of this flux and coalescence', states Isobel Armstrong, remarking on the language of the poem, 'is simultaneously of obliteration and preservation.'[50] Demogorgon's instructions to 'suffer woes which Hope thinks infinite' and at the same time 'to hope, till Hope creates / From its own wreck the thing it contemplates' are anticipated in the transpositions of Prometheus's plaint, despite its explicitly announced despair.

The sonic transformations of 'The Witch of Atlas' and *Prometheus Unbound*, then, act as a counterweight to the settled despair announced in what those poems, at crucial moments, say. The realisation, so to speak, of these transformations is never guaranteed, of course, since, above all, it is reliant on its noticing by the poems' readers. It is to what I call the interanimation of poem and reader that I now turn in the following chapter.

CHAPTER SIX

Poetry and the life of theory

Central to this book's attempt to develop an understanding of Shelley's view of the poetry of life and the life of poetry has been – as that way of putting it perhaps already intimates – an implicit insistence on the mutual interdependence of poetry and its readers. Without poetry, readers are subject to the vicissitudes of mere 'living on'; without readers, poetry does not live at all. I hope in this chapter to give a fuller account of what I want to call the interanimation of poetry and reading, and, in doing so, also to consider again the relation of poetry to 'theory'. This latter consideration is essential here because I have suggested throughout that Shelley's thinking about poetry and the 'apprehension of life' involves a reconception of poetry's relation to thinking such that, in particular, poetry's thinking involves something more than and different from the setting out in verse of pre-established theories.

I want to pursue these questions by turning here, at last, to 'The Triumph of Life'. In particular, I wish to take what may seem a slightly oblique approach to the question of Shelley's relation of poetry to theory by examining a particular instance of the relation to an esteemed theoretical forebear, namely, Bacon, in the poem. This approach is 'slightly oblique' because a more obvious interlocutor for Shelley's final examination of the relation between poetry and theory might seem to be 'the grim Feature' that is the remainder unconsumed by corruption of 'what was once Rousseau' (*SPP*, p. 489; ll. 190, 204). Moreover, this stunted remainder of Rousseau explicitly contrasts his writings with the songs of 'the great bards of old': 'I / Have suffered what I wrote, or viler pain!' (*SPP*, p. 492; ll. 274, 278–9). But it is, I hope to show, just before this point in the poem that Bacon, and not Rousseau, is claimed for poetry, and at precisely that moment that his theoretical achievements are celebrated. It is well known that fundamental to Shelley's high regard for Bacon was his admiration for his accomplishments as 'a poet', though what this means for Shelley's own poetry has been less well recognised. Claiming Bacon for poetry, as

I put it perhaps infelicitously a moment ago, does not involve here the articulation of an argument, or the explicit praise of Bacon's writing, or even the conscious appropriation of particular aspects of his writing. But it does involve the migration of Bacon's poetic thinking into the detailed orchestration of the movement of Shelley's verse.

Untheorised attention

In 1992, Kelvin Everest introduced a collection of essays to mark the bicentenary of Shelley's birth by opposing the theoretical readings of Shelley then prevalent, especially amongst American scholars, to 'acutely subtle and sympathetically inward' readings of Shelley's verse, characteristic, he claimed, of 'a native British tradition of untheorised attention to the precise workings and qualities of Shelley's poetry considered as a body of work which continues to live within a living literary culture.'[1] We may leave to one side the transatlantic dimension of this sketch of the state of Shelley criticism in the early 1990s. But just as it proves difficult to maintain any very strict distinction between American and British approaches to Shelley's work, so it turns out that it is difficult to keep 'theory' at arm's length for the essayists convened under Everest's editorship. To begin with, the first essay, Vincent Newey's attentive reading of *Alastor*, for instance, opens with a reflection on Freud's 'On Transience' that would hardly have been out of place in a more avowedly theoretical context.[2] To be sure, Newey's reference to Freud is not the springboard into a psychoanalytic reading of the kind that might have been ventured in a more avowedly theoretical context, and it remains the case that Everest's collection includes no deconstructive reading of Shelley for which Shelley's work is 'exemplary, both in terms of promoting the theory and illustrating it in a particular style of poetry'.[3] But it is true that Everest's own recourse to 'untheorised attention', and his own identification of certain scholars as practitioners of it, is already implicitly theoretical, for the lineaments of a theory of what that attention is, and not only exemplification of its workings, are, ultimately, what is presented in Everest's usefully insightful introduction.

Twenty years on from Everest's still valuable collection, it might, nevertheless, be felt that the slightly anxious concern with the status of 'theory' in the field of Shelley studies that Everest's preface displays has by now been dispelled and that new and different critical approaches (and controversies) have come to govern the terrain. But what certainly remains significant in Everest's introduction is instead the implicit opposition between theory and life. It is only, that is, once Shelley is the object of 'untheorised attention' that his work 'continues to live within a living literary culture'. Determining the specific relation between life and theory in Shelley's work, conceived as antagonistic by Everest, has proven remarkably fruitful. Recent work, as I discussed in Chapter 1, on Shelley's relation to early nineteenth-century science, has attempted to show him, on the basis of meticulous historical scholarship, as having been deeply involved with contemporary debates concerning the theory of life. The Shelley that emerges from the account developed, for example, in Sharon Ruston's *Shelley and Vitality* is, therefore, already theoretically engaged in a profound sense.

I also argued in Chapter 1 that Shelley in fact evinced a greater wariness about the possibility of a theory of life than is acknowledged in work that demonstrates his nonetheless undoubted interest in natural science. I wish to return to aspects of this argument in this chapter in order to develop the sense in which life is neither, in fact, straightforwardly amenable to theory, for Shelley, nor at the same time simply inimical to it. Despite the salutary recent emphasis on Romantic interest in, and in some cases elaboration of, scientific theories of life, it is well also to remember that many of Shelley's forebears, contemporaries and near-contemporaries did seek to articulate a distinction between life and the theory that would account for it. Preferring 'the lore which nature brings' to the 'barren leaves' of 'science and art' was, of course, central to Wordsworth's understanding of the 'wise passiveness' that we should allow to be cultivated in place of 'Our meddling intellect':

> Books! 'tis a dull and endless strife,
> Come, hear the woodland linnet,
> How sweet his music is; on my life
> There's more of wisdom in it.[4]

Wordsworth reanimates the dead metaphor by which he expresses his wager, 'on my life', since the wisdom that the woodland linnet teaches is the kind of knowledge that both lives and enlivens, in contrast to the merely 'endless strife' of books. The juxtaposition of life to theoretical analysis of it was similarly a central tenet of a number of German Romantic thinkers from Friedrich Schlegel to Ludwig Feuerbach. Feuerbach's statement, for instance, that 'life is a poet; the book, a philosopher' [*Das Leben ist ein Poet, das Buch ein Philosoph*], is anticipated by Wordsworth's dismissal of books in preference for the enlivening song of the linnet. And for Schlegel 'actual life' and 'pure philosophy' are starkly opposed, since the latter 'has nothing to do' with life.[5]

It should be emphasised, however, that Shelley's own version of the opposition between life and theory may be seen as quite sharply differentiated from Romantic versions of this opposition, such as those touched upon above. The emphasis for him, that is, is on our simple incapacity for both thinking about and living life at the same time, rather than on the irreducibility of life's fecundity to attempts to grasp it. Hume's is a relatively late version of the sceptical insistence that life dully, routinely goes on outside, while philosophers are worrying about it:

> In a word, human life is more governed by fortune than by reason; is to be regarded more as a dull pastime than as a serious occupation; and is more influenced by particular humour, than by general principles [...] While we are reasoning concerning life, life is gone; and death, though perhaps they receive him differently, yet treats alike the fool and the philosopher. To reduce life to exact rule and method, is commonly a painful, oft a fruitless occupation: And is it not also a proof, that we overvalue the prize for which we contend?[6]

In Shelley's final poem, 'The Triumph of Life', with which I am chiefly concerned in this chapter, Shelley presents a brilliant but negative variation on the opposition between life and theory as his scepticism apparently reaches its zenith. It is not, that is, thanks to the marvellous superfluity of life that no theory of it can (or ought) to be given, but instead life's eroding sway renders any attempt to grasp and formulate an account of it null.

I will turn to one particularly influential articulation of that account of 'The Triumph of Life', Paul de Man's, in a moment. But I want to be clear now that Shelley's denial, for example, in the preface to *Prometheus Unbound* that his poetry contains 'a reasoned system on the theory of human life' is not in the service of an irrationalist antagonism between life and theory, whether that antagonism is the result of life's richness or ultimate poverty. Moreover, the sceptical position that life is hardly worth the reasoning is itself difficult to maintain, at least in Hume's articulation of that position quoted above. The statement that '[w]hile we are reasoning concerning life, life is gone' expresses regret for that fact, rather than neutrally recording it. Both Shelley's poetry and poetics presuppose that life and its constant renewal are the necessary conditions of possibility for any theory not doomed to necrosis. And after all, for all of Wordsworth's putative rejection of 'Books', the 'impulse from a vernal wood' to which we ought to attend is nonetheless a teacher, and indeed 'May teach you more of man; / Of moral evil and of good, / Than all the sages can'.[7] Moreover, as Leon Chai has shown, the supposition of the theoretical necessity of the constant renewal of life was at least suggested, in fact, in one very early nineteenth-century attempt to elaborate a theory of life itself. Discussing Xavier Bichat's focus on digestion as an emblematic problem, so to speak, for any effort to establish a theory of life, Chai notes that, for Bichat, digestion focuses the question of what life is on the transition from non-vital to vital. Life, therefore, is not traceable to a principle but is instead this process of becoming vital. The consequences for theory of this realisation are profound, since it must shift its focus from seeking stable sources for vitality and instead 'find a more fluid conceptual repertory' to do justice to the ceaseless process of passage from non-vital to vital that is life.[8] Such a repertory, Chai suggests Bichat recognised, is not a theory in the traditional sense of a fixed set of definitions arranged around a stable conceptual core. This chapter pursues the suggestion that life's perpetual renewal must be mirrored by theory – and that that renewal, at once living and theoretical, is what Shelley's verse practice seeks to enact.

Process of erosion

Although Bichat's realisation that life is the process of the non-vital becoming vital, and the consequences of this realisation for the status of theory, form a useful starting point for discussion of Shelley's conception of the relation between life and theory, it has, as I mentioned above, long been thought that the lesson of Shelley's last, great poem, 'The Triumph of Life', is, in fact, the reverse of Bichat's view: life, that poem counsels, is the process instead of the passage from vital to non-vital. This is the interpretation of surely the most influential reading of 'The Triumph of Life' – and perhaps the most influential reading of any poem of Shelley's – Paul de Man's 'Shelley Disfigured'. De Man argues that the poem itself performs this erosive process, for in it, '[q]uestions of origin [...] always lead back to a new scene of questioning which merely repeats the quest and recedes in infinite regress'. Thus, the disarticulated articulation of the poem 'arrests the process of understanding'.[9] Indeed, this is in fact the situation not just for the poem's interpretation but was equally so for its writing. The answer to the first question posed by the poem's narrator emerges only after it has already, in fact, been multiply effaced. I attempt, here, to reproduce in type, with its always already imposed order, the chaos of Shelley's hand:

Half to m y self I said, and what is this
And ~~who is the mis tress of the mys tery~~?
is ~~she~~
~~And who she , and a __ voice made reply~~
~~And a voice said Life~~!
And who ~~the~~ mis tress of the mys tery
~~is~~
~~And a voice said Life~~ . . .
~~Life And life~~ . . .
(*BSM* I, f. 27v/171)

In the editorially established text, 'Life' emerges from beneath these multiple deletions only tentatively, between the forensic pincers of quotation marks and a sort of at once amputated and distended ellipses: 'But a voice answered . . "Life" . . .' (*SPP*, p. 489; l. 180). Yet perhaps in contrast to his own reading, and to the multiple evasions and qualifications of any outbreak of decisiveness in the poem itself, De Man concludes his account with this stark declaration:

> *The Triumph of Life* warns us that nothing, whether deed, word, thought or text, ever happens in relation, positive or negative, to anything that proceeds, follows, or exists elsewhere, but only as a random event whose power, like the power of death, is due to the randomness of its occurrence.[10]

Attempts to offer a critical encapsulation of 'The Triumph of Life' (such as this is, despite de Man's scepticism regarding the possibility of such a thing) are more often than not paradoxical in expression. First of all, the lesson that de Man draws from the poem – that nothing can be thought of as relating to anything else – is undermined by the fact that it is a lesson: if 'The Triumph of Life' 'warns us' of anything, then it must itself stand in a relation of warning to us.[11] This critical conclusion thus takes over, as it were, the paradoxical tenor that it explicitly identifies in the poem: what triumphs in 'The Triumph of Life' is 'the power of death'.

De Man, of course, was not the first to recognise this. For William Hazlitt, for example, this poem was typical of Shelley's delight in perplexity:

> The poem entitled 'The Triumph of Life', is in fact a new and terrific 'Dance of Death'; but it is thus Mr Shelley transposes the appellations of the commonest things, and subsists only in the violence of contrast [...] Any thing more filmy, enigmatical, discontinuous, unsubstantial than this, we have not seen; nor yet more full of morbid genius and vivifying soul.[12]

The commonest thing whose appellation is transposed is, of course, life, but Hazlitt's own commentary makes us wonder just how easily understandable the quality of living actually is, if one poem can be characterised by both its morbid genius and its vivifying soul. Hazlitt, indeed, despite his sometimes quite dismissive antipathy to Shelley's poetry, displayed a remarkably apt sense for the vitality of his verse even when the argument of his poems perversely (Hazlitt implies) renders life as death. Thus he declared elsewhere of Shelley's work that 'There is no *caput mortuum* of worn-out, thread-bare experience to serve as ballast to his mind; it is all volatile intellectual salt of tartar, that refuses to combine its evanescent, inflammable essence with any thing solid or any thing lasting.'[13] What this tacitly reveals is that while it may be lasting, a *caput mortuum* is nonetheless dead, whereas, implicitly, the evanescence of Shelley's verse is part of its life.

What both de Man's and Hazlitt's assessments of 'The Triumph of Life' seem, somewhat despite themselves, to suggest is the insecurity of any attempt to read the undecidability of 'Life' in this poem as betokening life's deathliness in any straightforwardly minatory way. Maureen N. McLane is right to say that this is 'a poem that neither recuperates nor decisively negates the promise of "life"'.[14] McLane's phrasing pays due heed to what she extols as de Man's withering demonstration of the miscarriage of 'optimistic readings' of the poem, while at the same time she abstains from the suggestion that a decisive negation of life's promise is what the poem delivers.[15] I wish to pursue the possibility that 'The Triumph of Life' does not decisively collapse 'the promise of "life"' into 'the power of death' by following Hazlitt's hint that the poem is animated by a 'vivifying soul' and examining the degree to which the poem's verse confirms or denies the morbidity of its discursive warning. Putting it this way already implies something significant about the power of verse: if it is possible for verse to confirm or deny argument, then verse is itself a kind of para-argument, a way of knowing, and not the ultimately trivial outer dress of argument or even compensation for acknowledged conceptual limitations.[16]

Dante's hail, Shelley's rain

But the particular stanzaic form of 'The Triumph of Life' might actually turn out to reinforce de Man's sense that the poem teaches us that life is a process of unstoppable erosion. Shelley's handling of terza rima has consistently been described in terms suggesting that this is in fact the case – especially when his terza rima is compared with Dante's. 'Dante's poetry', wrote Elizabeth Barrett to Robert Browning in 1845, 'seems to come down in hail, rather than in rain – but count me the drops congealed in one hailstone!', and whereas Dante's tercets congeal fluidity into solid units, each one drumming down, Shelley's instead flow into one another, rendering a solid form fluid.[17] Thus, Laurence Binyon, who thought that Christina Rossetti's *A Martyr* was really the only successful English poem in terza rima, was at best ambivalent about Shelley's efforts in this form, complaining that in 'The Triumph of Life' '[w]e miss the solidity and sureness with which in the *Commedia* each tercet swings into its place like stone on stone of some great building till the whole vast fabric is completed'.[18]

William Keach, in his *Shelley's Style*, certainly grants that Shelley's terza rima liquefies Dante's solid tercets. Thus he notes Shelley's frequent enjambment in this form, as well as, following Donald Reiman, his frequent reduction of stresses in the line of 'The Triumph of Life' from five to four in the service of greater rapidity.[19] Nevertheless, on the basis of detailed analysis of particular instances of Shelley's manipulation of stress, Keach dismisses the view that 'Shelley habitually and indiscriminately pursues speed as an end in itself'; moreover, he is also acutely attentive to the way that the verbal patterning of 'The Triumph of Life' is subtly recursive, rather than merely propulsive. This point is especially significant because it allows Keach to question the degree to which the poem's discursive emphasis on erosion, stressed in turn by de Man, is actually enacted in its verse. Thus, in particular, Keach is able to submit de Man's claim that the 'alignment between meaning and linguistic articulation' is 'random and superficial' to critical scrutiny through close attention to Shelley's use of rhyme.[20] Keach objects that de Man's description as merely accidental of the association created by the rhyme, for example, of 'billow' and 'pillow' in 'The Triumph of Life' 'is to obscure the process by which valuable constraints of meaning may be generated by, or discovered within, random verbal resources'.[21] Keach claims, therefore, that the instances of rhyming discernible, for instance, in 'The Triumph of Life' and elsewhere in Shelley's work suggest 'a compositional intelligence fully in touch with the arbitrariness of its expressive medium yet capable of shaping that arbitrariness into, as well as according to, precisely provisional "constraints of meaning"'.[22] As in my discussion in the previous chapter, Keach is thus able to argue that, in Shelley's manipulation and deployment of language, there is not dominant semantic sense and dominated, wholly accidental sonic material, but rather two tensely countervailing aspects of language at work. If anything, the relation of dependence between these two aspects is the other way around, as can be seen in Keach's description of 'The Triumph of Life' itself: 'Forgetting, obliteration and erasure are powerful forces in *The Triumph of Life*. But the articulation of these forces *depends upon* the counterforces of remembering, literation and repetition.'[23]

There are throughout 'The Triumph of Life' many examples of 'counterforces of remembering', in addition to the patterns of rhyme so closely studied by Keach. While, as Keach acknowledges, the poem's opening undeniably emphasises the swiftness of the sun's rising over the globe, the verse's instrumentation enacts a more involved, recollective development. For instance, the interpolation enacted in the move from 'c*rimson*' (*SPP*, p. 483; l. 6) to 'o*rison*' (l. 7) is a consolidating development of the most minute elements of verse even in their transposition. At the same time, the *r* and *s* and *n* of 'crimson' brought more closely together in 'orison' are also, conversely, dispersed throughout the part of the line in which that latter word appears, 'the Ocean's orison arose', where, furthermore, the movement of sound between words is aptly characterisable less as interpolation or transposition, and rather as susurrating osmosis.[24]

A comparable example of sonic development occurs slightly later in the opening passage, where the narrator describes the advent of the vision recounted in the rest of the poem:

the Deep
Was at my feet, and Heaven above my head
When a strange trance over my fancy grew
Which was not slumber, for the shade it spread

Was so transparent that the scene came through
As clear as when a veil of light is drawn
O'er evening hills they glimmer;
(*SPP*, p. 484; ll. 27–33)

The narrator describes his situation 'When a strange trance over my fancy grew'. The stress on both 'strange' and 'trance' serves to emphasise the internal verbal echo of that description, which is then re-echoed in 'fancy'. Here, sound appears to echo sense, since 'strange' grows into 'trance' and then into 'fancy', just as the 'strange trance' is described as growing, while the incantatory quality of the repeated stress on a closely echoing syllable seems to perform the entrancement described. And yet, the tendency of this pattern to cloud the fancy over which it grows and thus render it amnesiac, is offset by its resonance in the 'transparent' of line 31. Indeed, the fact that 'trance' recurs in 'transparent' is a good illustration of the density of Shelley's orchestration of sound and sense at once. The rejection of the suspicion that the 'strange trance' obfuscates the fancy through the insistence that the trance is itself 'transparent' is not only reinforced by the mere fact of the revisionary recollection of 'trance' in 'transparent', but, moreover, that we *hear through* 'transparent' the 'strange trance' of the earlier line puts into practice the at least prima facie perspicuity that the narrator claims for the vision whose emergence he is relating.

I have wanted by adducing these examples from early in 'The Triumph of Life' simply to add to the evidence of Shelley's manipulation of the recollective counterforces of sound in that poem. And I would like now to turn to a passage from later in the poem where the representatives of discursive theory meet 'the great bards of old' in order more fully to examine the relation it envisages between the 'thoughts of men' and poetic 'strain'. I set this discussion, in particular, in a slightly larger intellectual context than I have perhaps established so far in this chapter, while, by no means, leaving behind the minutiae of verse.

Bacon's leap

Not long after 'what was once Rousseau' has introduced himself to the poem's narrator, and thus, in fact, taken over the poem's narration from him, he draws our attention to a host of figures who illustrate the unseemly alliance of 'hoary anarchs, demagogue and sage' (l. 237). Having witnessed the procession of Voltaire and Kant along with the apparently enlightened despots who ruled during their lives, another, this time ancient pair of philosopher and ruler comes into view, before, in turn, Rousseau mentions the revolutionary and explicitly liberatory work of a more recent thinker who, revealingly, is not part of the procession. I quote the lines here in their uncompleted condition:

> "And near [ ] walk the [ ] twain.
> The tutor and his pupil, whom Dominion
> Followed as tame as vulture in a chain.—
>
> "The world was darkened beneath either pinion
> Of him whom from the flock of conquerors
> Fame singled as her thunderbearing minion;
>
> "The other long outlived both woes and wars,
> Throned in new thoughts of men, and still had kept
> The jealous keys of truth's eternal doors
>
> "If Bacon's spirit [ ] had not leapt
> Like lightening out of darkness; he compelled
> The Proteus shape of Nature's as it slept
>
> "To wake and to unbar the caves that held
> The treasure of the secrets of its reign—
>
> (*SPP*, pp. 491-2; ll. 260–73)

The relationship between Aristotle and Alexander had already attracted comment in antiquity, and, indeed, is directly pertinent to a number of extant works in the Aristotelian corpus itself, but the Norton editors cite in particular Bacon's remarks on Aristotle, whom he is represented here as superseding.[25] As many scholars have detailed, Shelley had a thorough knowledge of Bacon's works, and it is worth examining the moment where Bacon discusses Aristotle's relation to Alexander in conjunction with this passage specifically. Shelley owned and annotated a five-volume edition of Bacon's oeuvre, published in 1778.[26] He read *The Advancement of Learning*, in which Bacon comments on Aristotle and Alexander, along with its Latin translation, *De augmentis scientiarum*, and clearly knew them well, since he was able to identify additions to the former appearing in the latter.[27] It is in the Latin text that Shelley marks Bacon's comments on Aristotle and Alexander. I give that text, which Shelley highlighted in his copy, followed by the English version (which Bacon, as it happens, had written first) in brackets:

> Caeterum de viro tam eximio certe, et ob acumen ingenii mirabilii, Aristotele, crediderim facile hanc ambitionem eum a discipulo suo accespisse, quem fortasse aemulatas est; ut si ille omnes nationes, hic omnes opiniones subigeret, et monarchiam quondam in contemplationibus sibi conderet. [I will think of him that he learned the humour of his scholar, with whom it seemeth he did emulate, the one to conquer all opinions, as the other to conquer all nations.][28]

Shelley was evidently attracted to Bacon's critique of Aristotle's hegemony over thought that this way of putting the association of him with Alexander implies. Moreover, according to standard intellectual history, it was of course Bacon himself who was responsible for breaking the dominance of Aristotelian scholasticism, again as Shelley makes clear, by inaugurating the inductive and empirical procedures of modern scientific investigation, and thus invoking Bacon's description of Aristotle and Alexander in 'The Triumph of Life' prepares the ground, as it were, for Bacon's insurgent appearance in the following lines.

The passage of 'The Triumph of Life' from which the above quoted description of '[t]he tutor and his pupil' are taken is clearly concerned with uncomfortable accommodations between thinking and power more generally, and I want to return to its thematic interest below. But although the standard intellectual history is undoubtedly invoked in 'The Triumph of Life'' narrative of the transition from Aristotelian scholasticism to Baconian investigation, it is imperative also to recognise that, for Shelley, Bacon does not simply count as one, even if the first, of a range of enlightened philosophers. It is worth turning briefly to Shelley's characterisation of Bacon's distinctly poetic powers before examining more fully the specific influence of his description of Aristotle on Shelley's verse:

> Lord Bacon was a poet. His language has a sweet and majestic rhythm, which satisfies the sense, no less than the almost superhuman wisdom of his philosophy satisfies the intellect; it is a strain which distends, and then bursts the circumference of the hearer's mind, and pours itself forth together with it into the universal element with which it has perpetual sympathy. All the authors of revolutions in opinion are not only necessarily poets as they are inventors, nor even as their words unveil the permanent analogy of things by images which participate in the life of truth; but as their periods are harmonious and rhythmical and contain in themselves the elements of verse; being the echo of the eternal music. (*SPP*, pp. 514–15)

This description is enormously significant for Shelley's conception of poetry's relation to reason. One view of the relation of poetry to reason casts the former as a response to the limitations of the latter. Thus, for instance, C. E. Pulos remarked, in his consideration of Shelley's view of Plato as a poet, that '[a]s a sceptic', Montaigne, a decisive source for Shelley's scepticism, 'esteemed the "poetry" of Plato as the reaction of human nature to the unknown and unknowable'.[29] According to such a view, poetry (or 'poetry') is consolation for the failure of reason to yield knowledge. Something of this is perhaps initially traceable in the above passage from 'A Defence of Poetry', but although Shelley contrasts the satisfaction of the sense produced by the rhythm of Bacon's language with the satisfaction of the intellect by his philosophy, any neat separation of the sensible (or, indeed, sensual) and intellectual is quickly disabled. Bacon's language is a 'strain' whose radically expansive effect is on the 'hearer's' – and not 'reader's', as Mary Shelley's inoculating revision would have it – '*mind*'. Shelley further emphasises that it is not just the imagery of a writer like Bacon that is necessary to the revolution in opinions that he would effect, but the degree to which his writing contains the 'elements of verse'. That such writing must be at least in an elementary degree *verse* means that any attempt to account for Shelley's identification of Bacon as a poet on the basis of his valorisation of his imagery alone is condemned to insufficiency in its accommodation to a loose notion of poetry as the deployment of colourful images.[30]

It is thus thanks to the quite specific linguistic brilliance of his writings that Bacon is, for Shelley, a poet, and it is the linguistic brilliance of the description of Aristotle and Alexander in *De augmentis scientiarum* in particular that finds its echo in the lines from 'The Triumph of Life' quoted above. What we might call after Shelley the distending strain of Bacon's syllepsis, 'ut si ille omnes nationes, hic omnes opiniones subigeret', is taken up and startlingly expanded in a rare flight (in this poem) of feminine rhymes on 'Dominion', 'pinion' and 'minion'.[31] Each of these terms echoes the sound of the words for what Alexander and Aristotle respectively dominate ('nationes' and 'opiniones'). But whereas the effect of Aristotle's conquest is to subjugate opinions under his rule, the vital insurgency of Bacon's critique of the earlier philosopher is evident in the music of the verse's movement, even before explicit mention is made of Bacon himself a few lines later. Just as the poem tells of the domination of opinion by Aristotle, so the already tautly poised 'nationes' and 'opiniones' burst out of Bacon's text to cascade down the rhymes of Shelley's terza rima.

Let it be clear that I do not suppose Shelley had his copy of Bacon's works open before him as he composed this passage, nor, even, that this highlighted excerpt of Bacon was explicitly before his mind. 'I don't say that a poet must necessarily be conscious of all this.' But I do say that the perpetual linguistic renewal effected in and necessary to poetry is displayed here, immediately prior to the explicit account of the complementary philosophical renovation performed by Bacon. And I do say that Shelley's estimation of Bacon as a poet must be taken quite literally, and thus that the lines of Shelley's verse are as liable to echo the minute verbal details and sonic patternings of Bacon's writing as they are those of any other, more routinely recognised, poet. Aristotelian scholasticism characterised by its oppressive inertia is, in the very moment of its characterisation, countered by the productive movement of a Baconian thinking that is properly described as poetic.

The intervention of excitement

It is thanks, crucially, to Bacon's verbal virtuosity that he stands, for Shelley, in a quite different lineage from the one sketched in standard accounts of intellectual history. In 'A Defence of Poetry', as we saw in the previous chapter, Shelley is willing to grant that the achievements of Locke, Gibbon and other enlighteners must be given their due, but those achievements pale into relative insignificance when compared to those of another set of figures to which Bacon, surprisingly, is seen to belong:

> But it exceeds all imagination to conceive what would have been the moral condition of the world if neither Dante, Petrarch, Boccaccio, Chaucer, Shakespeare, Calderon, Lord Bacon, nor Milton, had existed; if Raphael and Michael Angelo had never been born; if the Hebrew poetry had never

> been translated; if a revival of the study of Greek literature had never taken place; if no monuments of antient sculpture had been handed down to us; and if the poetry of the religion of the antient world had been extinguished together with its belief. The human mind could never, except by the intervention of these excitements, have been awakened to the invention of the grosser sciences, and that application of analytical reasoning to the aberrations of society, which it is now attempted to exalt over the direct expression of the inventive and creative faculty itself. (*SPP*, p. 530)

Bacon's inclusion alongside Milton, Calderón, Shakespeare and others in this important passage is yet further testimony to the precise nature of Shelley's esteem for him as a poet. To be sure, Shelley also speaks of Dante and Shakespeare in particular as philosophers, and he no doubt thought the other figures listed here might be similarly categorised, but it is important to recognise that they are philosophers and poets in the same sense, displaying the same fine grain of linguistic genius as Bacon must also be held, by Shelley, to display.

The above passage from 'A Defence of Poetry' is, in fact, a crucial statement of Shelley's view of the relation of poetic 'excitements' to the apparently more sober business of 'analytical reasoning'. If it is true that the 'forms [of art] are rational, because reason is essential to both the organization and operation of art', it is also true, Shelley would add, that art is essential both to the organisation and operation of reason.[32] Thus, it 'exceeds all imagination to conceive' what the world would have been like had not the poets and artists listed above existed – a statement in which the fact that it would be left to *imagination* to attempt to *conceive* of a world without Dante and company is itself significant, for imagination is no mere adjunct to conception but basic to it. Furthermore, the lordly demeanour of 'analytical reasoning' in its attempt to 'exalt' over the 'inventive and creative faculty' is dangerously inappropriate because, after all, it was itself invented in response to the intervention of artistic excitements. The verbal echo of 'intervention' and 'invention' is instructive in this regard, because it suggests that the power of invention lies neither, as the grosser sciences might have it, with analytical reasoning, nor, indeed, entirely within the range of any individual human mind, because it must be prompted by interventions from without. Of course, these interventions are the product of human artistry, but we are asked to try to imagine what the world would have been without any one of the figures and cultural forms listed, such that none of them is uniquely privileged. The very profusion of the above passage – listing the pinnacles of artistic achievement from Dante to ancient sculpture – betokens the fact, as Shelley sees it, that excitements of this kind must be constantly renewed, and analytical reasoning's implied presumption that it can do without constantly renewed artistic excitements is deathly.

We can further draw out what is at stake in this argument about the relation of excitement to reasoning if we compare it to one of the most intriguing insights in Immanuel Kant's *Critique of Judgement* (1790) (which, it seems, Shelley did not know).[33] Kant argues that cognitive judgement – that is, the kind of judgement that results in knowledge, or, in Kant's specific usage of the term, 'experience' – is somehow prepared for or anticipated by aesthetic judgement – that is, the kind of judgement that estimates appearances as beautiful or ugly but which is not, according to Kant, experience in his sense and which does not actually produce knowledge.[34] In fact, Kant speculates that there was a time at which all cognition was preceded or accompanied by delight. 'It is true', he remarks, in section VI of the Introduction to the *Critique of Judgement*,

> that we no longer notice any decided pleasure in the comprehensibility of nature, or in the unity of its divisions into genera and species, without which the empirical concepts, that afford us our knowledge of nature in its particular laws, would not be possible. Still it is certain that the pleasure appeared in due course, and only by reason of the most ordinary experience being impossible without it has it become gradually fused with simple cognition, and no longer arrests particular attention.[35]

In a fashion notably similar to Shelley's considerations of the habitual nature of experience, Kant observes that the pleasure once taken in the comprehensibility of nature now 'no longer arrests particular attention' because the experience which it founds has become routine. Such pleasure would be a decided intervention in our experience of the kind envisaged by Shelley since it would (but does not) arrest attention.

In spite of this view that there is an important analogy or affinity between cognitive and aesthetic judgement, and as if in confirmation of the point that the accompaniment of cognition with delight is a thing of the past, it is central to Kant's aesthetics, as I mentioned above, that cognition and delight are to be distinguished. Shelley's conception of the relation between aesthetic delight and cognitive judgement is similar to Kant's intimation that the latter had once been accompanied by the former. What it is important to emphasise here, however, is that Shelley, in contrast to Kant, insists on the need for their connection to persist. Where Kant had ultimately tried to establish the analogy between cognitive and aesthetic judgement as that which both brought them together and – by dint of the fact that analogy is *only* analogy – kept them apart, Shelley, conversely, views the 'excitements' associated with the names of Dante, Petrarch, Boccaccio et al., as abidingly essential to the proper functioning of 'the grosser sciences'. It is thus the case for Shelley that, as Simon Jarvis has stated, 'poetry lies buried alive in systems of imaginary disenchantment, suppressed and stigmatized, or supplementary and aesthetic, certainly, but in truth one condition of their practicability and intelligibility alike'.[36] As I argued in the preceding chapter, the systems in which poetry lies buried alive are 'imaginary' both in the sense that they wrongly suppose themselves disenchanted and, as Jarvis here also makes clear, because they rely on imagination, and not just rationality, in order to function. Shelley's avowal of the need for poetry to continue to animate the systems of thought that would kill it off is the reason why he does not complain of the attempt on the part of 'analytical reasoning' to reason analytically but does indeed complain all the more strongly of its attempt to dominate 'the direct expression of the inventive and creative faculty itself' (*SPP*, p. 530). Thus, he agrees with Kant that delight plays a fundamental role in cognition but goes further than Kant by maintaining that the forgetting of delight by a cognition that has become habitual is detrimental to that cognition itself.

Shelley's complaint against the imperialist tendencies of that cognition which has announced its independence from delight also makes it clear that, however crucial to the proper functioning of the human mind poetic and artistic excitements may be, they are nevertheless acutely vulnerable to being devoured by the children they have begotten. We examined Shelley's conception of the battle waged between different visions of language in the previous chapter, where, in particular, I stressed Shelley's refusal to submit to a view of language in which the sounds of words would be at most decorative, if not wholly trifling. It is important to emphasise here that this battle is waged over time. It is a process of, in John W. Wright's phrase, '[s]emantic entropy', by which 'the elements of cognitive and emotive organization tend through time, like all other forms of energy, toward disorganization of the relationships once unified or integrally apprehended: imagined and felt, to use Shelley's terms'.[37] This tendency toward disorganisation of the elements of cognitive and emotive organisation is identified in Drummond's account of trains of ideas. In that account, Drummond rejects the view he ascribes to Locke that ideas are subject to voluntary recall, illustrating this rejection, significantly, by giving the example of a forgotten word in some lines of poetry: its recollection, he points out, is by no means an act of will and depends rather on the mode of attention characterising the initial reception of the lines in question. Drummond's example is significant because it suggests (and would have suggested to Shelley) that poetry's power is variable, that its potential recollection depends on its initial force and that it stands in need of renewal. The initial idea in a train of ideas, Drummond moreover suggests, excites the mode of attention upon which it then depends. 'This principal idea', he writes, 'continues to prolong the duration of its dependent train always in proportion to the degree of attention, which it itself has excited until some new perception give another turn to the course of our thoughts.'[38]

For Shelley, however, it is not simply that poetry, in particular, is subject to displacement by other sensations but rather that it is prone to the evisceration of sensation itself. Yet poetry's vulnerability to the process of abstraction is not a straightforward flaw in it, the undesirability of the outcome of such a process notwithstanding. Were poetry invulnerable to becoming abstract because it stands in no need of renewal, then it would lose its vitality. The life of poetry is thus mortal – but this in turn is not to say that it is simply doomed to die. In Shelley's translation of *The Banquet of Plato*, Diotima is reported as describing how even though each human being is 'said to live, and be the same from youth to old age', that life is in fact a constant and semi-paradoxical process of becoming new by loss and change. Nonetheless, mortal nature still 'seeks, as far as it is able, to become deathless and eternal', a desire it can only accomplish, Diotima immediately makes clear, by 'generation'.[39] The consequence of this is that while mortal being can become immortal, it is then immortal in a quite different manner to the immortality of beings immortal, as it were, to begin with. Diotima states this important distinction in the following way:

> In this manner, every thing mortal is preserved: not that it is constant and eternal, like that which is divine; but that in the place of what has grown old and is departed, it leaves another new like that which it was itself. By this contrivance, O Socrates, does what is mortal, the body and all other things, partake of immortality; that which is immortal, is immortal in another manner.[40]

Helen Small has argued that, in this dialogue, 'Plato has almost nothing to say about mortality as death-relatedness [...] His concern is rather with mortal life as the determining structure within which we exist and think.'[41] If mortality is not chiefly understood as life which is terminated in death but rather defined by it and thus given determining structure, then Diotima's distinction between mortal immortality and immortal immortality is not as incomprehensible as it might initially appear.

A comparable evocation of the relation between mortal and immortal immortality is to be found in the second (uncompleted) stanza of the late poem, 'The Zucca':

> Summer was dead, but I yet lived to weep
> The instability of all but weeping;
> And on the Earth lulled in her winter sleep
> I woke, and envied her as she was sleeping.
> Too happy Earth! over thy face shall creep
> The wakening vernal airs, until thou, leaping
> From unremembered dreams, shalt [ ] see
> No death divide thy immortality.
> (Hutchinson, p. 665; ll. 9–16)

The explicit point of the stanza is to contrast the unwanted wakefulness of the poem's speaker with the Earth's 'winter sleep'. The speaker's wakefulness paradoxically does not betoken his life in any emphatic sense, as opposed to the death in winter of the earth, but rather, it is implied, the fact that he '*yet* lived' suggests the inappropriate, mournful perpetuation of his life as death-in-life. The Earth, by contrast, appears to enjoy immortal immortality, for it, 'leaping / From unremembered dreams, shal[l] see / No death divide [its] immortality.' But it is not, in fact, that the Earth is an immortal immortal and the speaker simply mortal. On the contrary, the Earth's life is a renewed, reproduced mortality, whereas the speaker's is a bad immortality. The Earth may wake 'From unremembered dreams', but that does not mean that those dreams did not occur, nor does its failure to 'see' the division of its immortality by death mean that the interpolation of winter did not happen. Indeed, the stanza's suspicion of undivided life is discernible in what is here a slightly eerie characterisation of spring as somewhat furtive or even licentiously intimate ('over thy face shall creep / The wakening vernal airs'), whereas the Earth, having slept, will not creep, but leap back to life. In any case, this discontinuity between the gradual effect of spring and Earth's sudden return to life is emphasised, moreover, by the fact that whereas the two preceding pairs of *a*/*b* rhymes had expanded the rhyme word in the *a* position by making it a participle in the *b* line ('weep'/'weeping'; 'sleep'/'sleeping'), lines 13 and 14 preserve the rhyme pattern with terms that are not only lexically unrelated but, in fact, semantically opposed: 'creep'/'leaping'.[42]

Earth's immortality, then, is not undivided. Crucial to its life is the fact that it stops and starts, that there are pauses in its progress, in contrast to the undivided and therefore deathly life of the poem's speaker. Pauses are fundamental to the life of poetry. It is, for example, the 'just and harmonious arrangement of the pauses' of another significant verse form, the Spenserian stanza, that attracted Shelley to it in *Laon and Cythna*, where, for example, Cythna-as-Laone's eulogy to freedom and equality is described thus:

> She, like a spirit through the darkness shining,
> In tones whose sweetness silence did prolong,
> As if to lingering winds they did belong,
> Poured forth her inmost soul: a passionate speech
> With wild and thrilling pauses woven among,
> Which whoso heard, was mute, for it could teach
> To rapture like her own all listening hearts to reach.
> (*Poems* II, p. 157; canto fifth, stanza LII, ll. 2274–80)

The flow of Laone's speech – described in the following stanza as 'as a mountain stream' (LIII, l. 2281) – is tempered by pauses which are not emptiness but 'wild and thrilling'. And while the comparison with 'lingering winds' might seem to invoke perpetuation, rather than pausing, lingering invokes a departure from the normal or expected course of things, a hiatus in it. The risk, moreover, that a pause might turn out to be a finish cannot be evaded if the monotony of perpetuated living on is ever to be broken in favour of something new, as the counterpoising of lingering and pausing in the tenth stanza of the poem's dedication hesitantly intimates:

> Is it, that now my inexperienced fingers
> But strike the prelude of a loftier strain?
> Or, must the lyre on which my spirit lingers
> Soon pause in silence, ne'er to sound again
> Though it might shake the Anarch Custom's reign
> (ll. 82–6)

The living line

Any life that is perpetual living on without pause is unliveable. We cannot inhale forever; the heart must start and stop if it is to beat at all. And a poem without breaks is no poem. I have implied so far that Shelley sees an analogy between the necessary pauses of life and those of poetry, but I want to attempt now to establish a closer affiliation between the lives of readers and those of poems than I have so far done. It might be objected to the kind of account that I have been advancing, not just in this chapter, but throughout, that while poems might legitimately be thought of as enlivening, they need not be alive. I want to address this objection by way of examining a passage of 'The Triumph of Life' which immediately follows the one inspired by Bacon that I discussed above. And I do want to argue, as it happens, that the kinds of poetic excitements envisaged in it – the 'living melody' of the poets – are in fact both enlivening and living. Moreover, they are living by virtue of being enlivening, and vice versa, since they only live through their reception by living beings, whose feeling of life, in turn, they promote. Here are the lines, beginning with the indication of the poets in the procession of Life by 'what was once Rousseau':

> "See the great bards of old who inly quelled
>
> "The passions which they sung, as by their strain
> May well be known: their living melody
> Tempers its own contagion to the vein
>
> "Of those who are infected with it—
> (*SPP*, p. 492; ll. 274–8)

Commentary on these lines has emphasised the contrast between the poets and Rousseau, who remarks that '"I / Have suffered what I wrote, or viler pain! – // And so my words were seeds of misery – / Even as the deeds of others"' (ll. 278–81). Thus, Rousseau's works have both a biographical basis and an immediate effect ('misery') on the lives of others, in contrast to the controlled passions of the bards. But how can it then be said that the bards' poetry is 'living' if it lacks these connections (both in origin and destination) with actual lives? On the one hand, the contrast with Rousseau is not perhaps as stark as might initially be thought. That the bards 'inly quelled' their passions does not result in the obliteration of those passions, but, quite the contrary, this action of inly quelling itself 'by their strain / May well be known'. The knowledge in question here is not, as in Rousseau's case, a detailed biographical account, and thus not knowledge, whatever its subsequent effects may be, that is nonetheless simply waiting to be discovered, but one that must be relived. This is brought into view, first of all, by senses available to the word 'strain' as it is used here. First, 'strain' is potentially painful exertion, of the kind that might be expected to result from the inward quelling of passion. Second, it may also denote 'a musical sequence of sounds; a melody, tune', a sense clearly supported by the context of the above lines. (These first two senses of 'strain', incidentally, are also at play in Wordsworth's lines in the first stanza of 'The Solitary Reaper', 'Alone she cuts and binds the grain / And sings a melancholy strain', where the strain of the highland lass's work is echoed in her song.)[43] Third, a 'strain' is also progeny, a tribe, family, or line of descendants. This final sense is crucial, not just because Shelley had considered the familial 'Homer and his brethren' as an alternative for 'the great bards of old' (*SPP*, p. 492, n. 4), but moreover because what this sense of the 'strain' points to is the role of those coming after the bards in recognising the significance of their song, of, that is, their 'strain' in the second sense above.

What is known in the strain is not simply the possession of those that sing it, but instead has to be relived in everyone that experiences it: '"their living melody / Tempers its own contagion to the vein / Of those who are infected with it"'. The figure of contagion and infection requires some consideration here. It should be noted that infection is ambivalent in Shelley's work. In 'A Defence of Poetry', for instance, he criticises the 'weak attempt to teach certain doctrines' during 'periods of the decay of social life, [when] the drama sympathizes with that decay'. Such attempts, he writes, 'are usually no more than specious flatteries of some gross vice or weakness with which the author in common with his auditors are infected' (*SPP*, p. 520). But two years earlier, writing to Peacock, the interlocutor of 'A Defence of Poetry', from Bologna, Shelley could imagine infection quite otherwise. He remarks, in the important context of a reflection on the physical vulnerability of painting, prompted by a visit to the Academia delle Belle Arte where a number of paintings had been damaged by French troops, that although paintings must physically perish, 'The poet embodies them in his creation, the systems of philosophers are modelled to gentleness by their contemplation, opinion that legislator is infected with their influence' (9 November 1818, *Letters* II, p. 53).

Indeed, this indecision about the nature of contagion is fitting, since contagion can never be decisively appropriated. It is never anyone's in particular and, moreover, Shelley is fond of deploying the word 'own' ('own contagion') in contexts where it is acutely unresolved whose 'own' it is. This equivocation regarding possession is suggested not just by the semantic equivocation of these lines, but in the decisions as to their scansion that they demand of their readers. So far, these reflections have been broadly thematic in orientation, focusing on the implications of Shelley's characterisation of the bards' 'living melody' as a 'strain' knowable to its recipients. But the lines make the demand for that living recognition perfomatively, as well as insisting upon it discursively. The question I am interested in here might seem diminutively technical but is, in fact, crucial to Shelley's claim that the works of the bards are 'living melody': how are we to read these lines and do they themselves contain a clear answer to this question?

This is a pertinent consideration because the lines pose a specific set of problems to straightforward realisation of them according to the established pattern of the rising ten- or eleven-syllable line. To begin with, is Rousseau's instruction, 'See', stressed, as might be felt since it introduces a shift in attention and, moreover, because the dash at the end of the preceding line might be taken to reinforce the importance of indication at this point? If 'See' is stressed, does that entail that the next strong stress comes on 'bards', with their qualification as 'great' receiving concomitantly less emphasis? Or is 'See' somewhat glided over to arrive at a spondaic summit of the line in 'great bards'? How are we to handle 'melody' exactly, with its forestress and unstressed final syllable at the end of the line? (This is perhaps an especially important question, for we are to face it again at the conclusions of lines 280 and 282 with 'misery' and 'company'.) And what are we to make of the word immediately following 'melody' after the enjambed line ending, 'Tempers'? Is this a cunning metrical joke, with its initial inversion, shunting stress to the fore, when what the word denotes is restraint and accordance with established patterns?

These questions invite alternative answers (I have answered them alternatively for myself on different readings of these lines). Any answer must be tenable, but the point is that such answers nevertheless reveal themselves to be provisional in the sense, in part, that they rely on a mutual modification of text and reading. What is involved here is captured well in an account of one of the most Shelleyan of recent poems, John Wilkinson's *The Speaking Twins*. Simon Jarvis remarks on the presence of 'The Triumph of Life' in Wilkinson's poem, and comments in particular on lines 21 to 28 of Shelley's poem, where the phrases 'before me fled / The night; behind me rose the day; the Deep / Was at my feet' briefly establish a set of six-syllable rising groups in contrast to the rising ten- and eleven-syllable lines that predominate. The significance of this counterbalancing effect is explained by Jarvis in the following way:

> What this reminds us of is the instability of the idea of metre itself. Metre is always suspended between induction and deduction, description and prescription, because it is always something which you have both to induce empirically from the verse material in front of you (otherwise you could just decide that it was in any metre you liked) and also something which you have to *do* to the verse material in front of you (a metrical performance does not result simply from obeying the ordinary phonological rules for the organization of intonational patterns in everyday speech, but is, on the contrary, always an attempt performatively to reconcile two often conflicting sets of requirements: the requirement of intelligibly organized phonology and the requirement that the line count as an instance satisfying a set of underlying rhythmic constraints). There is a necessary circle here: you cannot make the poem work metrically without making a decision about

> its metre, but you cannot make a decision about its metre without already having made it work metrically.[44]

It might be added to this account that the mutual modification of metre and reader required by the reading of metrical verse is itself liable to be modified each time the living individual reader is brought before the lines – and each time that reader's reading is brought into dialogue with those of others. That is not to say that since any given reading is not determinable according to proofs that it is merely relative; it is instead to point to the fact that the reading of verse relies on the kind of living realisation both discursively imagined and performatively demanded in the lines about the great bards cited above. There is a schema of mutual dependence in these lines such that they both beget a lineage ('their strain') and depend on it for their realisation. Poetry is un-self-sufficient because, as Wordsworth simply said and as Shelley recognised, '[p]oems [...] cannot read themselves'.[45] The consequence of this constraint for poetry is radical: 'If it has not entered a single mind, a poem does not yet exist.'[46]

Importantly, the inability of poems to read themselves does not mean that, in their reliance on being read, they are simply at the mercy, so to speak, of their readers. Clive Scott claims that 'in reading, we assimilate the text to our own physiology', but assimilation in this instance is not like other kinds of physiological assimilation.[47] Our physiology, in reading, has to fit itself to poetry, just as much as poetry must be fitted to it. While the reader's initial attitude, as it were, toward the poem may be like that toward any other object, the poem is taken into the body and borrows the very means by which it is kept alive. The poem is indeed only lent the reader's breath, but it is in the intimacy of this relationship that poetry takes over, becoming the subject dealing, now, with the reader.[48]

This mutuality marks out the tempering of 'living melody' from the forms of compulsion envisaged in the lines surrounding the description of the bards.[49] As we have seen, both Alexander and Aristotle are agents of dominion;[50] Bacon similarly 'compelled / The Proteus shape of Nature's as it slept', but it is important to note that his action is, in contrast to Aristotle's inert enthronement in the minds of men, inspired by a republican desire to open up the hoard of secrets collected during nature's 'reign'. The quelling of the bards' passions within themselves involves a different kind of compulsion again. The contrast is most usually drawn with Rousseau here, who, rather than first controlling his passions, 'suffered what I wrote' and thus spelled 'misery'. The quelling of the bards' passions did not, of course, lead to the non-communication of them. Indeed, in this context concerned not just with writers but, especially when we return to the account offered by the shade of what was once Rousseau of 'what I wrote', with the act of writing itself, is it not possible to hear in 'inly quelled' 'ink well', and thus a hint that the very process of writing was in fact central to the quelling and the transmission through literary tradition of the passions which the bards 'sung'?[51] Crucially, though, that act of quelling does not ossify the bards' passions but enables the 'strain' of the bards to become 'living melody', to take on a life of its own, which exists, as it were, not simply in the writing of the bards, but between the bards themselves, their texts, and their readers.

Living melody, in this sense, 'Tempers its own contagion to the vein / Of those who are infected with it'. Although Godwin's argument near the end of *Political Justice* that we may hope, one day, to exert voluntary control even over the circulation of our blood might be thought of as one of his more eccentric speculations,[52] it is important to notice that it is precisely undecided whether the consequence of the fact that 'living melody / Tempers its own contagion to the vein / Of those who are infected with it' is an alteration chiefly in 'living melody' or in the vein it infects. Living melody both relies on the circulation of blood in the veins of those by whom it is received, yet it may also quicken their pulses. Lines of living melody are not just lines of written verse but lines as they run, like veins, through the living readers of that verse.

Coda

At the end of 'The Triumph of Life', the narrator of the poem quotes himself asking the question that Shelley had also asked in 'On Life':

' [...] —thus, on the way
   Mask after mask feel from the countenance
And form of all, and long before the day

   'Was old, the joy which waked like Heaven's glance
The sleepers in the oblivious valley, died,
   And some grew weary of the ghastly dance

   'And fell, as I have fallen by the way side,
   Those soonest, from whose forms most shadows past
And least of strength and beauty did abide.'—

   'Then, what is Life?' I said ... the cripple cast
His eye upon the car which now had rolled
   Onward, as if that look must be the last,

And answered.... 'Happy those for whom the fold
   Of

(*SPP*, pp. 499–500; ll. 535–8)

In order to ask this question, the questioner must know enough of 'Life' to be aware that it is something he does not know about, though he wishes to know about it. In this way, this question, like any question, draws at least minimally on past experience concerning which it demands further information and explanation. But in so far as it is a question at all, 'Then, what is Life?' looks to an answer that is to come. The 'Then' that introduces the question, in fact, announces the at once retrospective and prospective movement of questioning. Having witnessed all this, I then require an explanation; having made that requirement clear, only then will the explanation come.

Obvious enough as these facts about the act, or, better, the direction of questioning undoubtedly are, it is well to be reminded of them here. For the end of this poem is profoundly concerned with, and of course enacts, the frustration of the hope for synoptic circumspection declared in the question – a frustration that applies both to those who fall by the wayside and the readers of this uncompleted masterpiece. The cripple's attempt to fix his eye 'upon the car which now had rolled / Onward' hints at the impossibility, in fact, of establishing a stable point of view, since the cripple's eye is 'upon' something that itself refuses to keep still as it rolls 'Onward'. As many commentators have remarked, the attempt discursively to grasp life in this poem is overwhelmed by the unstoppable perpetuation of life itself. There is no ending to speak of here, other than the poem's curtailment in Shelley's death.

The question, then, is left pendant and unanswerable, as it was in the passage from 'On Life' with which this book began and to which, now, I should like to return:

> What is life? Thoughts and feelings arise, with or without our will and we employ words to express them. We are born, and our birth is unremembered and our infancy remembered but in fragments. We live on, and in living we lose the apprehension of life. How vain is it to think that words can penetrate the mystery of our being. Rightly used they may make evident our ignorance to ourselves, and this is much. For what are we? Whence do we come, and whither do we go? Is birth the commencement, is death the conclusion of our being? What is birth and death? (*SPP*, p. 506)

Read alongside the narrator's question at the end of 'The Triumph of Life', this passage, in its repeated questioning, can in fact look more fretfully uncertain than concertedly inquiring. Is it then possible that the 'apprehension of life' is not, in fact, life's plenitudinous realisation, but the anxiety, foreboding, and uncertainty that inexorably besets the process of living? Is this a possibility – itself anxiously suppressed by this book, if truth be told, until here, at its conclusion – that actually overwhelms any attempt finally to recuperate the apprehension of life in the face of living on? The two sentences following the declaration 'We live on, and in living we lose the apprehension of life', which declare the vanity of verbally defining 'the mystery of our being' and console us with our ability to know our ignorance, are in fact short-lived attempts to allay the anxiety involved in asking 'what is life?', to stop worrying, before the worrisome questions press in again. The loss of the apprehension of life in living on is hardly to be regretted, but magnanimously put down to experience.

The *OED* advances the following definitions for 'apprehension' (its eleventh and twelfth for this term) in the sense being discussed here: 'The representation to oneself of what is still future; anticipation; *chiefly* of things adverse'; and, somewhat but not altogether more emphatically, 'Fear of what may happen; dread'. The *OED* itself has a mild case of anxious uncertainty in proffering its definition of these senses of 'apprehension'. Even before it is admitted that the 'anticipation' involved here is '*chiefly* of things adverse' – an italicization that trembles uncertainly between emphatic declaration and cautious restraint – the fact that apprehension is 'representation to oneself of what is *still* future' (my emphasis) hints at the nervousness attendant upon having to go on waiting for an outcome that might reasonably have been expected (or hoped) already to be past.

It is notable that Shelley barely uses 'apprehension' in anything like the sense outlined here. Ellis's concordance, in fact, gives no instances at all of him using the word to mean 'anticipation' or '[f]ear of what may happen'.[1] And while Shelley does say of Victorio in 'The Wandering Jew' – as he is about to throw himself into the sea in despair at the frustration of his love for Rosa – that 'No apprehension paled his cheek, / No sighs from his bosom break, / No terror dimmed his eye' (*Poems* I, p. 74; canto IV, l. 1124–6), the emphasis here is on Victorio's sternly noble acceptation of his fate, rather than on the quite conventional characterisation of apprehension as inducing pallor. To be sure, the sense of apprehension as anxiety was abundantly available to Shelley. I discussed in Chapter 4 Shelley's reception of the juxtaposition of apprehension and comprehension by Shakespeare's Theseus, but there are many instances of 'apprehension' as '[f]ear of what may happen' throughout Shakespeare's works. Likewise, while the sense of 'apprehension' as the at the once both sensible and intellectual recognition of truths not fully available to mere reason is crucially developed amongst Shelley's more immediate forebears and contemporaries, it is also used by them quite prominently to evoke a state of anxious, often dramatic tension.

To take just one example from Wordsworth's oeuvre, *The Excursion* deploys 'apprehension' and its cognates as both intellectual-sensible grasping and anxious foreboding. Book I, for instance, describes how 'many a Tale / Traditionary' had fostered the imagination of the Wanderer, 'And gave the Mind that apprehensive power / By which she is made quick to recognize / The moral properties and scope of things.'[2] The imagination of 'apprehensive power' here is close to the sense of 'apprehension' developed by Shelley. It makes the mind 'quick', a term that evokes both the speed that it has thus acquired and also, of course, its animation. And it is, moreover, a special kind of recognition to which apprehension tends. It leads to recognition not just of matters of fact but to the 'moral properties and scope of things', where 'scope' has its older sense as 'an end in view; an object, purpose, aim' (*OED*, 'scope, n.2', sense 2(a)). It is worth pointing out that apprehensive power's particular atunement to the 'scope of things' in this sense already suggests the crucially prospective aspect of apprehension. But in the next book of *The Excursion* apprehension is prospective in the sense that it is fearful anticipation of what lies vaguely before, not the apprehending, but rather the apprehensive person. Thus when the Solitary tells the tale of his expedition to find the Pensioner lost in a storm in his search for fuel on the hills, the Pensioner, found at last, is characterised by his lassitude:

> We spake – he made reply, but would not stir
> At our entreaty; less from want of power
> Than apprehension and bewildering thoughts.[3]

We might struggle to maintain any very firm distinction between 'want of power', on the one hand, and 'apprehension and bewildering thoughts', on the other, here, since the Pensioner – described earlier, incidentally, as 'slow and torpid' (II.753) – does after all fail to get up from underneath his bed of heather in response to his rescuers' salutation. The sense, though, that apprehension and want of power both overlap and are yet distinct from one another is crucial to the understanding of apprehension as anxiety. I emphasised earlier that, for Shelley, drawing in turn on a long-established philosophical and literary tradition, apprehension is an intellectual operation that is at once emphatically sensuous. Apprehension-as-anxiety is certainly sensible, but only to the degree that the senses are enervated.[4] The Pensioner has the power to get up, but that power is so disordered as to root him, instead, to the spot.

Is it, then, that Shelley's juxtaposition of 'the apprehension of life' and 'living on' is only a tendentious valorisation of momentary insight that in fact cannot but submit to time and tide? And does calling that momentary insight 'apprehension', despite the apparent absence from Shelley's work of the use of this term to mean anxiety or anticipation, betray the anxious anticipation that Shelley, in fact, is seeking to suppress? Shelley's emphasis on the eviscerating, stupefying effect of habit on people as they 'grow up' might seem to support such an interpretation. What he wishes to recover, that is, is the experience of a life somehow prior to our fall into the onward progress of living; what transpires, however, is that that act of recovery is impossible, and that that impossibility is tacitly, unconsciously recognised by him.

But the apprehension of life is, as I sought to emphasise at the beginning of this book, not simply opposed to 'living on', not simply opposed, that is, to what we might call the onward process of daily life. On the contrary, Shelley hopes that the 'apprehension of life' might transform 'living on', rather than simply stand in ineluctable but also ineffectual opposition to it. That hope is its ethical and political character, a character which is at the same time thoroughly poetic. For it is part of the poet's task not just to apprehend, but poets' language, as the famous definition of 'A Defence of Poetry' has it, 'marks the before unapprehended relations of things, and perpetuates their apprehension' (*SPP*, p. 512).

The suggestion that the onwardness of life, so to speak, is not just to be despaired of is, in fact, discernible in the progress of the argument of 'On Life' itself. It is in that essay, as most commentators have wanted to stress, that Shelley outlines his commitment to a philosophical position derived in part from Drummond's *Academical Questions*. But we should attend not to only to Shelley's summary of that position, but to his account of his arrival at it as well. 'The most refined abstractions of logic', he remarks, 'conduct to a view of life which, though startling to the apprehension, is in fact that which the habitual sense of its repeated combinations has extinguished in us.' The startled apprehension is, of course, clearly juxtaposed against 'the habitual sense of [life's] repeated combinations', but the view of life which is found to be so startling to the apprehension is one to which logic 'conduct[s]' us. Startled apprehension is, that is to say, the result not of an immediate flash of insight, but of the development and eventual emergence of a view of life that is quite contrary to the creeping envelopment of life by habit. Explaining his arrival at the view that 'nothing exists but as it is perceived', Shelley likewise states that '[i]t is a decision against which all our persuasions struggle, and we must be long convicted, before we can be convinced that the solid universe of things is "such stuff as dreams are made of"'. The long conviction that yields this conclusion is necessarily the product of living on, despite the fact that in reinvigorating – startling – the apprehension it might well be taken to restore the apprehension of life that Shelley earlier seemed to suggest was destroyed by living on. Again, later promoting 'the intellectual system', Shelley states that

> [e]xamined point by point and word by word, the most discriminating intellects have been able to discover no train of thoughts in the process of

> its reasoning, which does not conduct inevitably to the conclusion that has been stated. (*SPP*, p. 507)

Shelley's emphasis on the 'train of thoughts in the process of its reasoning' and what it may be taken 'to conduct inevitably to' might be viewed as standard features of the articulation of argument, but here they crucially indicate the importance of living on to Shelley's conception of the newly awakened apprehension, for there is no long conviction or inevitable conduction without living on. Minutely detailed attention, far removed from the torpor of mechanically repeated and habitual operations of reasoning, takes its course in onward life, 'point by point and word by word'. The relation between apprehension of life and living on is not as merely and absolutely inimical as may initially appear to be the case.

This recuperation of living on, however, does seem to run somewhat counter to Shelley's explicit disavowal of change in his definition (if so it may be called) of man in 'On Life', where he declares that

> man is a being of high aspirations 'looking both before and after', whose 'thoughts that wander through eternity', disclaim alliance with transience and decay, incapable of imagining to himself annihilation, existing but in the future and the past, being, not what he is, but what he has been, and shall be. (*SPP*, p. 506)

That Shelley has recourse to quotation (from Shakespeare and then from Milton) when arguing that man looks 'both before and after' and has 'thoughts that wander through eternity' is significant, since in quotation Shelley is looking back to earlier writers and also, in recalling these quotations, allowing his thoughts to range over poetic history. But change is not disavowed at this point in 'On Life' in order instead to insist upon the sheer permanence and invariance of the human soul. The chiastic structure of 'existing but in the future and the past, being, not what he is, but what he has been and shall be', where future, past, past ('what he has been'), future ('and shall be'), certainly disturbs the predictable sequence of past, present, and future, but the insistence that man exists in the future and the past nevertheless relies upon the assumption that man is subject to change. Shelley's rejection of 'transience and decay', of 'change and extinction' in this passage is not predicated upon a belief in the fixed condition of man's soul, but, on the contrary, upon a rejection of the prospect that man might ultimately be reduced to the absolutely unchanging state of 'nothingness and dissolution' (the phrase, according to the Norton editors, above which Shelley subscribed 'change and extinction', deleting neither). It is, furthermore, revealing that central to Belial's contrast of 'intellectual being' with annihilation in the section of *Paradise Lost* from which Shelley quotes in the passage above is a view of life as characterised by 'sense and motion', as opposed to the condition of being 'swallowed up and lost / In the wide womb of uncreated night'. Belial's view of life is moving in more ways than one.

Shelley's avoidance of 'apprehension' as 'anticipation; *chiefly* of things adverse' is best read, then, not as bad faith, not as a weak attempt to suppress the anxiety of life. Rather, the 'apprehension of life' is to be the hopeful yet fragile anticipation of things auspicious. Familiar life is not simply to be denigrated – to be 'hated', as Yeats thought Shelley hated life – but to be transformed. In 'A Defence of Poetry' Shelley remarks on the effects of the abolition of slavery and the emancipation of women, events that are at once political and poetic:

> It was as if the statues of Apollo and the Muses had been endowed with life and motion and had walked forth among their worshippers; so that earth became peopled by the inhabitants of a diviner world. The familiar appearance and proceedings of life became wonderful and heavenly; and a paradise was created as out of the wrecks of Eden. And as this creation itself is poetry, so its creators were poets; and language was the instrument of their art: 'Galeotto fù il libro, e chi lo scrisse.' The Provençal Trouveurs, or inventors, preceded Petrarch, whose verses are as spells, which unseal the inmost enchanted fountains of the delight which is in the grief of Love. (*SPP*, p. 525)

The 'inhabitants of a diviner world' that 'peopled' the earth were, of course, the animated statues of Apollo and the Muses. But, especially as the passage develops, it becomes clear that they are also the people of the earth, which itself becomes 'a diviner world' thanks to the creative power of poetry at work in it. Life becomes no less familiar, nor does it cease to proceed, as it becomes 'wonderful and heavenly'. That wonder, though, is hardly established once and for all, since this passage's past tense reveals that the paradise created out of the wrecks of Eden has again been wrecked. But it may, in turn, again be hoped for. The apprehension of life need not be lost to living on, nor, at best, represent a temporary refuge from it. Through its cultivation, onward life may instead be anticipated neither with fear nor with indifference, but with wonder.

Notes

INTRODUCTION

1 John Keats, *Endymion*, in *The Poems of John Keats*, ed. Miriam Allott (London: Longman, 1970), pp. 169–70; book II, ll. 153–9.

2 Laura Quinney, *Literary Power and the Criteria of Truth* (Gainesville, FL: University Press of Florida, 1995), p. 114. Quinney's discussion focuses in particular on Shelley's use of 'splendour', pp. 113–15.

3 Jacques Derrida, 'Living On', trans. James Hulbert, in Harold Bloom, Paul de Man, Jacques Derrida, Geoffrey Hartman and J. Hillis Miller, eds., *Deconstruction and Criticism* (London: Continuum, 1979), pp. 62–142, at p. 110.

4 The full record can be found by searching for 'Shelley' and 'life' in the online catalogue of the Pierpont Morgan Library, http://corsair.themorgan.org. See also Brooke Hopkins' suggestion that the essay from which the passage I have been discussing is taken, known as 'On Life', might more accurately be titled 'On "Life"'. Brooke Hopkins, 'Teaching "On Life": An Introduction to Shelley's Skeptical Poetics', in Spencer Hall, ed., *Approaches to Teaching Shelley's Poetry* (New York: Modern Language Association of America, 1990), pp. 111–13, at p. 111.

5 John Middleton Murry, *The Problem of Style* (Oxford University Press, 1922), p. 28. Murry is thinking of Baudelaire's claim in his *Fusées* that '[d]ans certains états de l'âme presque surnaturels, la profondeur de la vie se révèle tout entière dans le spectacle, si ordinaire qu'il soit, qu'on a sous les yeux. Il en devient le symbole.' Charles Baudelaire, *Œuvres complètes*, ed. Claude Pichois, 2 vols. (Paris: Gallimard, 1975), vol. I, p. 659. I thank an anonymous reviewer for Cambridge University Press for putting me on the track of this quotation.

6 *Studies in Words*, 2nd edn (Cambridge University Press, 1967), p. 287. The whole of Lewis's chapter on 'life' is valuable (see pp. 269–305; the section on 'Life: "What I Like"' is pp. 285–9), though note the reticence right at the outset, expressed in his book in connection with no other word in quite the same way, about addressing this particular topic: 'It is for biologists and philosophers to discuss "what life is"; we have the less ambitious task of examining what people mean by the word life, or, more strictly, some of the different things they may mean' (p. 269).

7 A. N. Whitehead, *Science and the Modern World* (London: Fontana, 1975), p. 106.
8 Whitehead, *Science and the Modern World.* The effort to restore a proper recognition of this 'part of the main structure of [Shelley's] mind' had a rich history in the wake of Whitehead. Two prominent works responding to the challenge issued by Whitehead were, for example, Carl Grabo's *A Newton Among Poets: Shelley's Use of Science in 'Prometheus Unbound'* (New York: Copper Square, 1930) and Desmond King-Hele's *Shelley: His Thought and Work*, 3rd edn (London: Macmillan, 1984), especially Chapter 8, 'A Newton Among Chemists?', pp. 155–68.
9 See, for a recent instance, Richard Holmes's *The Age of Wonder: How the Romantic Generation Discovered the Beauty and Terror of Science* (London: Harper Press, 2008), p. xv and the accompanying note, p. 498, where Holmes acknowledges a range of pioneers of the term 'Romantic science'.
10 This critique is most forcefully articulated, for instance, by Murray Krieger: 'I prefer to maintain that, from the early versions of organicism on, far from being an antagonistic intrusion, the *variety* side of the *unity-in-variety* motto is built into organicism's sense of itself and requires a fuller reading of it by us.' Murray Krieger, *A Reopening of Closure: Organicism Against Itself* (New York: Columbia University Press, 1989), p. 50. Charles I. Armstrong's *Romantic Organicism: From Idealist Origins to Ambivalent Afterlife* (Houndmills: Palgrave Macmillan, 2003) ambivalently takes up Krieger's suggestion (see, e.g., pp. 185–6 for the ambivalence); and Denise Gigante, in her *Life: Organic Form and Romanticism* (New Haven, CT: Yale University Press, 2009) attempts to show how Christopher Smart's *Jubilate Agno*, for example, instantiates 'an *open* organic form' (p. 49) and also attempts to revive the prospects of 'Romanticism as a shared intellectual project' (p. 3).
11 Sharon Ruston, *Shelley and Vitality* (Houndmills: Palgrave Macmillan, 2005). On Shelley's proximity to Lawrence's position, see, for example, pp. 86 and 92, and, on the connections between radical physiology and radical politics more generally, see p. 53 and passim. Shelley, incidentally, put himself under Lawrence's care on two occasions (once in 1815 and again in 1818). For brief accounts of Shelley's various dealings with Lawrence, see, for instance, James Bieri, *Percy Bysshe Shelley: A Biography* (Baltimore, MD: Johns Hopkins University Press, 2008), pp. 266, 311, and, for Lawrence's recommendation that Shelley desist from poetic composition, 'imaginative effort being considered bad for recuperation', see pp. 383–4.
12 Gigante, *Life*, pp. 7–23, on epigenesis, and pp. 84 and 104–5, on epigenesist poetics.
13 Gigante, *Life*, p. 164.
14 Gigante, *Life*, pp. 182, 175.
15 Already in 1949, for example, Fogle scorned the idea of Shelley's work as 'a rhymed manual of natural science'. Richard Harter Fogle, *The Imagery of Keats and Shelley: A Comparative Study* (Hamden, CT: Archon, 1962), pp. 217–18.

16 For a brief overview of these, questions see Ross Wilson, 'Introduction', in Ross Wilson, ed., *The Meaning of 'Life' in Romantic Poetry and Poetics* (New York: Routledge, 2009), pp. 1–12, at pp. 4–9.

17 Michel Henry, 'Ce que la science ne sait pas', in *Phénoménologie de la vie*, 4 vols. (Paris: Presses Universitaires de France, 2003–4), vol. IV: *Sur l'éthique et la religion* (2004), pp. 41–51, at p. 46 (my translation). Mauspassant's character is Rosalie, 'the happy curmudgeon', in Guy de Maupassant, *A Life*, trans. Roger Pearson (Oxford University Press, 1999), and her statement is the last line of the book (p. 240 in Pearson's translation).

18 Whitehead, *Science and the Modern World*, pp. 105, 106. Whitehead's apparently casual statement that Shelley 'can simply make nothing' of the 'secondary qualities' fundamental to science is in fact wryly literal: secondary qualities reduce real aspects of experience to nothing.

19 Henry himself, in fact, also allows a limited, 'purely methodological', role to scientific reduction; the problem for him is that scientific reduction has been granted 'an ontological signification' instead. Henry, 'Ce que la science ne sait pas', p. 47.

20 W. B. Yeats, 'The Philosophy of Shelley's Poetry', in *Essays and Introductions* (London: Macmillan, 1961), pp. 65–95, at p. 94.

21 Thomas Mann, 'On Goethe's Werther', trans. Elizabeth Corra, in Victor Lange, ed., *The Sufferings of Young Werther and Elective Affinities* (New York: Continuum, 1990), p. 2, quoted by Richard Eldridge, *Literature, Life, and Modernity* (New York: Columbia University Press, 2008), p. 50. See also James I. Porter's subtle treatment of a related set of questions: 'Is it possible to love life while despairing of life – to love a life one despairs of, or to love life even when it is felt that, objectively, life lacks all intrinsic value?' James I. Porter, 'Love of Life: Lucretius to Freud', in Shadi Bartsch and Thomas Bartscherer, eds., *Erotikon: Essays on Eros, Ancient and Modern* (University of Chicago Press, 2005), pp. 113–41, at p. 116.

22 Eldridge, *Literature, Life, and Modernity*, p. 53.

23 Richard Holmes suggests that, thanks to the quarrel between them, Shelley felt that his friendship with Hogg 'was one more example of an intimate emotional relationship that had failed him' and that, moreover, he came to think that Hogg had deserted him, rather than the other way around. See *Shelley: The Pursuit* (London: Quartet, 1976), p. 93. Both Holmes (p. 91) and Bieri (*Percy Bysshe Shelley*, p. 180) emphasise the passionate nature of Shelley and Hogg's relationship.

24 Stephanie Nelson, 'Shelley and Plato's *Symposium*: The Poet's Revenge', *International Journal of the Classical Tradition*, 14 (2007): 100–29, at p. 106. Nelson quotes Shelley's translation (underlining his departure from the Greek) from James A. Notopoulos, *The Platonism of Shelley: A Study of Platonism and the Poetic Mind* (New York: Octagon Books, 1969), pp. 414–60, at p. 421.

25 There is a similar thought, perhaps, in Byron's remembrance of John Edleston in canto 2 (stanza 95) of *Childe Harold's Pilgrimage*:

Thou too art gone, thou lov'd and lovely one!
Whom youth and youth's affection bound to me;
Who did for me what none beside have done,
Nor shrank from one albeit unworthy thee.
What is my being? thou hast ceas'd to be!

The Complete Poetical Works of Lord Byron, ed. Jerome J. McGann, 7 vols. (Oxford: Clarendon Press, 1980–93), vol. II, p. 75. References to Byron's works will be to this edition.

26 William Godwin, *Enquiry Concerning Political Justice*, 3rd edn, ed. Isaac Kramnick (Harmondsworth: Penguin, 1976), pp. 770–7, at p. 775.

27 Godwin, *Political Justice*, p. 774.

28 *Ibid.*

29 Maureen N. McLane, *Romanticism and the Human Sciences: Poetry, Population, and the Discourse of the Species* (Cambridge University Press, 2000), p. 212.

30 *Ibid.*

31 On Shelley and Adorno, see, in particular, Robert Kaufman's essays, 'Legislators of the Post-Everything World: Shelley's *Defence* of Adorno', *ELH*, 63 (1996): 707–33, and 'Intervention & Commitment Forever! Shelley in 1819, Shelley in Brecht, Shelley in Adorno, Shelley in Benjamin', in Michael Scrivener, ed., *Reading Shelley's Interventionist Poetry, 1819–1820* (2001), available online at www.rc.umd.edu/praxis/interventionist/ (accessed 21 December 2011).

32 Christian Knudsen, 'Intentions and Impositions', in Norman Kretzman, Anthony Kenny and Jan Pinborg, eds., *The Cambridge History of Later Medieval Philosophy: From the Rediscovery of Aristotle to the Disintegration of Scholasticism 1100–1600* (Cambridge University Press, 1982), pp. 479–95, at p. 487. Note, however, that Bonaventure insisted that apprehension alone is insufficient and needs always to be complemented by 'natural judgement'. See Timothy C. Potts, 'Conscience', in *Ibid.* pp. 687–704, at p. 697.

33 Potts, 'Conscience', p. 695.

34 See *OED*, 'apprehension', senses 4–12.

35 *Hamlet*, II.ii.306. Works of Shakespeare are quoted from *The Complete Works*, ed. Stanley Wells and Gary Taylor (Oxford: Clarendon Press, 1988). Terence Hawkes, *Shakespeare and the Reason: A Study of the Tragedies and the Problem Plays* (London: Routledge & Kegan Paul, 1964), p. 30. See also Hawkes's 'Hamlet's Apprehension', *MLR*, 55 (1960): 238–41.

36 Hassel, Jnr. gives an extremely valuable account of 'apprehension' as suggesting 'either transcendent knowing or transcendent foolishness' in, especially, theological usage around Shakespeare's time. See R. Chris Hassel, Jnr. *Shakespeare's Religious Language: A Dictionary* (London: Continuum, 2005), p. 22, and, for a slightly fuller account of the connection in Puritan writing between 'apprehension' and the 'application' of Christ to oneself, see M. van Beek, *An Enquiry into Puritan Vocabulary* (Groningen: Wolters-Noordhoff, 1969), pp. 61–2. I am grateful to Peter Womack for drawing my attention to Hassel's book.

37 There is an account of apprehension's relation to the succession of ideas in the mind in Godwin, *Political Justice*, pp. 366–7. Also, though he does not use the term 'apprehension', William Drummond's discussion of attention in *Academical Questions* (London: Bulmer, 1805), vol. 1, pp. 15–16, is likewise significant in this connection.

38 Veena Das, *Life and Words: Violence and the Descent into the Ordinary* (Berkeley, CA: University of California Press, 2007), p. 39.

39 Susan Stewart, 'What Praise Poems Are For', *PMLA*, 120 (2005): 235–45, at p. 238.

40 Susan J. Wolfson, *Formal Charges: The Shaping of Poetry in British Romanticism* (Palo Alto, CA: Stanford University Press, 1997), p. 3. It should be clear from this quotation that Wolfson's paramount concern is with the ethical and political 'charges' of poetic form. See also Simon Jarvis's contention that the 'materialism' of Wordsworth's poetry (compare to the 'physical qualities' of poetry invoked by Stewart) is fundamental to 'thinking's attempt to do justice, both ethically and cognitively, to the qualitative complexity of experience'. Simon Jarvis, *Wordsworth's Philosophic Song* (Cambridge University Press, 2006), p. 55. I discuss Jarvis's work further below.

41 Wolfson, *Formal Charges*, p. 4. Compare to Richard Cronin's assessment of *The Mask of Anarchy* and 'The Witch of Atlas': 'both poems are fully available only to the reader willing to understand Shelley through his techniques, not to the reader who tries to disentangle the poem from its techniques.' 'The poem "means" its techniques, its language and its genre are not vehicles of the poem's meaning but expressions of it: the idea is fully integrated with the word.' Richard Cronin, *Shelley's Poetic Thoughts* (London: Macmillan, 1981), pp. 75 and 76. Despite Susan Stewart's description of poetry as 'conveying' knowledge, she would not, I think, dissent from this way of putting the relation between technique and meaning.

42 *Formal Charges* testifies throughout to the fact that this is not what Wolfson intends; I am merely pointing out that this way of putting it might be taken to suggest that it is (see the note above on the problem with Susan Stewart's description of poetry's conveying knowledge).

43 Jarvis, *Wordsworth's Philosophic Song*, pp. 3–4.

44 Simon Jarvis, 'Thinking in Verse', in James Chandler and Maureen N. McLane, eds., *The Cambridge Companion to British Romantic Poetry* (Cambridge University Press, 2008), pp. 98–116, at pp. 98–9.

45 Simon Jarvis, 'Musical Thinking: Hegel and the Phenomenology of Prosody', *Paragraph*, 28 (2005): 58–71, at p. 69. Two remarks should, perhaps, be made here. First, central to Jarvis's rethinking of 'thinking' is the revisionary reading of Descartes's philosophy found in the work of Jean-Luc Marion and Michel Henry (an example of which was discussed above). See, for example, Michel Henry, *The Genealogy of Psychoanalysis*, trans. Douglas Brick (Palo Alto, CA: Stanford University Press, 1993), especially Chapter 1, 'Videre Videor', pp. 11–40. Second, and in keeping with the recovery in the work of Marion and Henry of an overlooked but fundamental aspect of the philosophical

tradition, Jarvis 'warns us against assuming that the idea of poetry as vitally connected to philosophy and to cognition more broadly is a late invention' (*Wordsworth's Philosophic Song*, p. 16). Here, Jarvis articulates this warning by setting out an important trend in eighteenth-century poetics, though, as he amply testifies elsewhere, this idea is much older than that. See Jarvis, 'Thinking in Verse', but also, for example, Colin Macleod, 'Homer on Poetry and the Poetry of Homer', in *Collected Essays* (Oxford: Clarendon Press, 1983), pp. 1–15 (especially pp. 6–7).

46 Theodor W. Adorno, *Minima Moralia: Reflections from Damaged Life*, trans. E. F. N. Jephcott (London: Verso, 1974), p. 80.

47 See also, in addition to 'Musical Thinking', Simon Jarvis, 'The Melodics of Long Poems', *Textual Practice*, 24 (2010): 607–21 (especially pp. 611–12).

48 See, in particular, the collection of essays, Susan J. Wolfson, ed., *'Soundings of Things Done': The Poetry and Poetics of Sound in the Romantic Ear and Era* (2008), available online at http://romantic.arhu.umd.edu/praxis/soundings/index.html (accessed 17 December 2011). The essays by Wolfson, James Chandler, and Garrett Stewart in particular contain valuable reflection on the role of sound in Shelley's verse.

49 Peter de Bolla, 'What Is a Lyrical Ballad? Wordsworth's Experimental Epistemologies', in Alexander Regier and Stefan H. Uhlig, eds., *Wordsworth's Poetic Theory: Knowledge, Language, Experience* (Houndmills: Palgrave Macmillan, 2010), pp. 43–60, at pp. 48–9. Drawing on a close acquaintance over many years with Shelley's manuscripts, Nancy Moore Goslee has addressed the written appearance of Shelley's work (especially 'The Triumph of Life') in *Shelley's Visual Imagination* (Cambridge University Press, 2011). See pp. 202–8 in particular.

50 Eric Griffiths, *The Printed Voice of Victorian Poetry* (Oxford: Clarendon Press, 1989), pp. 12–13.

51 'May or may not be thought of as "theatrical"', that is, because of the complexity of *Prometheus Unbound*'s relationship to the theatre. For a recent treatment, see Jacqueline Mulhallen, *The Theatre of Shelley* (Cambridge: Open Book, 2011), Chapter 5, pp. 147–76.

52 For wide-ranging accounts of the relation of Shelley's work to scepticism, including especially its British empiricist form, see (among many others): C. E. Pulos, *The Deep Truth: A Study of Shelley's Scepticism* (Lincoln, NE: University of Nebraska Press, 1954); Earl R. Wasserman, *Shelley: A Critical Reading* (Baltimore, MD: Johns Hopkins University Press, 1971), especially pp. 3–128; Lloyd Abbey, *Destroyer and Preserver: Shelley's Poetic Skepticism* (Lincoln, NE: University of Nebraska Press, 1979), which claims to advance on Pulos's account in particular; Angela Leighton, *Shelley and the Sublime: An Interpretation of the Major Poems* (Cambridge University Press, 1984), especially pp. 25–72; and Donald H. Reiman, *Intervals of Inspiration: The Skeptical Tradition and the Psychology of Romanticism* (Greenwood, FL: Penkevill, 1988), pp. 1–52.

I POETRY AND THE THEORY OF LIFE

1 Jasper Griffin, *Homer on Life and Death* (Oxford: Clarendon Press, 1980), p. 213 (and p. 212 for 'death').

2 Griffin notes, for instance, that life is described in Homer by a number of revealing set phrases: 'seeing the light of the sun', 'having one's limbs full of movement', etc. The variety of life, so to speak, that these phrases conjure is significant, because death, by contrast, is emptiness (*Homer on Life and Death,* p. 44). Griffin states that he aims in general to qualify the assessment of Walter Marg, in 'Zur Eigenart der Odyssee', *Antike und Abendland* 18 (1973): 1–14, that the *Iliad* is the poem of death: instead, for Griffin, it is 'the poem of life and death: of the contrast and transition between the two' (*Homer on Life and Death,* p. 95). Note, however, that Griffin alludes approvingly to Marg's assessment later, when he states that the '*Iliad* is a poem of death' (*Homer on Life and Death,* p. 143).

3 Griffin (*Homer on Life and Death,* p. 44) does not give a source for these descriptions, and, though he is explicitly discussing the *Iliad,* the clearest association of life with 'seeing the light of the sun' is in fact in the fifth of the Homeric Hymns, 'To Aphrodite', where Anchises asks of Aphrodite, 'Only have a kindly heart, and grant that I may be a man outstanding among the Trojans, and make my future offspring healthy, and myself to live long and well, seeing the light of the sun [ὁρᾶν φάος ἠελίοιο] and enjoying good fortune among the peoples, and to reach the doorstep of old age.' *Homeric Hymns, Homeric Apocrypha, Lives of Homer,* trans. Martin L. West (Cambridge, MA: Harvard University Press, 2003), p. 167 (Greek, p. 166, l. 105). Shelley began a translation of this Homeric hymn (as 'Hymn to Venus') but did not get as far as Anchises' appeal to Aphrodite (*Poems* II, pp. 345–7). I have not been able to trace an instance of Homer explicitly depicting life with a phrase translatable as 'having one's limbs full of movement' as such, though he does, for instance, describe how Paris struck Euchenor 'and forthwith his spirit [θυμὸς] departed from his limbs, and hateful darkness gat [sic] hold of him', which nicely encapsulates Griffin's point about the opposition between life and death-as-emptiness. See Homer, *The Iliad,* trans. A. T. Murphy, 2 vols. (Cambridge, MA: Harvard University Press, 1960), vol. II, p. 53 (Greek, p. 52, book XIII, ll. 671–2).

4 Shelley is misremembering slightly the line 'All are but parts of one stupendous whole' from Pope's *An Essay on Man,* Epistle I, l. 267. *The Poems of Alexander Pope,* ed. John Butt (London: Methuen, 1963), p. 514.

5 P. M. S. Dawson, *The Unacknowledged Legislator: Shelley and Politics* (Oxford: Clarendon Press, 1980), argues that Shelley would still have understood didactic poetry as poetry about 'practical matters, which could serve the purposes of a textbook on the subject' (pp. 212–13), yet Shelley's explicit declarations on this question do, in fact, seem to suggest something close to the later sense of 'didactic poetry' as poetry with a direct moral or political purpose in particular. For example, writing to Thomas Hookham in early 1813 about the expected date of completion for *Queen Mab,* he remarks that, 'The notes to Q.M. will be long & philosophical. I shall take that opportunity which I judge to be

a safe one of propagating my principles, which I decline to do syllogistically in a poem. A poem very didactic is I think very stupid' (26 January 1813, *Letters* I, p. 350). Thus, a 'poem very didactic' would be one in which 'principles' are syllogistically propagated. But note also, incidentally, that, writing to Hogg a fortnight later, Shelley remarks of *Queen Mab* that 'The didactic is in blank verse' (7 February 1813, *Letters* I, p. 352). See David Duff's treatment of the 'dialectic' between Romanticism's anti-didacticism and 'its own fashion for moralizing [...] and [...] philosophizing and polemicizing in verse' in Duff, *Romanticism and the Uses of Genre* (Oxford University Press, 2009), pp. 95–118, at p. 98. Duff comments that Shelley's expressed abhorrence for didactic poetry in the preface to *Prometheus Unbound* 'was, in part, a reaction against his own earlier work, notably his "philosophical poem" *Queen Mab*' (*Romanticism and the Uses of Genre*, p. 97).

6 Grabo, for example, complains of how '[t]here has been much talk of Shelley's exquisite lyricism and very little of Shelley's hard intellectual meaning' (*A Newton Among Poets*, p. vii), thus intellectually disenfranchising lyric. Grabo does acknowledge that an understanding of the science in *Prometheus Unbound* will not yield a fully adequate commentary: for that, the Platonic and neo-Platonic allusions in the poem would have to be deciphered as well (p. xi).

7 Roy Fuller, 'The Osmotic Sap: The Text of a Lecture Given in Oxford on May 6', *Times Literary Supplement*, 14 May 1971, pp. 559–61.

8 Fuller, 'The Osmotic Sap', p. 560.

9 *Ibid.*

10 Compare the opening statement of Christopher Ricks's *Milton's Grand Style* (London: Oxford University Press, 1963), p. 1: 'Like many years, 1958 saw the publication of a stern letter from Dr. F.R. Leavis.'

11 F. R. Leavis, *Revaluation: Tradition and Development in English Poetry* (Harmondsworth: Penguin, 1972; first publ. 1936), p. 172.

12 Chris Baldick states that '[h]ostility towards science, and fear of its growth, is a constant and indeed constitutive element of the English literary-critical tradition from Arnold through to the Leavises'. See *The Social Mission of English Criticism, 1848–1932* (Oxford: Clarendon Press, 1983), p. 199.

13 F. R. Leavis, Letter to the Editor, *Times Literary Supplement*, 21 May 1971, p. 593.

14 *Ibid.*

15 William Keach, *Shelley's Style* (London: Methuen, 1984), pp. 213–14, at p. 213.

16 Letter to the Editor, *Times Literary Supplement*, 28 May 1971, p. 620. I learnt of Prynne's letter (and thence of Leavis's letter and Fuller's lecture to which both responded) from Jeremy Noel-Tod's blog, *The Lyre: British Poetry News*, available online at http://thelyreonline.blogspot.com/2009/12/sir.html, 4 December 2009 (accessed 15 September 2011).

17 King-Hele, *Shelley*, p. 155.

18 See, for example, Gigante, *Life*, p. 203. But Gigante is rightly careful to qualify Shelley's poetry as 'an *aesthetic* inquiry into life' (p. 155; my emphasis) and states that 'fiction can go places that science cannot' (p. 162).
19 King-Hele, *Shelley*, p. 155.
20 Ruston, *Shelley and Vitality*, p. 182.
21 *Ibid.*
22 Ruston, *Shelley and Vitality*, p. 103, and see the sensitive reading of the line and metre in the visitation of the furies in *Prometheus Unbound*, Act I (p. 108). Comparable assumptions are also behind Jacqueline Mulhallen's contention that a successful staging of *Prometheus Unbound* today would have to update systematically its scientific references and allusions. See *The Theatre of Shelley*, p. 241.
23 See, incidentally, Philip Connell's discussion of Shelley's association of Malthus and Paley on the grounds that both 'couched their arguments in the language of liberal Anglican theodicy' in his *Romanticism, Economics, and the Question of 'Culture'* (Oxford University Press, 2001), p. 212.
24 Drummond, *Academical Questions*, pp. 20–1.
25 See, for example, Jeffrey N. Cox, *Poetry and Politics in the Cockney School: Keats, Shelley, Hunt and their Circle* (Cambridge University Press, 1998), p. 143, and Kim Wheatley, *Shelley and His Readers: Beyond Paranoid Politics* (Columbia, MO: University of Missouri Press, 1999), pp. 110–15, for an account of the relation between Shelley's imagination of his audience in the Preface to *Prometheus Unbound* and the poem's reception on the part of conservatively minded reviewers.
26 'On Christianity' (1817), in *Prose*, pp. 246–71, at p. 266.
27 Byron, *Poetical Works*, vol. V (1986), canto VII, stanzas 4 and 6. For Wasserman's comments, see *Shelley*, p. 59, though note he mistakenly ascribes Byron's lines to canto III of *Don Juan*.
28 Eric Lindstrom, '"To Wordsworth" and the "White Obi": Slavery, Determination, and Contingency in Shelley's *Peter Bell the Third*', *Studies in Romanticism*, 47 (2008): 549–80, at p. 549). Compare to Quinney's excellent reading of the late, short lyric, 'When passion's trance is overpast', particularly of the concluding lines, 'All things revive in field or grove / And sky and sea, but two, which move / And form all others – life and love' (*SPP*, p. 470, ll. 12–15). Quinney comments that '[t]he charms of generalization have here exerted themselves through a strange logic, since it is in the absence of life that things "revive." Totalised entities confront one another in a mutually exclusive relation. "All things" survive but love and life – which are all, in another sense' (*Literary Power*, p. 97).
29 Henry, 'Ce que la science ne sait pas', p. 49 (my translation).
30 Henry 'Ce que la science ne sait pas', p. 46.
31 Cathy Caruth, 'Parting Words: Trauma, Silence, and Survival', in Carol Jacobs and Henry Sussman, eds., *Acts of Narrative* (Palo Alto, CA: Stanford University Press, 2003), pp. 44–61, at p. 51; the quotation from Freud's *Beyond*

the Pleasure Principle is on the same page but appears above with my emphasis added.

32 Compare Susan J. Wolfson's insight that the rhymes of the first four lines of *The Mask of Anarchy* are in fact anticipated in the first line's '"as*lee*p" (itself oozing suggestively out of the initial *As I*).' 'As I lay asleep in Italy / There came a voice from over the Sea, / And with great power it forth led me / To walk in the visions of Poesy' (*Poems* III, p. 36; ll. 1–4). See Wolfson, *Formal Charges*, p. 197.

33 See 'alas, int. and n.', *OED*.

34 I owe this point to Ian Patterson, who raised it in response to my discussion of this poem in a paper, 'Departure into Life: Percy Shelley and Overliving', delivered at a colloquium on the work of Cathy Caruth at the Centre for Research in the Arts, Social Sciences, and Humanities, Cambridge (11 March 2011).

35 For an informative and subtle reading of the poetic form and grammar of the final lines of 'England in 1819', see Wolfson, *Formal Charges*, pp. 204–6.

36 It might be worth pointing out that I realise that the sense of 'idling' which I use here would not have been available to Shelley; the first use of 'idling' in this sense (still cautiously handled with quotation marks) is to be found in R. T. Nicholsen's *Book of Ford* (1916) according to the *OED*, 'idling, *n.*'.

37 See, for example, Hutchinson's title: 'Fragment: "Alas, this is not what I thought life was!"' (Hutchinson, p. 633).

38 Dante Alighieri, *The Vision; or Hell, Heaven, and Purgatory, of Dante Alighieri*, trans. H. F. Cary, 3 vols. (London: Taylor & Hessey, 1814).

39 Compare to Fogle's view that '[t]he rapid flow of his swift-moving forms and essences is usually set in a motionless and solid frame' (*The Imagery of Keats and Shelley*, p. 55). This isn't quite right, of course, not least because the distinction between form and frame requires explanation; rather, as we have seen here, in the instance of 'Alas, this is not what I thought life was', it is more the case that the propulsive movement of Shelley's verse often turns out to be recursive but that this recursion nonetheless maintains a formal openness.

40 This is an anonymous translation, from *The First and Fourth Books of the Odes of Horace, Translated into English Verse* (London, 1799), p. 10, but see also, for example, Philip Francis's *The Odes, Epodes, and Carmen Seculare of Horace*, 2 vols. (London, 1743), vol. I, p. 23: 'Or Oak, or Brass with triple Fold / That hardy Mortal's daring Breast enroll'd'; and Christopher Smart's 'prose interpretation', *The Works of Horace, Translated into Verse*, 4 vols. (London, 1767), vol. I, p. 14: 'His breast was encompassed with oak and triple brass, who first ventured a frail ship to the merciless ocean.'

41 Homer, *The Iliad and Odyssey of Homer, Translated into English Blank Verse*, trans. William Cowper, 2 vols. (London: Johnson, 1791), *Iliad*, XI.429–30.

42 Edward Young, *The Complaint; or, Night Thoughts on Life, Death, & Immortality* (London: Dodsley, 1742), p. 12.

43 John Hollander, 'The West Wind and the Mingled Measure', *Daedalus*, 111 (1982): 131–48, at p. 145. Hollander's essay addresses in particular the figure of the Aeolian harp. For an explanation of 'transumption', see Hollander, 'Appendix: The Trope of Transumption', in *The Figure of Echo: A Mode of Allusion in Milton and After* (Berkeley, CA: University of California Press, 1981), pp. 133–49.

2 LIVING LOSING LIFE

1 John Locke, *An Essay Concerning Human Understanding*, ed. Peter H. Nidditch (Oxford: Clarendon Press, 1975), pp. 151–2.

2 But compare Thomas Parnell's 'A Night-Piece on Death': 'The flat smooth Stones that bear a Name / The Chissels slender help to Fame / (Which e'er [*sic*] our Sett of friends decay / Their frequent Steps may wear away)', in *Poems on Several Occasions* (London, 1722), p. 154. Parnell is satirising the pretensions to lasting fame of memorial inscription, but the wearing away of the chiselled name is compensated for, as much as it is caused by, the many visits of friends to the tomb of the deceased.

3 David Hume, *An Enquiry Concerning Human Understanding*, ed. L. A. Selby-Bigge, 3rd edn, rev. by P. H. Nidditch (Oxford: Clarendon Press, 1975), p. 16.

4 See, for example, Trudy Govier, 'Variations on Force and Vivacity in Hume', *Philosophical Quarterly*, 22 (1972): 44–52; Wayne Waxman, 'Impressions and Ideas: Vivacity as Verisimilitude', *Hume Studies*, 19 (1993): 75–88; Francis W. Dauer, 'Force and Vivacity in the *Treatise* and the *Enquiry*', *Hume Studies*, 25 (1999): 83–99.

5 Govier, 'Variations on Force and Vivacity', p. 46. Dauer, for instance, insists that 'force' and 'vivacity' be taken together as a 'technical term – call it "Humean force and vivacity"' ('Force and Vivacity', p. 85), although, despite the effect this has of drawing these terms closer to verisimilitude, he understands this somewhat differently from Govier's 'lifelikeness' and 'clarity'. Of course, the division proposed by Dauer between ordinary and Humean senses of terms would be problematic for Hume in particular, who was especially alive to the relation between ordinary and philosophical language; see, for example, David Hume, 'Of Essay Writing' (1742), in *Essays, Moral, Political, and Literary*, ed. Eugene F. Miller, rev. edn (Indianapolis, IN: Liberty Fund, 1987), pp. 533–7, at pp. 534–5.

6 The letter that Shelley refers to in the second sentence, in which he announces to Peacock his party's arrival at the end of its journey, was sent by him on 6 April 1818 (*Letters* II, p. 3).

7 Howard Mills remarks on Peacock's recognition of the humour in Shelley's letters to him; Mills, *Peacock: His Circle and His Age* (Cambridge University Press, 1969), p. 78. Michael Rossington offers a reading of this letter, similar to that developed above, in his account of 'Shelley's "writing back" to the republican moment of Marlow from a continental European vantage-point';

Rossington, 'Shelley's Republics', in Heather Glen and Paul Hamilton, eds., *Repossessing the Romantic Past* (Cambridge University Press, 2006), pp. 63–79, at pp. 63–4. Likewise, Thomas R. Frosch sees it as exemplifying the 'general anxiety of self-knowledge' often discernible in Shelley's writing; Frosch, *Shelley and the Romantic Imagination: A Psychological Study* (Cranbury, NJ: Associated University Presses, 2007), p. 294.

8 T. E. Hulme, 'Preface to Sorel's *Reflections on Violence*', in *Selected Writings*, ed. Patrick McGuinness (Manchester: Carcanet, 1998), pp. 173–9, at p. 177.

9 Compare Leigh Hunt's *The Story of Rimini: A Poem* in which the bower where Francesca, the poem's heroine, meets Paolo, the dashing and decent brother of the rather less delectable Giovanni to whom she has been married off, is described as 'A spot, that struck you like enchanted ground'. Leigh Hunt, *The Poetical Works of Leigh Hunt*, ed. H. S. Milford (Oxford University Press, 1923), p. 22, canto III, l. 436. After a 'sudden sense of wretchedness' draws the lovers back from repeating the consummation of their passion on a second occasion in 'The spot where they had last gone smilingly' (Hunt, *Poetical Works*, p. 27; canto IV, l. 34), 'She never ventured in that spot again' (*Poetical Works*, p. 27; canto IV, l. 49).

10 Information from the headnote to 'I visit thee but thou art sadly changed' in *Poems* I, p. 571. Bieri notes that Shelley and Mary 'resided nine months at Bishopsgate, the longest period they would live together *à deux*' (Bieri, *Percy Bysshe Shelley*, p. 312).

11 The line beginning in *Poems* I, 'After its wanderings' is, in the transcription offered in *BSM* XVII, 'After [?thier] wanderings found [?a] [?F]' with the (conjectured) words '[?brief]' and '[?years]' inscribed beneath the lower part of the line (126/135).

12 Michel de Montaigne, 'On Habit: and On Never Easily Changing a Traditional Law', in *The Complete Essays*, trans. and ed. M. A. Screech, rev. edn (London: Penguin, 2003), pp. 122–39, at p. 123.

13 Montaigne, 'On Habit', p. 131 (Montaigne, of course, cites Lucretius's Latin).

14 Godwin, *Political Justice*, p. 771.

15 Godwin, *Political Justice*, p. 773. But compare the following statement from 'Of Awakening the Mind' (the first of the *Enquirer* essays): 'Many things that, in the dark and unapprehensive period of youth, are attained with infinite labour, may, by a ripe and judicious understanding, be acquired with an effort inexpressibly inferior.' *The Enquirer: Reflections on Education, Manners, and Literature* (London: Robinson, 1797), Part I, p. 5.

16 Kenneth Neill Cameron, *Shelley: The Golden Years* (Cambridge, MA: Harvard University Press, 1974), pp. 95 and 151–5.

17 Hume, *Enquiry*, p. 44.

18 Hume, *Enquiry*, p. 42.

19 Rupert Read helped me expand this point when he responded to my paper 'Living Losing Life' presented to the Research Seminar, School of Philosophy, University of East Anglia, 11 February 2010.

20 Hume, *Enquiry*, pp. 28–9.

21 Hume, *Enquiry*, p. 32.

22 *Ibid.*
23 Hume, *Enquiry*, p. 45.
24 Michael Henry Scrivener, *Radical Shelley: The Philosophical Anarchism and Utopian Thought of Percy Bysshe Shelley* (Princeton University Press, 1982), p. 15.
25 *Ibid.*
26 Cian Duffy, *Shelley and the Revolutionary Sublime* (Cambridge University Press, 2005), p. 55. Duffy wishes in particular to argue that, however involuntary the response described by Shelley, and thus akin to conventional accounts of the operation of the sublime, what is involuntarily acknowledged is the 'touch of nature', rather than of God. Thus, 'Shelley's point [...] is that an "authentic record" of the natural sublime would acknowledge that the experience – "rightly" felt by an imagination freed from "custom" – leads not to a belief in God, but rather to an apprehension of the "Spirit of Nature"' (*Revolutionary Sublime*, pp. 55–6).
27 Compare Eusebes' comment on matter in 'A Refutation of Deism': 'But matter deprived of qualities, is an abstraction, concerning which it is impossible to form an idea. Matter, such as we behold it, is not inert. It is infinitely active and subtile' (*Prose*, p. 116).
28 Montaigne, 'On Habit', p. 129. That custom is capable of doing anything is a central plank in Shelley's response to the objection made to vegetarianism that humans quite happily eat meat: custom can get us used to anything, even if what we then become accustomed to has (as Shelley believes is the case with meat-eating) damaging effects on health and morals. See 'On the Vegetable System of Diet', in *Prose*, pp. 147–55, at p. 152. See also the 'accustomed prey' of the mind and of 'a young eagle' (which is a simile for the mind) in, respectively, 'Pantherlike Spirit! beautiful and swift' (*Poems* III; p. 331, l. 6) and 'Ode to Liberty' (*Poems* III, p. 388; l. 9).
29 For an important consideration of the view of autonomy advanced in 'Sonnet: Political Greatness' in relation to competing conceptions of the self in Shelley's thought, see Wasserman, *Shelley*, pp. 180–3.

3 MERE WHEELS OF WORK

1 David Simpson, *Wordsworth, Commodification and Social Concern: The Poetics of Modernity* (Cambridge University Press, 2009), pp. 114–15.
2 Simpson, *Wordsworth*, p. 57.
3 Lindstrom, '"To Wordsworth"', p. 549.
4 The editors of *Poems* I suggest (p. 454) that the opening of book VI, 'The Church-Yard Among the Mountains', of *The Excursion* (the 'Poet's Address to the State and Church of England') would in particular have been found objectionable by the Shelleys: 'Hail to the Crown by Freedom shaped – to gird / An English sovereign's brow! and to the throne / Wheron he sits! Whose deep foundations lie / In veneration and the people's love'. William Wordsworth, *The Excursion*, ed. Sally Bushell, James A. Butler and Michael C. Jaye (Ithaca, NY: Cornell University Press, 2007), p. 196; book VI, ll. 1–4.

5 Simpson, *Wordsworth*, p. 231. Compare Lear's question on the heath to 'Poor naked wretches': 'How shall your houseless heads and unfed sides, / Your looped and windowed raggedness, defend you / From seasons such as these?' *King Lear*, Act III, scene 4, ll. 30–2.

6 Cameron was thus right to emphasise the continuity between Shelley's early and mature work, noting in particular that the Gothic novels 'deal with the theme of the undying mortal, a theme which continued to fascinate Shelley'. Kenneth Neill Cameron, *The Young Shelley: Genesis of a Radical* (London: Gollancz, 1951), p. 35. The 'undying mortal', this chapter argues, is also the unliving mortal according to Shelley.

7 Scrivener, *Radical Shelley*, pp. 212–13.

8 This widely noted assessment was recorded by Mary Shelley on 14 September 1814, in *The Journals of Mary Shelley*, ed. Paula R. Feldman and Diana Scott-Kilvert, 2 vols. (Oxford University Press, 1987), vol. I, p. 25.

9 See also 'A Defence of Poetry': 'The abolition of personal slavery is the basis of the highest political hope that it can enter into the mind of man to conceive' (*SPP*, p. 523). Dawson (*The Unacknowledged Legislator*, p. 18) notes that agitation for abolition reached its zenith during Shelley's adolescence and that the borough of Horsham (in which Field Place, his family's home, lies) was strongly abolitionist.

10 Lee argues that while Romantic writers 'may seem to be using the terms "slavery" and "freedom" in abstract and even universal ways, [...] the terms are, in fact, grounded in the historical specificity of the transatlantic trade and plantation slavery'. Debbie Lee, *Slavery and the Romantic Imagination* (Philadelphia, PA: University of Pennsylvania Press, 2002), p. 30. I do not necessarily contest this assessment in Shelley's particular case, other than to point out that Shelley is also concerned with slavery in the ancient world and to add the caveat that the terms he uses in his condemnation of commerce may well be 'grounded in' debates surrounding the campaign for the abolition of the transatlantic slave trade and their aftermaths, but that does not mean that they are always best explained by tracing them to those debates. Compare Coleridge's opposition to commerce as enslavement, which strongly anticipates (as we will see below) Shelley's characterisation of commercial production, discussed by Joan Baum, *Mind-Forg'd Manacles: Slavery and the English Romantic Poets* (North Haven, CT: Archon Books, 1994), pp. 139–40, and Baum's broad claim that Shelley's sympathies (along with Wollstonecraft's) were 'for all victims of tyranny' (p. 221, n.8), which, of course, Lee would hardly deny.

11 Titus Lucretius Carus, *The Nature of Things: A Didactic Poem*, trans. John Mason Good, 2 vols. (London: Longman, Hurst, Rees, & Orme, 1805), vol. I, p. 51, book I, ll. 192–5 (Latin), book I, ll. 218–22 (Good trans.). For an informative account of Good's translation, which was all but certainly known by Shelley, see Michael A. Vicario, *Shelley's Intellectual System and its Epicurean Background* (London and New York: Routledge, 2007), Chapter 4, pp. 121–52.

12 Judith Butler, *Frames of War: When Is Life Grievable?* (London: Verso, 2009), pp. 23 and 19.

13 Leigh Hunt, 'Bacchus and Ariadne' (1819), in Hunt, *Poetical Works*, p. 46, ll. 101–3.

14 Note that earlier, on first discovering Theseus's flight, Ariadne 'as a dead thing, down falls' (Hunt, 'Bacchus and Ariadne', *Poetical Works*, p. 45; l. 44). It is not that Hunt's descriptions are inconsistent – that at one moment she is 'as a dead thing' and the next a 'living thing' – but rather that she is agonisingly poised, in life, between life and death.

15 Dawson, *The Unacknowledged Legislator*, p. 78, emphasises Shelley's abhorrence in these lines for mere expediency on the part of politicians, and particularly for the 'split between [...] the devotion to liberty of Whig ideology and the party politics and boroughmongering of Whig practice'.

16 See James Grahame's sparklingly acerbic condemnation of Malthus's conception of 'nature under the disguise of a rich man's porter unchaining a fat mastiff at a beggar'. Grahame, *An Enquiry into the Principle of Population*Edinburgh1816 (,), p. 33, quoted by C. E. Pulos, 'Shelley and Malthus', *PMLA*, 67 (1952): 113–24, at p. 117. Identifying a similar distortion fundamentally at work in Malthus's argument, Geraldine Friedman suggests that 'Malthus transforms life science into the study of death' because society (or, rather, in his own terms, 'nature'), as he imagines it, is a mechanistic system in which human life is reified. See Geraldine Friedman, 'Section Introduction: Romanticism and Life Science – Questions of Method', *European Romantic Review*, 18 (2007): 205–11, at p. 211. David Collings captures well this sense of the reification of human life fundamental to Malthus and identified by Friedman when he remarks that Malthus's insistence on moral continence is aimed not at the abolition of disaster but rather at 'incorporating scarcity into the most intimate aspects of everyday life. The overriding purpose of uncovering the principle of population is not to defeat it but to impose the logic of the market upon ordinary people [...] Ironically enough, to become a moral person, one must embrace one's own dehumanization.' See Collings, 'The Discipline of Death: Knowledge and Power in *An Essay on the Principle of Population*', *European Romantic Review*, 18 (2007): 223–30, at p. 226.

17 Robert Southey, *Wat Tyler: A Dramatic Poem* (written 1794; surreptitiously published 1817), in *Robert Southey: Later Poetical Works, 1811–1838*, ed. Lynda Pratt and Tim Fulford, 4 vols. (London: Pickering & Chatto, 2012), vol. III: *Poems from the Laureate Period, 1813–1823*, pp. 467–506, at p. 473 (Act I, ll. 111–12, 113–18). Compare to John Ball's insistence that 'Abundant is the earth' (p. 484; Act II, l. 85) in the course of his exhortation to ask 'wherefore should that man, / No worthier than myself, thus lord it over me, / And bid me labour, and enjoy the fruits?' (p. 484; Act II, ll. 77–9) and again, later, his question, 'Why then these vain distinctions? – bears not the earth / Food in abundance?' (p. 504; Act III, ll. 213–14). Shelley mentions *Wat Tyler* in letters to Charles Ollier (11 June 1821) and Claire Clairmont (16 June 1821) (*Letters* II, pp. 298 and 302), where he holds out little hope that an injunction will be granted him to suppress a pirated edition of *Queen*

Mab because a similar application to suppress the unauthorised *Wat Tyler* has recently been refused Southey. In a letter to Leigh Hunt, as Editor of *The Examiner* (22 June 1821), likewise on the topic of the pirated *Queen Mab*, Shelley remarks that *Wat Tyler* was likely written 'with the same unreflecting enthusiasm' as characterised his poem, though he does make clear his abiding opposition to religion and monarchy and commitment to 'freedom' (*Letters* II, p. 305). In the advertisement prefixed to the play in 1837, Southey, somewhat by contrast, justified *Wat Tyler*'s publication with his imprimatur by stating that he hoped 'it may not be supposed that I think it any reproach to have written it, or that I am more ashamed of having been a republican, than of having been a boy'. The advertisement begins by stating that he has 'learnt to appreciate and to defend the institutions of my country'. See Southey, *Later Poetical Works*, p. 462.

18 The Longman editors note the echo of Malthus's pessimistic assumption of the inevitability of human want for 'the unhappy persons who in the great lottery of life have drawn a blank' (*Poems* III, p. 417, note to l. 263). See T. R. Malthus, *An Essay on the Principle of Population*, ed. Geoffrey Gilbert (Oxford University Press, 2008), p. 85. Malthus's repeated portrayals of nature according to metaphors drawn from human culture perhaps betray the fact that 'nature' is in fact the operation of vested interest in society.

19 George Gordon, Lord Byron, *The Complete Poetical Works of Lord Byron*, ed. Jerome J. McGann, 7 vols. (Oxford: Clarendon Press, 1980–93), vol. II, p.41; canto I, ll. 887–8.

20 Timothy Morton, *Shelley and the Revolution in Taste: The Body and the Natural World* (Cambridge University Press, 1994), p. 172. Morton is commenting in particular on the portrayal of a regal banquet and its nauseating effects on its honouree (*Poems* I, pp. 291–2; canto III, ll. 44–64).

21 Edward Duffy claims that '[t]hat he who reigns is the most abject of slaves is probably Shelley's most frequent paradox'. See Edward Duffy, *Rousseau in England: The Context for Shelley's Critique of the Enlightenment* (Berkeley, CA: University of California Press, 1979), p. 107.

22 The 'sunshine of a court' (usually 'basked' in) was, incidentally, a standard phrase for conveying disapproval (often somewhat milder than that which Shelley is expressing here) for the grandeur of court life. The lines, 'Virtue must be thrown off, 'tis a coarse garment / Too heavy for the sunshine of a court', spoken by Alphonso in John Dryden's play, *The Spanish Fryar; or, The Double Discovery* (London, 1681), IV.ii.21, contain the first instance I can find. But compare in particular the use of the phrase in Arthur Murphy's 1793 translation of the description of the waning of Crispus's influence in Tacitus's *Annals* (book III, section 30): 'In the decline of life, he retained the appearance of power without the reality; a reverse of fortune, which had been felt by Mæcenas, and which, by some fatality, is the usual end of all who bask in the sunshine of a court.' Tacitus, *The Works of Cornelius Tacitus: With an Essay on His Life and Genius*, trans. Arthur Murphy, 4 vols. (London: Robinson, 1793), vol. I, p. 198. Shelley wrote to Thomas 'Clio' Rickman to order an '[o]riginal

and translation, if possible, united' of Tacitus, among many other books, in 1812 (24 December 1812, *Letters* I, p. 344); whether or not the translation he received was Murphy's is not stated. See also James Bieri's claim that Shelley assimilated the prodigious reading he undertook around the turn of 1813 into his composition of *Queen Mab* (*Percy Bysshe Shelley*, p. 234). In *Queen Mab*, Shelley strengthens the implicit disapproval associated with this phrase in Dryden and in Murphy's Tacitus by casting courtly sunshine not only as a luxury reserved for some but, moreover, as inherently corrupting. For the continued importance of Tacitus to Shelley's thinking later in his career, see Michael Rossington's excellent account of the place Tacitus would come to assume in the republicanism of the *History of a Six Weeks' Tour* (published 1817), 'Rousseau and Tacitus: Republican Inflections in the Shelleys' *History of a Six Weeks' Tour*', *European Romantic Review*, 19 (2008): 321–33. (In addition to the *History*, Rossington also discusses Shelley's 'Otho', which I examined in the previous chapter.)

23 For 'commerce' as a key characteristic of both the European society into which Shelley was born and its self-image, see, for example, Fernand Braudel, *The Wheels of Commerce*, trans. Sîan Reynolds (Berkeley, CA: University of California Press, 1992) for a geographically and conceptually broad account; J. G. A. Pocock's assessment that 'the movement of history toward credit, commerce, and the market was defined as a movement toward culture but away from virtue', in *Virtue, Commerce, and History* (Cambridge University Press, 1985), p. 70; and Paul Langford, *A Polite and Commercial People: England, 1727–1783* (Oxford University Press, 1989), pp. 1–4 and passim; and, in particular, Langford's connection, anticipated by Shelley (among others), of commerce and war: 'Every war in this period was in essence a commercial war' (*A Polite and Commercial People*, p. 3). Also, for discussion of some examples of contemporary critiques of commerce, see Langford, *A Polite and Commercial People*, pp. 125 and 143, and Philip Connell, *Romanticism*, pp. 234–73.

24 Dawson proposes that Shelley does evince a certain sympathy for a bygone chivalric code, though he acknowledges that 'this approval is strictly relative' (*The Unacknowledged Legislator*, p. 50). In any case, Dawson's remark is suggested by a reading of 'An Address to the People on the Death of the Princess Charlotte' (*Prose*, pp. 229–39), where Shelley bemoans the effect of the national debt in bringing about a 'double aristocracy' (*Prose*, p. 235): in addition to the old aristocracy, which had some redeeming features such as, Shelley claims, bravery and honour, there is now another aristocracy wholly dependent on the grace and favour of the established order (*Prose*, pp. 235–6). Dawson also usefully differentiates Shelley's rejection of aristocracy from that found in Paine's work, because Paine fails to 'make provision for the freedom of the unborn from the authority of the living' (*The Unacknowledged Legislator*, p. 60).

25 See Denise Gigante's discussion of Schiller's condemnation of the mechanical nature of commercial society: the members of commercial society, according to Gigante, 'are, so to speak, the living dead' (*Life*, p. 26).

26 *Poems* I, p. 314, note to ll. 72–8. Dawson, for example, does take these lines as evidence (albeit the only evidence) of Shelley's knowledge of Smith (*The Unacknowledged Legislator*, p. 48), although he later talks of Shelley's attempt in his 'Speculations on Moarlas' to 'refute the view of Mandeville, Adam Smith, and others, according to which the general interest is better served by everyone pursuing their own interest rather than by altruism' (*The Unacknowledged Legislator*, p. 235). The passage of the 'Speculations' to which Dawson is referring is *Works*, vol. VII, pp. 73–4.

27 See the subsection in Hegel's treatment of self-consciousness, 'Independence and Dependence of Self-Consciousness: Lordship and Bondage', in G. W. F. Hegel, *Phenomenology of Spirit*, trans. A. V. Miller (Oxford University Press, 1977), pp. 111–18.

28 Compare to Byron on the ruins of Greece:

> Thy fanes, thy temples to thy surface bow,
> Commingling slowly with heroic earth,
> Broke by the share of every rustic plough:
> So perish monuments of mortal birth,
> So perish all in turn, save well-recorded Worth;
> (*Childe Harold's Pilgrimage*,
> *Poetical Works*, II, p. 72; canto II, ll. 805–9)

29 Godwin, *Political Justice*, pp. 392–3. See also the anticipation of this concern for the dehumanisation of slaves in Mary Wollstonecraft's question in *A Vindication of the Rights of Woman* (1792): 'Is one half of the human species, like the poor African slaves, to be subject to prejudices that brutalize them[?]'. Mary Wollstonecraft, *'A Vindication of the Rights of Men' and 'A Vindication of the Rights of Woman'*, ed. Sylvana Tomaselli (Cambridge University Press, 1995), p. 235.

30 A need well expressed, for example, by Elizabeth Kowaleski Wallace, *The British Slave Trade and Public Memory* (New York: Columbia University Press, 2006), pp. 35–6 and 207.

31 For an excellent account focusing on the vicissitudes of the understanding of 'humanity' in the debate surrounding abolition, especially in sentimental literature of the late eighteenth and early nineteenth centuries, see Lynn Festa, 'Humanity without Feathers', *Humanity*, 1 (2010): 3–27. I am grateful to Lyndsey Stonebridge for bringing this article to my attention.

32 Orlando Patterson, *Slavery as Social Death: A Comparative Study* (Cambridge, MA: Harvard University Press, 1982), p. 7. See book 1, section 4 of Aristotle's *Politics* on lifeless and living instruments, and the slave as 'an instrument for instruments'. Aristotle, '*The Politics' and 'The Constitution of Athens*', ed. Steven Everson (Cambridge University Press, 1996), p. 15.

33 For a development of the concept of 'social death' in this context, see Patterson, *Slavery as Social Death*, pp. 38–51.

34 Henri Wallon, *Histoire de l'esclavage dans l'antiquité* (Paris: Hachette, 1879), p. 408, quoted in Patterson, *Slavery as Social Death*, pp. 4–5.

35 Patterson, *Slavery as Social Death*, p. 45. And, though he does not mention Patterson's related work, Eric L. Santner's elaboration of the category of

'undeadness' is significant here (and informs my discussion in diverse ways in what follows). Santner describes what he calls 'the dimension of undeadness' as 'the space between real and symbolic death', a dimension he later describes, in terms similar to Patterson's, as 'this zero degree of social existence'. See *On Creaturely Life: Rilke, Benjamin, Sebald* (University of Chicago Press, 2006), pp. xx and 25 n. 40.

36 Compare to Coleridge's clearest definition of mechanism, which Shelley would not have known, although it echoes a number of Coleridge's works that were known to him: 'Thus we may say that whatever is organized from without, is a product of mechanism; whatever is mechanised from within, is a production of organization.' Samuel Taylor Coleridge, 'Theory of Life', *Shorter Works and Fragments*, ed. H. J. Jackson and J. R. de J. Jackson, 2 vols. (Princeton University Press, 1995), vol. I, pp. 481–557, at p. 511 (note).

37 Butler, *Frames of War*, p. 15.

38 Karl Marx, *Economic and Philosophical Manuscripts* (written 1844), in *Early Writings*, trans. Rodney Livingstone and Gregor Benton (Harmondsworth: Penguin), pp. 279–400, at p. 287.

39 Marx, *Economic and Philosophical*, p. 353.

40 Patterson, *Slavery as Social Death*, p. 5.

41 Geoffrey Hartman, *Wordsworth's Poetry, 1787–1814* (New Haven, CT: Yale University Press, 1964), p. 126. Hartman is discussing the character of Marmaduke, in Wordsworth's *The Borderers*, 'as a type of Wandering Jew'.

42 John Milton, *Paradise Lost*, ed. Alastair Fowler, 2nd edn (Harlow: Longman, 2007), p. 82, book X, ll. 773–5.

43 Emily R. Wilson, *Mocked with Death: Tragic Overliving from Sophocles to Milton* (Baltimore, MD: Johns Hopkins University Press, 2004), pp. 7, 41, and passim. Wilson's title, of course, comes from Adam's soliloquy mentioned above. I am grateful to Fred Parker for drawing my attention to this book. The question Shelley is asking, as to whether one would want to live life again, has received some attention from philosophers: see, for example, David Heyd, 'Is Life Worth Reliving?', *Mind*, 92 (1983): 21–37; for a useful overview of discussions of the quite different questions concerning whether one would want to live indefinitely into the future, see Chapter 7, 'Now or Never', in Helen Small's *The Long Life* (Oxford University Press, 2007), pp. 209–36.

44 Compare to the emphasis on 'still' in 'Sadak the Wanderer. A Fragment' (?1809), in which Sadak 'Strays [...] through the wild' and 'wanders', 'Still in weariness, and woe; / Pacing still the world's huge round' (*Poems* I, p. 7, ll. 26, 28, 32–3). In an early letter to Hogg, Shelley wrote that 'For the immoral "never to be able to die, never to escape from some shrine as chilling as the clay-formed dungeon which now it inhabits" is the future punishment which I believe in' (3 January 1811, *Letters* I, p. 35). The 'future punishment' here is just a perpetuation of the present condition, in an apparently monumental form ('some shrine') which is really akin to 'the clay-formed dungeon', the body, that the spirit inhabits. And, finally, compare to Shelley's punning on 'still' in relation to the condition of the wandering Jew the shift in emphasis

from a condition of torpor to one of being harried in Harold's song 'To Inez', where he characterises the 'secret woe / [...] corroding joy and youth' for him:

> It is that settled, ceaseless gloom
> The fabled Hebrew wanderer bore;
> That will not look beyond the tomb,
> But cannot hope for rest before.
> What Exile from himself can flee?
> To Zones, though more and more remote,
> Still, still pursues, where-e'er I be,
> The blight of life—the demon, Thought.
> (*Childe Harold's Pilgrimage*,
> *Poetical Works*, II, p.40; canto I, l. 853–60)

45 Jacques Derrida, 'Living On', trans. James Hulbert, in Harold Bloom, Paul de Man, Jacques Derrida, Geoffrey Hartman and J. Hillis Miller, eds., *Deconstruction and Criticism* (London: Continuum, 1979), pp. 62–142, at p. 63, and I am indebted to this essay, passim, in the comments on 'on' above.

46 Michel Foucault, *The History of Sexuality*, trans. Robert Hurley, 3 vols. (London: Penguin, 1978), vol. I: *An Introduction*, p. 142; Giorgio Agamben, *Homo Sacer: Sovereign Power and Bare Life*, trans. Daniel Heller-Roazen (Palo Alto, CA: Stanford University Press, 1998), p. 165. For treatments of 'biopolitics' in Romantic studies, see, for example, Sara Guyer's subtle reading of Agamben alongside Wordsworth in *Romanticism after Auschwitz* (Palo Alto, CA: Stanford University Press, 2007), pp. 68–70; and Hilary Strang's consideration of the 'politics of common life' in Mary Shelley's work, 'Common Life, Animal Life, Equality: *The Last Man*', *ELH*, 78 (2011): 409–31.

47 Butler, *Frames of War*, p. 29. Note that Butler distances her concept of the precariousness of life from Agamben's concept of 'bare life', since she reads Agamben as stressing the emergence of 'bare life' in a 'space of exception' (Agamben, *Homo Sacer*, p. 164 and passim) outside of the juridical space of the State, whereas, for her, the precariousness of life is precisely what is legislated by the State.

48 Butler, *Frames of War*, pp. 24–5; see also p. 21.

49 Agamben, *Homo Sacer*, p. 1. For further information on the ancient Greek sense of the distinction between *zoē* and *bios*, see section I (by Pierre Hadot) of the entry on 'Leben' in Joachim Ritter and Karlfried Gründer, eds., *Historisches Wörterbuch der Philosophie*, 13 vols. (Basel: Schwabe, 1980), vol. V, columns 52–103.

50 Though there is no mention in Shelley's letters or Mary Shelley's journal of this dialogue (see Appendix VIII, 'Shelley's Reading', in *Letters* II, pp. 467–88, which collates these sources; the entry for Plato is on p. 482), James A. Notopoulos is certain that Shelley read the *Protagoras* at Oxford with Hogg in the 'harsh and un-English' anglicised version of André Dacier's French translation of Plato. See Notopoulos, *The Platonism of Shelley*, pp. 33, 36, and 75 (and for the estimation of the English Dacier, see p. 396). Notopoulos also

takes the phrase 'to know themselves' in l. 212 of 'The Triumph of Life' as a translation of γνῶθι σεαυτόν from *Protagoras*, 343b, which is perhaps a bit of a stretch.

51 On the significance to Shelley's understanding of liberty of imagination as a faculty extending the self beyond the self, see Jonathan Mendilow, 'Shelley's Philosophy of Liberty', *Journal of Libertarian Studies*, 6 (1982): 169–80, at pp. 170–1.

4 HAPPIER FORMS

1 G. W. F. Hegel, *Aesthetics: Lectures on Fine Art*, trans. T. M. Knox, 2 vols. (Oxford: Clarendon Press, 1975), vol. I, p. 29. Translation modified in the light of Hegel, *Werke*, ed. Eva Moldenhauer and Karl Markus Michel, 20 vols. (Frankfurt: Suhrkamp, 1971), vol. XIII: *Vorlesungen über die Ästhetik*, vol. I, p. 48.

2 Hegel, *Aesthetics*, vol. I, p. 29.

3 *Ibid.*

4 *Ibid.*

5 *Ibid.*

6 *Ibid.*

7 J. M. Bernstein, *Against Voluptuous Bodies: Late Modernism and the Meaning of Painting* (Palo Alto, CA: Stanford University Press, 2006), p. 224.

8 Bernstein, *Against Voluptuous Bodies*, pp. 224–5.

9 Bernstein, *Against Voluptuous Bodies*, p. 225.

10 *Ibid.*

11 Theodor W. Adorno and Max Horkheimer, *Dialectic of Enlightenment*, trans. John Cumming (London: Verso, 1997), p. 235. Translation modified in the light of *Dialektik der Aufklärung: Philosophische Fragmente* (1944), in Theodor W. Adorno, *Gesammelte Schriften*, ed. Rolf Tiedemann and Gretel Adorno, 20 vols. (Frankfurt: Suhrkamp, 1970), vol. III (1981), p. 269.

12 Hegel, *Aesthetics*, vol. II, p. 964 (Hegel's emphases).

13 Hegel, *Aesthetics*, vol. II, p. 960.

14 Hegel, *Aesthetics*, vol. II, p. 961.

15 Compare Cian Duffy's discussion of 'revolution and the natural sublime', *Revolutionary Sublime*, pp. 29–37 and see pp. 53–4.

16 Lucretius, *Nature of Things*, p. 335, book II, ll. 1029–38 (Latin), book II, ll. 1042–50 (Good trans.). Lucretius's poem is itself about the entirety of the universe, as Good remarks in his 'Life of Lucretius', 'The subject he had selected, though the noblest, was the most profound, as well as the most comprehensive, that can ever engage the attention of the human mind; nor is there any title by which it could be designated so pertinently as that selected by himself, THE NATURE OF THINGS. It embraces the whole scope of natural, metaphysical, and moral philosophy; and to execute with any great degree of success, required a knowledge almost, if not altogether, universal' ('Life of Lucretius', in Titus Lucretius Carus, *The Nature of Things: A Didactic Poem*,

trans. John Mason Good, 2 vols. [London: Longman, Hurst, Rees, & Orme, 1805], pp. xix–ciii, at p. xxxix.

17 For Hume's discussion of miracles see, of course, section X, 'Of Miracles', in the *Enquiry*, pp. 109–31.

18 Good suggests that 'no critic of modern times has more justly appreciated the style and talents of Lucretius than Mr. Hume' ('Life of Lucretius', vol. I, p. xlvi). For a brief but useful account of the influence of Lucretius on Hume's thinking, see Eric Baker, 'Lucretius in the European Enlightenment', in Stuart Gallespie and Philip Hardie, eds., *The Cambridge Companion to Lucretius* (Cambridge University Press, 2007), pp. 274–88, at pp. 279–81, though note that Peter Loptson downplays the philosophical importance of Lucretius to Hume. Peter Loptson, 'Hume and Ancient Philosophy', *British Journal for the History of Philosophy*, 20 (2012): 741–72, at p. 761.

19 Henri Meschonnic, *La Rime et la vie* (Lagrasse: Verdier, 1989), p. 187 (my translation). Meschonnic is commenting on the sentences from Shelley's 'A Defence of Poetry' that follow above. And note Meschonnic's expansion on this idea: 'Poetry must transform the world; it transforms our relation to the world or it is not poetry, but a poetization.' Henri Meschonnic, *Vivre poème* (Liancourt: Dumerchez, 2006), p. 12.

20 Milton, *Paradise Lost*, p. 76, book I, ll. 254–5. Shelley, in fact, slightly misquotes this to read that the mind can make a heaven or hell 'of', rather than 'in', itself.

21 Harold Bloom, *Shelley's Mythmaking* (New Haven, CT: Yale University Press, 1959), p. 105.

22 Bloom, of course, had his own reservations about *Shelley's Mythmaking* in retrospect. For a brief account of these, see Peter de Bolla, *Harold Bloom: Towards Historical Rhetorics* (London and New York: Routledge, 1988), p. 10.

23 Ruston, *Shelley and Vitality*, p. 185.

24 Georges Faure notes the frequency of variations on the *i* sound in these and immediately surrounding lines, in 'He', 'bees', 'will', 'reflected', 'illume', 'in', and even 'lake' and 'ivy'. He does not, though, comment on the specific modulation on 'bees' that interests me. See *Les Éléments du rythme poétique en anglais moderne: esquisse d'une nouvelle analyse et essai d'application au 'Prometheus Unbound' de P. B. Shelley* (The Hague: Mouton, 1970), p. 275.

25 In addition to Faure, see, for a summary of the versification of this song, *Poems* II, p. 517, n.11, where it is noted that the triplet pattern of the spirits' songs is varied by couplets and an unrhymed line 10, apart from in the song of the Fourth Spirit, where line 10 is 'picked up in the closing couplet'. However, there is no 'closing couplet' but, instead, another triplet: 'Nurslings of immortality! – / One of these awakened me, / And I sped to succour thee.' What occurs here, in fact, in the picking up of 'be' in the rhymes of the final triplet (not couplet) is at once the extreme attenuation of the triplet pattern – 'be' seems initially isolated – and its sublation in a concluding pattern of a triplet whose rhyme was already anticipated. Louise Propst, incidentally, observes

that in Shelley's stanzaic lyrics (such as we may take the songs of the spirits to be) unrhymed lines are very rare. Louise Propst, *An Analytical Study of Shelley's Versification*, University of Iowa Humanistic Studies, vol. 5, no. 3 (University of Iowa Press, 1933), p. 41. Note also Chris Foss's account of 'deferred rhyme' as distracting 'the drive toward signification in that the focus on meaning is in this dimension of the text distracted by the search for rhyming partners (which becomes a competing order to that of logical meaning)'. Chris Foss, 'Shelley's Revolution in Poetic Language: A Kristevan Reading of Act IV to *Prometheus Unbound*', *European Romantic Review*, 9 (1998): 501–18, at p. 508.

26 And note, by the way, Hunt's view of bees as inherently songful in 'The Nymphs' (1818), a poem much admired by Shelley: 'And fragrant-living bee, / So happy, that he will not move, not he, / Without a song' (Hunt, *Poetical Works*, p. 321; ll. 76–8). Compare too 'the rich bee rejoicing as he goes' in 'To John Keats' (1818) (Hunt, *Poetical Works*, p. 243; l. 5), but especially compare my discussion of the sound of 'bees' in the song of the Fourth Spirit above with the chime of 'bee', 'happy', 'he' and only then with the rhyme-word 'he' in Hunt's lines from 'The Nymphs'. For Shelley's significant admiration of this poem as 'truly poetical, in the intense and emphatic sense of the word' and as 'executed with the fullest and most flowing lyrical power', see his letters to Hunt of 22 March 1818 and 14–18 November 1819 (*Letters* II, pp. 2–3 and 152).

27 Faure, *Les Éléments du rythme*, p. 272 (my translation). Faure also comments on the re-gathering and reordering of the group *l*, *p*, *s* of 'lips' in 'slept' in the first line (*Les Éléments du rythme*, p. 273).

28 Compare Judith Chernaik's commentary on this aspect of 'To Constantia' in *The Lyrics of Shelley* (Cleveland, OH: Case Western Reserve University Press, 1972), pp. 53–4.

29 John Wilkinson, 'Following the Poem', in *The Lyric Touch: Essays on the Poetry of Excess* (Cambridge: Salt, 2007), pp. 195–211, at p. 196.

30 Wilkinson, 'Following the Poem', p. 210.

31 Laura Wells Betz, '"At Once Mild and Animating": *Prometheus Unbound* and Shelley's Spell of Style', *European Romantic Review*, 21 (2010): 161–81 p. 172.

32 Godwin, *Political Justice*, pp. 370–1.

33 Godwin, *Political Justice*, p. 370.

34 See Ross Wilson, 'Clare's Indistinct Array', *Romanticism*, 17 (2011): 148–59, for a comparable treatment of kinds of indistinctness in the verse of John Clare.

35 Edward Duffy, *Rousseau in England: The Context for Shelley's Critique of the Enlightenment* (Berkeley, CA: University of California Press, 1979), p. 110. Compare Rousseau's characterisation of 'reverie' as the product of the 'unhindered and untroubled' mind at the beginning of the second walk in *Reveries of the Solitary Walker*, trans. Russell Goulbourne (Oxford University Press, 2011), p. 11.

36 Wilkinson, 'Following the Poem', p. 210.

37 Gilbert Highet takes this passage from the Preface to *Prometheus Unbound* as the occasion for his reflections on how the landscape of Rome in the early nineteenth century was spread with 'huge fields, [...] which are at a great distance revealed as being, not fields, but the overgrown floors of temples and baths; [...] hills which covered buried palaces'. Gilbert Highet, *Poets in a Landscape* (Harmondsworth: Penguin, 1959), p. 221.

38 Chernaik, *The Lyrics of Shelley*, p. 168.

39 Jonathan Bate, *The Song of the Earth* (London: Picador, 2000), pp. 90, 91.

40 Bate, *Song of the Earth*, pp. 91–2.

41 See also Thomas R. Frosch's psychoanalytic reading of the poems to Jane, in which he asserts that '*With a Guitar. To Jane* dreams of sublimating sexual desire and aggression into art, but it ultimately reveals art to be an instrument of eros and aggression.' Thomas R. Frosch, '"More Than Ever Can Be Spoken": Unconscious Fantasy in Shelley's Jane Williams Poems', *Studies in Philology*, 102 (2005): 378–413, at p. 401.

42 G. Rostrevor Hamilton, 'Shelley's Own', *English*, 5 (1945): 149–53, at p. 151.

43 Perhaps it is worth noticing here that the description of the guitar as a 'slave' is a quite radical revision of two earlier alternatives which are semantically related to one another: 'take / This sweet This child of slave of music for the sake'. *BSM* XIX, 105 reverso/204.

44 Plato, *Meno*, trans. by G. M. A. Grube, in *Plato: Complete Works*, ed. John M. Cooper with D. S. Hutchinson (Indianapolis, IN: Hackett, 1997), pp. 870–97, at pp. 880–6. Notopoulos thinks that Shelley came across the story of the slave boy in the 'Platonic potpourri' of Coleridge's *Biographia* (*The Platonism of Shelley*, p. 158); he also suggests that the 'unremembered world' in the lines 'I do not feel as if I were a man, / But like a fiend appointed to chastise / The offences of some unremembered world' from *The Cenci* (*SPP*, p. 179; Act IV, scene I, ll. 160–2) and the mention of 'obscure remembrances' in *Peter Bell the Third* (*SPP*, p. 354; part fifth, l. 418) are echoes of the doctrine of the pre-existence of the soul as outlined in the *Meno*. For Coleridge's mention of the slave episode, see *Biographia Literaria*, ed. James Engell and W. Jackson Bate (Princeton University Press, 1983), p. 251.

45 Bate, *Song of the Earth*, p. 92.

46 Lucretius, *Nature of Things*, vol. I, p. 135; book II, ll. 823–7 (Latin), book II, ll. 887–91 (Good trans.). Shelley described Lucretius's poetry to Hogg, incidentally, as 'full of irresistible energy of language as well as the profoundest truth' (6 July 1817; *Letters* I, 545).

47 Lucretius, *Nature of Things*, vol. p. 147, book I, 906–13 (Latin), book I, 969–76 (Good trans.). Compare the Loeb translation, which stays closer to Lucretius's play on *ignes et lignum* but doesn't achieve Good's play on different words made up of precisely the same letters, when it asks the reader to consider 'how the same elements a little changed in their relations create fires and firs'. Titus Lucretius Caro, *De rerum natura*, trans. W. H. D. House, rev. Martin Ferguson Smith (Cambridge, MA: Harvard University Press, 1992), p. 75.

48 Garrett Stewart, *Reading Voices: Literature and the Phonotext* (Berkeley, CA: University of California Press, 1990), p. 167.

49 Richard Lovelace, *The Poems of Richard Lovelace*, ed. C. H. Wilkinson (Oxford: Clarendon Press, 1930), p. 38. The poem immediately following 'Orpheus to Beasts' in *Lucasta*, 'Orpheus to Woods', begins 'Hark! O hark! you guilty trees', thus rendering explicit the hints at the aural of the other poem (*Poems, ibid.*).

50 Compare to Günther Anders's view that music 'is nowhere and everywhere it is heard'. Günther Anders, 'Spuk und Radio', *Anbruch*, 12 (1930): 65–6, at p. 65, quoted in Veit Erlmann, *Reason and Resonance: A History of Modern Aurality* (New York: Zone, 2010), p. 319.

51 Clive Scott and T. V. F. Brogan, 'Terza Rima Sonnet', in Alex Preminger and T. V. F. Brogan, eds., *The New Princeton Encyclopedia of Poetry and Poetics* (Princeton University Press, 1993), p. 1271. S. C. Wilcox, however, discerned in Shelley's ode 'a form of both movement and suspension akin to Spenser's quatorzains', thus taking the Spenserian sonnet to be characterised by the kind of forward and recursive movement which Scott and Brogan find to be more or less absent from it. Wilcox, like Scott and Brogan, clearly emphasises the more than merely onward movement of 'Ode to the West Wind', both in his positive comparison to Spenser's sonnets and in his comment on the thematic development of odes that '[a]n ode grows, not by mere expansion, but concentrically from a conceptual core'. S. C. Wilcox, 'The Prosodic Structure of "Ode to the West Wind"', *Notes and Queries*, 18 February 1950, pp. 77–8, at p. 77.

52 *BSM* V, pp. 136–7 (both reverse) (285 and 287).

5 SOUNDS OF AIR

1 For a useful collection of these responses to Theseus, see Jonathan Bate, ed., *The Romantics on Shakespeare*, rev. edn (Harmondsworth: Penguin, 1997). In his *Shakespeare and the English Romantic Imagination*, Bate, referring in particular to Woodhouse's gloss on a letter of Keats to John Taylor, notes that Theseus's lines were often treated 'as if they were Shakespeare's *Poetics*' and, most importantly, that the Romantic conception of 'imagination' was very much forged in relation to the Shakespearean uses of that term. Bate also acknowledges Blake's frustration with the apparently general ignorance of the fact that Theseus is *condemning* imagination. Jonathan Bate, *Shakespeare and the English Romantic Imagination*, rev. edn (Oxford University Press, 1992), pp. 172, 4 and 128 respectively.

2 Shelley's scattered references to *A Midsummer Night's Dream* do not directly address this speech, though they do demonstrate a detailed knowledge of the play. When Leslie Stephen remarked on a passage of *Hellas* that it, 'like so many in Shelley, shows that he had Shakespeare in his mind without exactly copying him', he captures well, I think, the mode of influence of Theseus's

speech on him. See Leslie Stephen, 'Godwin and Shelley' (1879), in *Hours in a Library*, 3 vols. (London: Folio Society, 1991), vol. III, pp. 59–93, at p. 81).

3 Isobel Armstrong, *Language as Living Form in Nineteenth-Century Poetry* (Brighton: Harvester, 1982), p. 113. Armstrong's reading of *Prometheus Unbound* in her Chapter 4, 'Shelley's Perplexity', pp. 113–40, has considerably influenced the reading of that poem I advance below.

4 Paul A. Olson, '*A Midsummer Night's Dream* and the Meaning of Court Marriage', *ELH*, 24 (1957): 95–119, at p. 97. I am grateful to Tony Gash for having suggested the relevance of this essay to my discussion.

5 Compare the distinction between the denigration of the 'mere' body and the celebration of 'the body that loves and plays' in *Queen Mab* established by Scrivener, *Radical Shelley*, p. 71.

6 Compare Charles Lamb's review of Wordsworth's *The Excursion* (1814), the poem, of course, that provoked the opprobrium of the Shelley circle (see pp. 67–8 above) which was merely entrenched by the publication of *Peter Bell* five years later. Lamb sardonically remarks of the judgement of those who would censure Wordsworth's poetry as childish because it often has children as its subject: 'how apprehensive! how imaginative! how religious!' Robert Woof, ed., *William Wordsworth: The Critical Heritage*, vol. I: 1793–1820 (London and New York: Routledge, 2001), p. 415.

7 Adam Smith, whose life Shelley had praised to his father as 'characterised by the strictest morality', describes prudence as a cautious reticence: the prudent man 'is not always frank and open', although, naturally, he does always speak the truth when he speaks at all. See Part VI, section I, 'Of the Character of the Individual So Far as It Affects His Own Happiness; or, Of Prudence', in Adam Smith, *The Theory of Moral Sentiments*, 6th edn, 2 vols. (London, 1790), vol. II, p. 55. See, on Smith as a morally upstanding Deist, Shelley's letter to Timothy Shelley of 6 February 1811, *Letters* I, p. 46.

8 Strictly speaking, the reduction of exceptional humans to the status of animals is an explicit concern only of *Philoctetes* and *Othello*, whereas *Agamemnon* (perhaps more conventionally) addresses the specifically human flaw of arrogating a divine right, as evident in Agamemnon's decision to step on the purple carpet on his return to Argos. Note, nevertheless, the frequency with which Cassandra is described as an animal (e.g., ll. 1063, 1064 and 1093–4), her retort that Clytemnestra and Aegisthus are wild animals (ll. 1258–9) and the Chorus's similar assessment (l. 1251). See Aeschylus, *Agamemnon*, trans. Richmond Lattimore, in *Greek Tragedies*, ed. David Grene and Richmond Lattimore, 3 vols., 2nd edn (University of Chicago Press, 1991), vol. I, pp. 5–60.

9 See Gary Farnell's comment on *Adonais*, 'a work whose very title [...] clearly signals its shaping rhetorical and affective investment in the possibility of an "anagrammatic" annunciation. Shelley invokes the determining force, indeed the magic of names to save the "*Author of Endymion, Hyperion, Etc.*" (as the subtitle of *Adonais* has it paraphrastically) from precisely that kind of nonexistence as is at present implied by the end of logocentrism; namely, the sheer

senselessness of death.' Gary Farnell, 'Rereading Shelley', *ELH*, 60 (1993): 625–50, at p. 629. Farnell does not comment on the fact that the titles of Keats's works specified by Shelley, '*Endymion, Hyperion*', are sonically very similar, both bearing a stress on their second syllables, both permitting (or inviting) elision of their potentially penultimate syllable, and rhyming, of course, on '-ion'. The sonic character of these titles is crucial to the 'magic' salvation hoped for from them.

10 Compare Nietzsche's characterisation of utilitarian moralities as 'prudence, prudence, prudence, mingled with stupidity, stupidity, stupidity' in Friedrich Nietzsche, *Beyond Good and Evil: Prelude to a Philosophy of the Future*, trans. R. J. Hollingdale, rev. edn (London: Penguin, 1990), p. 119.

11 Quinney, *Literary Power*, p. 107.

12 Quinney, *Literary Power*, p. 89.

13 Connell, *Romanticism*, pp. 210–33.

14 On Shelley's suspicion of 'the view that progress is steady and continuous', see Mendilow, 'Shelley's Philosophy of Liberty', p. 172.

15 In addition to this contrast between Rousseau and Voltaire in particular, Shelley also compares Rousseau and Gibbon in his and Mary Shelley's 'Letters Written in Geneva' (1817). In the third letter, probably written exclusively by Percy, he recalls an episode in which he and Byron visited Gibbon's grave: 'My friend gathered some acacia leaves to preserve in remembrance of him [Gibbon]. I refrained from doing so, fearing to outrage the greater and more sacred name of Rousseau; the contemplation of whose imperishable creations had left no vacancy in my heart for mortal things.' *Prose*, p. 220.

16 Notopoulos also finds reference to the 'reveries of Plato' in Pierre-Jean-Georges Cabanis's *Rapports du physique et du moral de l'homme* (1802), and, moreover, shows that the image of Plato as dreamer, though having its roots in the Middle Ages, is prominent in other eighteenth-century French rationalists, citing in particular Pierre Bayle's *Dictionary* (1697) and Voltaire's 'Plato's Dream' (1756).

17 See, among many examples, Susan Hawk Brisman's still valuable '"Unsaying His High Language": The Problem of Voice in *Prometheus Unbound*', *Studies in Romanticism*, 16 (1977): 51–86, especially her attempt to articulate a Promethean principle of language opposed to a Hermetic one; Keach, *Shelley's Style*, pp. 1–41, notably his argument that Shelley's 'strongest confidence in language derives from exactly the same source as his deepest anxiety about it' (p. 33); Stuart Peterfreund, *Shelley Among Others: The Play of the Intertext and the Idea of Language* (Baltimore, MD: Johns Hopkins University Press, 2002), especially pp. 25–34; David S. Ferris, *Silent Urns: Romanticism, Hellenism, Modernity* (Palo Alto, CA: Stanford University Press, 2000), pp. 144–57, for an intricate account of the discontinuity between the uttering and content of Prometheus's curse (especially pp. 146–8); and Foss, 'Shelley's Revolution', pp. 504–8 in particular.

18 Compare to the following statement from the fragment 'On Learning Languages' of around 1816: 'The generous and inspiriting examples of

philosophy and virtue you desire intimately to know and feel, not as mere facts detailing names and dates and motions of the human body, but clothed in the very language of the actors – that language dictated by and expressive of the passions or principles which governed their conduct. Facts are not what we want to know in poetry, in history, in the lives of individual men, in satire or in panegyric' (*Prose*, p. 164). Note in particular that, despite the rejection of 'facts', we still, according to Shelley, 'want to know' something in poetry, etc., – a knowing which he allies with feeling, characterising both as 'intimate'.

19 Michael O'Neill, '"Driven as in Surges": Texture and Voice in Romantic Poetry', *The Wordsworth Circle*, 38 (2007): 91–3, at p. 91. One might add to the resonances noted by O'Neill that between 'recurrence' and 'influence', and point out, moreover, that O'Neill's remarks themselves reverberate with the echoes he finds in Shelley, seeing in sound the 'ground and foundation' of the order of thoughts.

20 Wolfson, who acknowledges her debt to O'Neill's remarks, likewise suggests that the relation of 'Sounds' and 'found' offers a demonstration of the vanity of translation upon which Shelley goes on to insist in the same paragraph of 'A Defence of Poetry'. Susan J. Wolfson, 'Sounding Romantic: The Sound of Sound', in Susan J. Wolfson, ed., *'Soundings of Things Done': The Poetry and Poetics of Sound in the Romantic Era and Ear* (2008), available online at http://romantic.arhu.umd.edu/praxis/soundings/wolfson/wolfson.html (accessed 11 March 2013), p. 13.

21 O'Neill, commenting on the lines spoken by The Earth in Act IV of *Prometheus Unbound*, 'Language is a perpetual Orphic song, / Which rules with daedal harmony a throng / Of thoughts and forms, which else senseless and shapeless were' (*Poems* II, pp. 639–40, Act IV, ll. 415–17), goes on to state that 'song fights an endless battle with, and yet is enabled by, all that is "senseless and shapeless"'. O'Neill, '"Driven as in Surges"', p. 91.

22 'Byron and Shelley on the Character of Hamlet', *New Monthly Magazine and Literary Journal*, 29 (1830): 327–36.

23 'Byron and Shelley', p. 330.

24 *Ibid.*

25 Stuart Peterfreund, 'Shelley, Monboddo, Vico, and the Language of Poetry', *Style*, 15 (1981): 382–400, at p. 383.

26 *Ibid.* And it is worth noting that, like O'Neill's finding of the 'ground and foundation' of thought in sound, Peterfreund's prose forms its own echo chamber here, where the 'notion' of the sound /l/ as liquid is associated with the 'motion' of a river.

27 Peterfreund, 'Shelley, Monboddo', p. 396.

28 Raymond D. Havens, 'Structure and Prosodic Pattern in Shelley's Lyrics', *PMLA*, 65 (1950): 1076–87, at p. 1086. Havens' idea of 'that sense of fitness which we all possess, heightened and intensified until it becomes creative' is, of course, related to Shelley's 'faculty of approximation to the beautiful' which exists 'in excess' in poets ('A Defence of Poetry', *SPP*, p. 512).

29 I am drawing here on the description of the relation between 'distinct consciousness' (understood as 'reflective consciousness') and 'reason' (understood as 'the very element or condition of possibility of these "symphonic" operations [viz., what 'Byron' dismisses as mechanical contrivances]') in Jarvis's reading of this conversation. Jarvis, 'Thinking in Verse', p. 101. See also the account of thinking as 'making explicit' and the alternative to it in Jarvis, 'Musical Thinking', especially pp. 58–9 and 67–9.

30 The scholarship treating Shelley's relation to Dante is, of course, vast. For an early (but still usefully compact) overview, see Oscar Kuhns, 'Dante's Influence on Shelley', *MLN*, 13 (1898): 161–5; for a fuller and more recent discussion, focusing on 'The Triumph of Life' in particular but taking into account much previous consideration of Shelley's relation to Dante, see Ralph Pite, Chapter 5, '"The Lucifer of that starry flock": Shelley in *Purgatorio*', in *The Circle of Our Vision: Dante's Presence in English Romantic Poetry* (Oxford: Clarendon Press, 1994), pp. 161–98.

31 Shelley comments on Catholicism and its excesses in a number of places in his work. Not all of these remarks, however, are as resolutely critical as Bryan Shelley in his otherwise useful account would appear to suggest. See Bryan Shelley, *Shelley and Scripture: The Interpreting Angel* (Oxford: Clarendon Press, 1994), pp. 77–95. For instance, Shelley at least expresses sympathy with the Catholic doctrine of Purgatory in his 'An Address, to the Irish People': 'I know no men of thought and learning who do not consider the Catholic idea of purgatory, much nearer the truth than the Protestant one of eternal damnation. Can you think that the Mahometans and the Indians, who have done good deeds in this life, will not be rewarded in the next. The Protestants believe that they will be eternally damned – at least they swear that they do. – I think they appear in a better light as perjurers, than believers in a falsehood so hateful and uncharitable as this' (*Prose*, p. 16).

32 Tillotama Rajan, *The Supplement of Reading: Figures of Understanding in Romantic Theory and Practice* (Ithaca, NY: Cornell University Press, 1990), p. 281.

33 Wilhelm von Humboldt, *Humanist without Portfolio: An Anthology of the Writings of Wilhelm von Humboldt*, trans. Marianne Cowan (Detroit, MI: Wayne State University Press, 1963), p. 280, quoted by Rajan, *Supplement of Reading*, pp. 28 and 96. Gerald L. Bruns, incidentally, usefully glosses this statement of Humboldt's: 'Language is not an artifact of the spirit but the very form in which the life of the spirit is realized. [...] [L]anguage does not simply articulate the already formed contents of man's interior; on the contrary, it is the activity by which man's inner life takes on form and meaning.' Gerald L. Bruns, *Modern Poetry and the Idea of Language: A Critical and Historical Study* (New Haven, CT: Yale University Press, 1974), p. 65.

34 Rajan, *Supplement of Reading*, p. 278.

35 Jerrold E. Hogle, *Shelley's Process: Radical Transference and the Development of His Major Works* (Oxford University Press, 1988), p. 20 and compare to, for example, p. 278.

36 Bloom, *Shelley's Mythmaking*, p. 174.

37 Glenn O'Malley's *Shelley and Synesthesia* (Evanston, IL: Northwestern University Press, 1964) is still valuable here. Although he does not discuss 'The Sensitive-Plant' extensively, he nevertheless does draw attention to the 'music-odor comparison', e.g., p. 17.

38 Compare Coleridge, of course, on the 'despotism of the eye', in *Biographia Literaria*, p. 107.

39 Although Richard Cronin insightfully remarks that this stanza 'effects an uneasy conjunction between the surreal and the real', I am not sure I agree that 'fled and gone' is a 'colloquialism'. See Cronin, *Shelley's Poetic Thoughts*, p. 66. The only instance of 'fled and gone' that I have managed to find in the *OED*, from Ralph Cudworth's *Intellectual System* (1678), is likewise reliant on its difference from 'dead and gone': 'That Soul and Life that is now fled and gone, from a lifeless Carcase, is only a loss to that particular Body or Compages of Matter, which by means thereof is now disanimated.' For Cudworth, in this quotation, it is not the 'Soul and Life' that is dead and gone, but rather it, in contrast to the body it has left, is alive. Note also the slight strain of Cudworth's syntax in following through this distinction: the soul, surely, has not 'gone, from a lifeless Carcase', because, as long as it remains in the body, the body lives, but rather that since the soul has departed from the body it (only) then becomes lifeless; and note also the oddity involved in thinking that the flight of the soul is the 'means' by which the body is 'disanimated', as if that were an end in the teleological, rather than merely terminal, sense. It is unlikely, incidentally, that Shelley read any of Cudworth's works and so will not have encountered this interesting anticipation of his use of 'fled and gone'.

40 Compare Lucretius' account of how shared elements (i.e. letters) produce different meanings and sounds in different contexts in his verse, discussed in the previous chapter (p. 111).

41 Stewart, *Reading Voices*, p. 164. 'Hymn to Intellectual Beauty' quoted from the 'B' text. The 'A' text reads, similarly: 'Love, hope and self-esteem like clouds depart – / And come, for some uncertain moments lent.–'

42 Stewart, *Reading Voices*, p. 166.

43 Kipperman, *Beyond Enchantment: German Idealism and English Romantic Poetry* (Philadelphia, PA: University of Pennsylvania Press, 1986), p. 169.

44 Stanley Cavell, *In Quest of the Ordinary: Lines of Skepticism and Romanticism* (University of Chicago Press, 1988), Chapter 3, 'Texts of Recovery', pp. 50–75.

45 Betz, '"At Once Mild and Animating"', p. 164.

46 Compare 'A Sabbath Walk', written around the same time (late 1811 to early 1812), in which Christian rites are 'idle prayers' and 'senseless mummeries' (*Poems* I, p. 200; l. 48).

47 David Ferris reads this account of the words of Christ as centrally important to the portrayal of Prometheus's struggle to avoid a similar fate. Ferris, *Silent Urns*, p. 152.

48 Betz, '"At Once Mild and Animating"', p. 163.
49 Also noted by Stewart, *Reading Voices*, p. 162.
50 Armstrong, *Language as Living Form*, p. 114.

6 POETRY AND THE LIFE OF THEORY

1 Kelvin Everest, 'Preface', in 'Percy Bysshe Shelley: Bicentenary Essays', ed. Kelvin Everest, *Essays and Studies*, n.s. 45 (1992), vii–ix, at pp. viii–ix. Everest did pick out William Keach as an American scholar notable for his attention to 'the quality of [Shelley's] achievements simply as a writer' (p. viii).
2 Vincent Newey, 'Shelley's "Dream of Youth": *Alastor*, "Selving" and the Psychic Realm', in 'Percy Bysshe Shelley: Bicentenary Essays', 1–23, at p. 1, n.1.
3 G. Kim Blank, 'A Shelley Survey: Which Shelley Now?', in G. Kim Blank, ed., *The New Shelley: Later Twentieth-Century Views* (Houndmills: Macmillan, 1991), pp. 242–7, at p. 247.
4 William Wordsworth, 'The Tables Turned', *'Lyrical Ballads' and Other Poems, 1797–1800*, ed. James Butler and Karen Green (Ithaca, NY: Cornell University Press, 1992), ll. 9–12; 'wise passiveness' is from the preceding poem in *Lyrical Ballads*, 'Expostulation and Reply', l. 24.
5 See Pierre Hadot, Ulrich Dierse, Hans Hübner, Rainer Piepmeier, Klaus Rothe, Richard Toellner and Joachim Vennebusch, 'Leben', in *Historisches Wörterbuch der Philosophie*, vol. V, cols. 52–103, at col. 81. It was this tendency of Romanticism's alleged resistance to 'defin[ing] indefinite life' that provoked Carl Schmitt's ire. See Carl Schmitt, *Political Romanticism*, trans. Guy Oakes (Cambridge, MA: MIT Press, 1986), p. 66. I have addressed Schmitt's critique in Wilson, 'Introduction', pp. 2–7.
6 David Hume, 'The Sceptic', in *Essays*, pp. 159–80, at p. 180. Tim Milnes emphasises the likely significance of Hume's statement that '[w]hile we are reasoning concerning life, life is gone'. See 'Centre and Circumference: Shelley's Defence of Philosophy', *European Romantic Review*, 15 (2004): 3–22, at p. 19.
7 Wordsworth, 'The Tables Turned', ll. 21–4.
8 Leon Chai, *Romantic Theory: Forms of Reflexivity in the Romantic Era* (Baltimore, MD: Johns Hopkins University Press, 2006), p. 111. Chai gives a richly morbid account of Bichat's work in the squalid conditions of the Hôtel-Dieu in Paris, where Bichat made many of the observations that formed the basis of his approach in his *Anatomie générale, appliquée à la physiologie et à la medicine* (1801).
9 Paul de Man, 'Shelley Disfigured', in Harold Bloom, Paul de Man, Jacques Derrida, Geoffrey Hartman and J. Hillis Miller, *Deconstruction and Criticism* (London: Continuum, 1979), pp. 32–61, at pp. 36–7.
10 De Man, 'Shelley Disfigured', p. 56.
11 See Rodolphe Gasché's account (to which I was alerted by Jarvis, *Philosophic Song*, p. 155) of de Man's paradoxically systematic defiance of relationality in Gasché, *The Wild Card of Reading: On Paul de Man* (Cambridge, MA: Harvard University Press, 1988), p. 5. Compare Orrin N. C. Wang's account

of the disingenuousness of aspects of de Man's reading in Wang, *Fantastic Modernity: Dialectical Readings in Romanticism and Theory* (Baltimore, MD: Johns Hopkins University Press, 1996), pp. 54–5.

12 William Hazlitt, review of Shelley's *Posthumous Poems*, in James E. Barcus, ed., *Shelley: The Critical Heritage* (London: Routledge & Kegan Paul, 1975), pp. 335–45, at p. 342.

13 William Hazlitt, from 'On Paradox and Commonplace', *Table Talk*, in Barcus, *The Critical Heritage*, pp. 284–6, at p. 285.

14 McLane, *Romanticism and the Human Sciences*, p. 222.

15 *Ibid.*

16 *Pace*, in this instance, Wang (*Fantastic Modernity*, p. 53): '"The Triumph of Life" works, then, as an aphasia, whereby its technical and poetic virtuosity overcompensate for a conceptual stutter of which the poem is intensely aware', if, of course, 'overcompensate' means, as it appears to mean, under-compensate, since 'technical and poetic virtuosity' are by no means fitted (so it is implied) to conceptual work of any kind. And see also the revealing testimony to the 'intensity and power' of the poem, which are denied any real importance in the same moment that they are noted, in Abbey (*Destroyer and Preserver*, p. 143): 'Can man achieve certain knowledge of anything? Through its self-destructive imagery, "The Triumph of Life" focuses this philosophical problem with an intensity and power surely unsurpassed in English Romanticism.'

17 Letter, 1 May 1845, in Daniel Karlin, ed., *Robert Browning and Elizabeth Barrett: The Courtship Correspondence, 1845–1846: A Selection* (Oxford University Press, 1990), p. 42.

18 Lawrence Binyon, '"Terza Rima" in English Poetry', *English*, 3 (1940): 113–17, at p. 115. George Saintsbury also contrasts Dante and Shelley on the same grounds, though he is commenting on Shelley's 'Prince Athanase' and not 'The Triumph of Life'. See George Saintsbury, *A History of English Prosody*, 3 vols. (New York: Russell & Russell, 1961), vol. III, p. 107.

19 Keach, *Shelley's Style*, p. 164.

20 Keach, *Shelley's Style*, pp. 184–200 (de Man quoted on pp. 184 and 185). There have, in addition to Keach's and the other responses already noted, been a number of other reactions to de Man's essay, but on this specific topic of the status of non-semantic aspects of language see also Thomas M. Greene's defence of Wordsworth's view of language (in 'Essays on Epitaphs, III') against de Man's strictures (in *The Rhetoric of Romanticism* (in which 'Shelley Disfigured' is reprinted)) in Greene's *Poetry, Signs, and Magic* (Newark, DE: University of Delaware Press, 2005), pp. 17–28 (especially p. 24). Andrew Welsh, incidentally, had earlier taken what he claims is his extension of Wordsworth's question regarding the nature of poetic language as the point of departure for his important study, *Roots of Lyric: Primitive Poetry and Modern Poetics* (Princeton University Press, 1978), especially p. 4.

21 Keach, *Shelley's Style*, p. 185. Keach has developed the implications – especially the political ones – of the central and contended role of 'arbitrariness' in

language theory in the period after Locke in William Keach, *Arbitrary Power: Romanticism, Language, Politics* (Princeton University Press, 2004).

22 Keach, *Shelley's Style*, p. 188. Compare, of course, Chapter 1's discussion of Shelley's 'creative intelligence' highlighted by J. H. Prynne in response to F. R. Leavis.

23 Keach, *Shelley's Style*, p. 192 (my emphasis).

24 Compare to Steven McCaffery on the perpetual and unpredictable volatility (and vitality) of letters in McCaffery, *Prior to Meaning: The Protosemantic and Poetics* (Evanston, IL: Northwestern University Press, 2001), pp. xix–xx.

25 William O. Scott also makes this connection. See 'Shelley's Admiration for Bacon', *PMLA*, 73 (1958): 228–36, at p. 229.

26 See David Lee Clark, 'Shelley and Bacon', *PMLA*, 48 (1933): 529–46, at p. 534, n. 23 for bibliographic information on Shelley's copy of Bacon.

27 Clark, 'Shelley and Bacon', p. 543.

28 Clark, 'Shelley and Bacon', p. 543. The English text from *The Advancement of Learning* is given in *SPP*, p. 491, n.9.

29 Pulos, *Deep Truth*, p. 72.

30 Scott ascribed Shelley's praise of Bacon as a poet to his discovery in his works of 'poetic material' in the form of 'highly congenial imagery' ('Shelley's Admiration for Bacon', p. 234). I do not deny that but assert in addition that Shelley viewed Bacon as a poet for more specific reasons still than this.

31 For the relative infrequency of feminine rhymes in 'The Triumph of Life', see Donald Reiman, *Shelley's 'The Triumph of Life': A Critical Study* (Urbana, IL: University of Illinois Press, 1965), p. 93 (and n. 12 for the locations of these rhymes in the poem). Louise Propst discusses feminine ending in 'To Jane', where it 'is apt to give rising rhythm a semblance of falling rhythm' (*An Analytical Study*, p. 13). She notes, too, that 'To a Sky-Lark' appears to deploy feminine ending but that, in fact, only two of twenty-one iambic hexameters have feminine endings in this poem (*An Analytical Study*, p. 14).

32 Jonathan Kertzer, *Poetic Argument: Studies in Modern Poetry* (Kingston, ON: McGill-Queen's University Press, 1988), p. 17. Shelley, therefore, hardly shares in the supposed 'romantic disavowal of reason' rejected, in turn, by Modernism (Kertzer, *Poetic Argument*, p. 22).

33 Shelley mentions Kant as a 'sage' in 'The Triumph of Life' (*SPP*, p. 490; ll. 236–7), but James Bieri records Hogg's opinion that, despite ordering a Latin translation of the *Critique of Pure Reason* in 1813, Shelley never studied Kant – an opinion which need not necessarily contrast with Mary Shelley's view that Kant would have been a major influence on her husband had he lived. See Bieri, *Percy Bysshe Shelley*, p. 718, n.13. Hugh Roberts also notes that 'we cannot say with any certainty' whether or not Shelley read Kant. See 'Shelley Among the Post-Kantians', *Studies in Romanticism*, 35 (1996): 295–329, at p. 304.

34 For somewhat differing treatments of this aspect of Kant's aesthetics, see Hannah Ginsborg, *The Role of Taste in Kant's Theory of Cognition* (New York: Garland, 1990) and Rodolphe Gasché, *The Idea of Form: Rethinking Kant's*

Aesthetics (Palo Alto, CA: Stanford University Press, 2003). Gasché claims that Kant does not view aesthetic judgement as, in fact, anterior to or preparatory for cognitive judgement but rather as 'para-epistemic' since what they achieve is 'cognition in general' and, thus, in Gasché's terms, 'a minimal mastery and minimal identification of something for which no determined concepts of the understanding are at hand' (*The Idea of Form,* p. 4). This account brings Kant closer to the version of this argument which I am going on to claim Shelley's 'A Defence of Poetry' articulates, although the minimalism of Kantian aesthetic judgement is still at odds with the paucity Shelley ascribes to cognition without recourse to the 'intervention of [those] excitements' he catalogues.

35 Immanuel Kant, *Critique of Judgement*, trans. James Creed Meredith, rev. and ed. Nicholas Walker (Oxford University Press, 2007), p. 22. For an excellent commentary on this aspect of Kant's theory of aesthetic judgement and its consequences, see J. M. Bernstein, *The Fate of Art: Aesthetic Alienation from Kant to Derrida and Adorno* (Cambridge: Polity, 1992), Chapter 1, 'Memorial Aesthetics: Kant's *Critique of Judgement*', pp. 17–65 and passim.

36 Jarvis, 'Thinking in Verse', p. 103. Compare to Notopoulos's comparison of Shelley and the Plato of the *Republic* on the related question of the role of poetry in education; Notopoulos notes that '[b]y supplanting reason with imagination Shelley makes poetry not a mere stage at a certain level of education, but education itself. Thus Plato and Shelley agree as to the function of poetry in education, but differ as to the primacy of reason or imagination in the educational process' (*The Platonism of Shelley*, p. 348).

37 John W. Wright, *Shelley's Myth of Metaphor* (Athens, GA: University of Georgia Press, 1970), p. 31.

38 Drummond, *Academical Questions*, vol. I, p. 16.

39 Notopoulos, *The Platonism of Shelley*, p. 446.

40 Notopoulos, *The Platonism of Shelley*, pp. 446–7.

41 Small, *The Long Life*, p. 32.

42 I realise, of course, that 'weep' and 'sleep' are different parts of speech: the former an infinitive ('but I lived yet to weep'); the latter a noun ('the Earth lulled in her winter sleep'). Significant as this difference is, what matters for my purposes above, however, is the more emphatic shift in relation between *a* and *b* rhyme words effected in 'creep' / 'leaping'. There is, alas, no room to expand on the intriguingly involuted rhymes of, in particular, stanzas 2 and 3 of 'The Zucca' here.

43 The association between the solitary reaper's working (including the exertion involved in it) and her singing is repeated, this time more explicitly, in the poem's final stanza: 'I saw her singing at her work / And o'er the sickle bending'. The senses of 'strain' cited above are from the *OED*.

44 Simon Jarvis, 'Unfree Verse: John Wilkinson's The Speaking Twins', in Peter Dayan and David Evans, eds., 'Rhythm in Literature After the Crisis in Verse', special issue of *Paragraph*, 33 (2010): 280–95, at pp. 286–7.

45 William Wordsworth, Preface to *Poems* (1815), in *Selected Prose*, ed. John O. Hayden (Harmondsworth: Penguin, 1988), pp. 372–86, at p. 376.

46 Jacques Roubaud, 'Prelude: Poetry and Orality', trans. Jean-Jacques Poucel, in Marjorie Perloff and Craig Dworkin, eds., *The Sound of Poetry/The Poetry of Sound* (University of Chicago Press, 2009), pp. 18–25, at p. 19. Compare Peter de Bolla's account of the fact that 'in the case of artworks made of language we must first read them before we are able to say anything at all about a response', which introduces his commentary on Wordsworth's 'We are Seven', in *Art Matters* (Cambridge, MA: Harvard University Press, 2002), p. 95.

47 Clive Scott, *The Poetics of French Verse: Studies in Reading* (Oxford: Clarendon Press, 1998), p. 98, and Chapter 2, 'The Reading of Verse', pp. 82–104 generally. See also the brief but illuminating discussion in Roubaud ('Prelude', p. 19) of the relation between what he calls the 'external' and 'internal' aspects of poetry: 'The external aspects of a poem are interpersonal. They are transmissible to practically anyone who speaks and reads the language in which a given poem is composed. The internal aspects are personal. They are in the mind of the reader-listener; essentially nontransmissible from one person to another; they are always in movement within memory: movement of images, of thoughts.'

48 See Vilma Mönckeberg, *Der Klangleib der Dichtung* (Hamburg: Classen & Goverts, 1946).

49 I therefore differ here from Vidyan Ravinthiran's otherwise fine reading of 'The Triumph of Life' in 'Dante and Shelley's Terza Rima', *Essays in Criticism*, 61 (2011): 155–72, at pp. 169–70. Ravinthiran discerns a growing suspicion of '"temperance" to *any* authority' in Shelley's work, and argues that, in the lines I am discussing, he 'uses Rousseau to articulate his ambivalence' toward the 'great bards of old' (p. 169). Leaving to one side the question of Shelley's 'use' of Rousseau, the view that Shelley is here 'express[ing] doubt about this numinous model of influence' – that is, the influence supposed to be exercised by the bards – ignores the ambivalence in fact inherent in Shelley's account of what 'tempering' actually involves here by reading it simply as the influence of the bards on later generations of readers and poets. It is not, that is, that the example of the bards is 'an image of constraining ideology', since it is not open to them as subjects to exercise constraint on their readers as objects.

50 Donald Reiman's edition of 'The Triumph of Life', incidentally, notes the word 'Srumfredevi' written above 'Dominion' in the manuscript of the above lines. This is Shelley's diminutive shorthand for Sir Humphry Davy, whom Reiman takes to be a potential contemporary inspiration for the imperious Aristotle, quoting the assessment of Davy's tenure of the presidency of the Royal Society from the eighth edition of the *Encyclopaedia Britannica* (1854): 'he lent himself to the petty cabals of a coterie during his possession of the chair. His ill-concealed partiality for the aristocracy of birth …; the presumptuous assumption in his own person, on some occasions, of a patrician haughtiness; and a neglect of the ordinary courtesies of society, procured him many enemies.' Quoted in Reiman, *Shelley's 'The Triumph of Life'*, p. 171.

51 In the manuscript, 'inly' is so inkily inscribed that it is almost illegible. The line 'See Homer & his brethren, men who quelled' is cancelled, with 'See the great bards of elder time [replaced with 'old'] who quelled' written underneath, but 'inly' is inscribed right at the end, overlapping the 'quelled' in the cancelled line. See *BSM* I (33 recto/193).

52 'Our involuntary motions are frequently found gradually to become subject to the power of volition. It seems impossible to set limits to this species of metamorphosis. Its reality cannot be questioned, when we consider that every motion of the human frame was originally involuntary. Is it not then highly probable, in the process of human improvement, that we may finally obtain an empire over every articulation of our frame? The circulation of the blood is a motion, in our present state, eminently involuntary. Yet nothing is more obvious than that certain thoughts, and states of the thinking faculty, are calculated to affect this process. Reasons have been adduced which seem to lead to an opinion that thought and animal motion are, in all cases, to be considered as antecedent and consequent.' Godwin, *Political Justice*, p. 774.

CODA

1 Frederick Startridge Ellis, *A Lexical Concordance to the Poetical Works of Percy Bysshe Shelley: An Attempt to Classify Every Word Found Therein According to its Signification* (London: Clarendon, 1892), p. 20.

2 Wordsworth, *The Excursion*, p. 53; book I, ll. 185–7.

3 Wordsworth, *The Excursion*, pp. 101–2; book II, ll. 854–6.

4 Two of the three examples cited by the *OED* for 'apprehensive, adj.' to illustrate the sixth sense (which is 'Now the most usual sense'), '[a]nticipative of something adverse; fearful of what may be about to happen', emphasise the enervated physicality of the apprehensive state.

Bibliography

Abbey, Lloyd, *Destroyer and Preserver: Shelley's Poetic Skepticism* (Lincoln, NE: University of Nebraska Press, 1979).

Adorno, Theodor W., *Gesammelte Schriften*, ed. Rolf Tiedemann and Gretel Adorno, 20 vols. (Frankfurt am Main : Suhrkamp, 1981), vol. III: *Dialektik der Aufklärung: Philosophische Fragmente.*

Minima Moralia: Reflections from Damaged Life, trans. E. F. N. Jephcott (London: Verso, 1974).

Adorno, Theodor W. and Max Horkheimer, *Dialectic of Enlightenment*, trans. John Cumming (London: Verso, 1997).

Aeschylus, *Agamemnon*, trans. Richmond Lattimore, in *Greek Tragedies*, ed. David Grene and Richmond Lattimore, 3 vols., 2nd edn (University of Chicago Press, 1991), vol. I, pp. 5–60.

Agamben, Giorgio, *Homo Sacer: Sovereign Power and Bare Life*, trans. Daniel Heller-Roazen (Palo Alto, CA: Stanford University Press, 1998).

Alighieri, Dante, *The Vision; or Hell, Heaven, and Purgatory, of Dante Alighieri*, trans. H. F. Cary, 3 vols. (London: Taylor & Hessey, 1814).

[Anonymous], *The First and Fourth Books of the Odes of Horace, Translated into English Verse* (London, 1799).

Aristotle, *'The Politics' and 'The Constitution of Athens'*, ed. Steven Everson (Cambridge University Press, 1996).

Armstrong, Charles I., *Romantic Organicism: From Idealist Origins to Ambivalent Afterlife* (Houndmills: Palgrave Macmillan, 2003).

Armstrong, Isobel, *Language as Living Form in Nineteenth-Century Poetry* (Brighton: Harvester, 1982).

Baker, Eric, 'Lucretius in the European Enlightenment', in Stuart Gillespie and Philip Hardie, eds., *The Cambridge Companion to Lucretius* (Cambridge University Press, 2007), pp. 274–88.

Baldick, Chris, *The Social Mission of English Criticism, 1848–1932* (Oxford: Clarendon Press, 1983).

Barcus, James E., ed., *Shelley: The Critical Heritage* (London: Routledge & Kegan Paul, 1975).

Bate, Jonathan, *Shakespeare and the English Romantic Imagination*, rev. edn (Oxford University Press, 1992).

ed., *The Romantics on Shakespeare*, rev. edn (Harmondsworth: Penguin, 1997).

The Song of the Earth (London: Picador, 2000).
Baudelaire, Charles, *Œuvres complètes*, ed. Claude Pichois, 2 vols. (Paris: Gallimard, 1975).
Baum, Joan, *Mind-Forg'd Manacles: Slavery and the English Romantic Poets* (North Haven, CT: Archon, 1994).
Beek, M. van, *An Enquiry into Puritan Vocabulary* (Groningen: Wolters-Noordhoff, 1969).
Bernstein, J. M., *Against Voluptuous Bodies: Late Modernism and the Meaning of Painting* (Palo Alto, CA: Stanford University Press, 2006).
The Fate of Art: Aesthetic Alienation from Kant to Derrida and Adorno (Cambridge: Polity, 1992).
Betz, Laura Wells, '"At Once Mild and Animating": *Prometheus Unbound* and Shelley's Spell of Style', *European Romantic Review*, 21 (2010): 161–81.
Bieri, James, *Percy Bysshe Shelley: A Biography* (Baltimore, MD: Johns Hopkins University Press, 2008).
Binyon, Lawrence, '"Terza Rima" in English Poetry', *English*, 3 (1940): 113–17.
Blank, G. Kim, 'A Shelley Survey: Which Shelley Now?', in G. Kim Blank, ed., *The New Shelley: Later Twentieth-Century Views* (Houndmills: Macmillan, 1991), pp. 242–7.
Bloom, Harold, *Shelley's Mythmaking* (New Haven, CT: Yale University Press, 1959).
Braudel, Fernand, *The Wheels of Commerce*, trans. Sîan Reynolds (Berkeley, CA: University of California Press, 1992).
Brisman, Susan Hawk, '"Unsaying His High Language": The Problem of Voice in *Prometheus Unbound*', *Studies in Romanticism*, 16 (1977): 51–86.
Bruns, Gerald L., *Modern Poetry and the Idea of Language: A Critical and Historical Study* (New Haven, CT: Yale University Press, 1974).
Butler, Judith, *Frames of War: When Is Life Grievable?* (London: Verso, 2009).
'Byron and Shelley on the Character of Hamlet', *New Monthly Magazine and Literary Journal*, 29 (1830), 327–36.
Byron, George Gordon, *The Complete Poetical Works of Lord Byron*, ed. Jerome J. McGann, 7 vols. (Oxford: Clarendon Press, 1980–93).
Cameron, Kenneth Neill, *The Young Shelley: Genesis of a Radical* (London: Gollancz, 1951).
Shelley: The Golden Years (Cambridge, MA: Harvard University Press, 1974).
Caruth, Cathy, 'Parting Words: Trauma, Silence, and Survival', in Carol Jacobs and Henry Sussman, eds., *Acts of Narrative* (Palo Alto, CA: Stanford University Press, 2003), pp. 47–61.
Cavell, Stanley, *In Quest of the Ordinary: Lines of Skepticism and Romanticism* (University of Chicago Press, 1988).
Chai, Leon, *Romantic Theory: Forms of Reflexivity in the Romantic Era* (Baltimore, MD: Johns Hopkins University Press, 2006).
Chernaik, Judith, *The Lyrics of Shelley* (Cleveland, OH: Case Western Reserve University Press, 1972).
Clark, David Lee, 'Shelley and Bacon', *PMLA*, 48 (1933): 529–46.

Coleridge, Samuel Taylor, *Biographia Literaria*, ed. James Engell and W. Jackson Bate (Princeton University Press, 1983).

'Theory of Life', in *Shorter Works and Fragments*, ed. H. J. Jackson and J. R. de J. Jackson, 2 vols. (Princeton University Press, 1995), vol. 1, pp. 481–557.

Collings, David, 'The Discipline of Death: Knowledge and Power in *An Essay on the Principle of Population*', *European Romantic Review*, 18 (2007): 223–30.

Connell, Philip, *Romanticism, Economics, and the Question of 'Culture'* (Oxford University Press, 2001).

Cowper, William, *The Iliad and Odyssey of Homer, Translated into English Blank Verse*, 2 vols. (London: Johnson, 1791).

Cox, Jeffrey N., *Poetry and Politics in the Cockney School: Keats, Shelley, Hunt and their Circle* (Cambridge University Press, 1998).

Cronin, Richard, *Shelley's Poetic Thoughts* (London: Macmillan, 1981).

Das, Veena, *Life and Words: Violence and the Descent into the Ordinary* (Berkeley, CA: University of California Press, 2007).

Dauer, Francis W., 'Force and Vivacity in the *Treatise* and the *Enquiry*', *Hume Studies*, 25 (1999): 83–99.

Dawson, P. M. S., *The Unacknowledged Legislator: Shelley and Politics* (Oxford: Clarendon Press, 1980).

De Bolla, Peter, *Art Matters* (Cambridge, MA: Harvard University Press, 2002).

Harold Bloom: Towards Historical Rhetorics (London and New York: Routledge, 1988).

'What Is a Lyrical Ballad? Wordsworth's Experimental Epistemologies', in Alexander Regier and Stefan H. Uhlig (eds.), *Wordsworth's Poetic Theory: Knowledge, Language, Experience* (Houndmills: Palgrave Macmillan, 2010), pp. 43–60.

De Man, Paul, 'Shelley Disfigured', in Harold Bloom, Paul de Man, Jacques Derrida, Geoffrey Hartman, and J. Hillis Miller, eds., *Deconstruction and Criticism* (London: Continuum, 1979), pp. 32–61.

Derrida, Jacques, 'Living On', trans. James Hulbert, in Harold Bloom, Paul de Man, Jacques Derrida, Geoffrey Hartman, and J. Hillis Miller, eds., *Deconstruction and Criticism* (London: Continuum, 1979; repr. 2004), pp. 62–142.

Drummond, William, *Academical Questions* (London: Bulmer, 1805).

Dryden, John, *The Spanish Fryar; or, The Double Discovery* (London, 1681).

Duff, David, *Romanticism and the Uses of Genre* (Oxford University Press, 2009).

Duffy, Cian, *Shelley and the Revolutionary Sublime* (Cambridge University Press, 2005).

Duffy, Edward, *Rousseau in England: The Context for Shelley's Critique of the Enlightenment* (Berkeley, CA: University of California Press, 1979).

Eldridge, Richard, *Literature, Life, and Modernity* (New York: Columbia University Press, 2008).

Ellis, Frederick Startridge, *A Lexical Concordance to the Poetical Works of Percy Bysshe Shelley : An Attempt to Classify Every Word Found Therein According to its Signification* (London: Clarendon, 1892).

Erlmann, Veit, *Reason and Resonance: A History of Modern Aurality* (New York: Zone, 2010).
Everest, Kelvin, 'Preface', in 'Percy Bysshe Shelley: Bicentenary Essays', ed. Kelvin Everest, *Essays and Studies*, n.s. 45 (1992), vii–ix.
Farnell, Gary, 'Rereading Shelley', *ELH*, 60 (1993): 625–50.
Faure, Georges, *Les Éléments du rythme poétique en anglais moderne: esquisse d'une nouvelle analyse et essai d'application au 'Prometheus Unbound' de P. B. Shelley* (The Hague: Mouton, 1970).
Ferris, David S., *Silent Urns: Romanticism, Hellenism, Modernity* (Palo Alto, CA: Stanford University Press, 2000).
Festa, Lynn, 'Humanity Without Feathers', *Humanity*, 1 (2010): 3–27.
Fogle, Richard Harter, *The Imagery of Keats and Shelley: A Comparative Study* (Hamden, CT: Archon, 1962).
Foss, Chris, 'Shelley's Revolution in Poetic Language: A Kristevan Reading of Act IV to *Prometheus Unbound*', *European Romantic Review*, 9 (1998): 501–18.
Foucault, Michel, *The History of Sexuality*, trans. Robert Hurley, 3 vols. (London: Penguin, 1978), vol. 1: *An Introduction*.
Francis, Philip, *The Odes, Epodes, and Carmen Seculare of Horace*, 2 vols. (London, 1743).
Friedman, Geraldine, 'Section Introduction: Romanticism and Life Science – Questions of Method', *European Romantic Review*, 18 (2007): 205–11.
Frosch, Thomas R., '"More Than Ever Can Be Spoken": Unconscious Fantasy in Shelley's Jane Williams Poems', *Studies in Philology*, 102 (2005): 378–413.
Shelley and the Romantic Imagination: A Psychological Study (Cranbury, NJ: Associated University Presses, 2007).
Fuller, Roy, 'The Osmotic Sap: The Text of a Lecture Given in Oxford on May 6', *Times Literary Supplement*, 14 May 1971, pp. 559–61.
Gasché, Rodolphe, *The Idea of Form: Rethinking Kant's Aesthetics* (Palo Alto, CA: Stanford University Press, 2003).
The Wild Card of Reading: On Paul de Man (Cambridge, MA: Harvard University Press, 1988).
Gigante, Denise, *Life: Organic Form and Romanticism* (New Haven, CT: Yale University Press, 2009).
Ginsborg, Hannah, *The Role of Taste in Kant's Theory of Cognition* (New York: Garland, 1990).
Godwin, William, *The Enquirer: Reflections on Education, Manners, and Literature* (London: Robinson, 1797).
Enquiry Concerning Political Justice, 3rd edn (1798), ed. Isaac Kramnick (Harmondsworth: Penguin, 1976). First published 1793.
Goslee, Nancy Moore, *Shelley's Visual Imagination* (Cambridge University Press, 2011).
Govier, Trudy, 'Variations on Force and Vivacity in Hume', *Philosophical Quarterly*, 22 (1972): 44–52.
Grabo, Carl, *A Newton Among Poets: Shelley's Use of Science in 'Prometheus Unbound'* (New York: Copper Square, 1930).

Greene, Thomas M., *Poetry, Signs, and Magic* (Newark, DE: University of Delaware Press, 2005).
Griffin, Jasper, *Homer on Life and Death* (Oxford: Clarendon Press, 1980).
Griffiths, Eric, *The Printed Voice of Victorian Poetry* (Oxford: Clarendon Press, 1989).
Guyer, Sara, *Romanticism after Auschwitz* (Palo Alto, CA: Stanford University Press, 2007).
Hadot, Pierre, Ulrich Dierse, Hans Hübner, Rainer Piepmeier, Klaus Rothe, Richard Toellner and Joachim Vennebusch, 'Leben', in Joachim Ritter and Karlfried Gründer, eds., *Historisches Wörterbuch der Philosophie*, 13 vols. (Basel: Schwabe, 1980), vol. V, cols. 52–103.
Hamilton, G. Rostrevor, 'Shelley's Own', *English*, 5 (1945): 149–53.
Hardt, Michael, and Antonio Negri, *Multitude: War and Democracy in the Age of Empire* (London: Penguin, 2006).
Hartman, Geoffrey, *Wordsworth's Poetry, 1787–1814* (New Haven, CT: Yale University Press, 1964).
Hassel, R. Chris, Jnr., *Shakespeare's Religious Language: A Dictionary* (London: Continuum, 2005).
Havens, Raymond D., 'Structure and Prosodic Pattern in Shelley's Lyrics', *PMLA*, 65 (1950): 1076–87.
Hawkes, Terence, 'Hamlet's Apprehension', *MLR*, 55 (1960): 238–41.
Shakespeare and the Reason: A Study of the Tragedies and the Problem Plays (London: Routledge & Kegan Paul, 1964).
Hazlitt, William, 'On Paradox and Commonplace', *Table Talk*, in James E. Barcus, ed., *Shelley: The Critical Heritage* (London: Routledge & Kegan Paul, 1975), pp. 284–6.
Review of Shelley's *Posthumous Poems*, in James E. Barcus, ed., *Shelley: The Critical Heritage* (London: Routledge & Kegan Paul, 1975), pp. 335–45.
Hegel, G. W. F., *Aesthetics: Lectures on Fine Art*, trans. T. M. Knox, 2 vols. (Oxford: Clarendon Press, 1975).
Phenomenology of Spirit, trans. A. V. Miller (Oxford University Press, 1977).
Werke, ed. Eva Moldenhauer and Karl Markus Michel, 20 vols. (Frankfurt: Suhrkamp, 1971), vol. XIII: *Vorlesungen über die Ästhetik*.
Henry, Michel, 'Ce que la science ne sait pas', in *Phénoménologie de la vie*, 4 vols. (Paris: Presses Universitaires de France, 2003–4), vol. IV: *Sur l'éthique et la religion* (2004), pp. 41–51. First published 1989.
The Genealogy of Psychoanalysis, trans. Douglas Brick (Palo Alto, CA: Stanford University Press, 1993).
Heyd, David, 'Is Life Worth Reliving?', *Mind*, 92 (1983): 21–37.
Highet, Gilbert, *Poets in a Landscape* (Harmondsworth: Penguin, 1959).
Hogle, Jerrold E., *Shelley's Process: Radical Transference and the Development of His Major Works* (Oxford University Press, 1988).
Hollander, John, *The Figure of Echo: A Mode of Allusion in Milton and After* (Berkeley, CA: University of California Press, 1981).
'The West Wind and the Mingled Measure', *Daedalus*, 111 (1982): 131–48.

Holmes, Richard, *The Age of Wonder: How the Romantic Generation Discovered the Beauty and Terror of Science* (London: Harper Press, 2008).

Shelley: The Pursuit (London: Quartet, 1976).

Hopkins, Brooke, 'Teaching "On Life": An Introduction to Shelley's Skeptical Poetics', in Spencer Hall, ed., *Approaches to Teaching Shelley's Poetry* (New York: Modern Language Association of America, 1990), pp. 111–13.

Hulme, T. E., 'Preface to Sorel's *Reflections on Violence*', in *Selected Writings*, ed. Patrick McGuinness (Manchester: Carcanet, 1998), pp. 173–9.

Hume, David, *An Enquiry Concerning Human Understanding*, ed. L. A. Selby-Bigge, 3rd edn, rev. P. H. Nidditch (Oxford: Clarendon Press, 1975).

Essays, Moral, Political, and Literary, ed. Eugene F. Miller, rev. edn (Indianapolis, IN: Liberty Fund, 1987).

Hunt, Leigh, *The Poetical Works of Leigh Hunt*, ed. H. S. Milford (Oxford University Press, 1923).

Hurley, Michael D., 'The Audible Reading of Poetry Revisited', *British Journal of Aesthetics*, 44 (2004): 393–407.

Jarvis, Simon, 'The Melodics of Long Poems', *Textual Practice*, 24 (2010): 607–21.

'Musical Thinking: Hegel and the Phenomenology of Prosody', *Paragraph*, 28 (2005): 58–71.

'Prosody as Cognition', *Critical Quarterly*, 40 (1998): 3–15.

'Thinking in Verse', in James Chandler and Maureen N. McLane, eds., *The Cambridge Companion to British Romantic Poetry* (Cambridge University Press, 2008), pp. 98–116.

'Unfree Verse: John Wilkinson's The Speaking Twins', in Peter Dayan and David Evans, eds., 'Rhythm in Literature After the Crisis in Verse', special issue of *Paragraph*, 33 (2010): 280–95.

Wordsworth's Philosophic Song (Cambridge University Press, 2006).

Kant, Immanuel, *Critique of Judgement*, trans. James Creed Meredith, rev. and ed. Nicholas Walker (Oxford University Press, 2007).

Karlin, Daniel, ed., *Robert Browning and Elizabeth Barrett: The Courtship Correspondence, 1845–1846: A Selection* (Oxford University Press, 1990).

Kaufman, Robert, 'Intervention & Commitment Forever! Shelley in 1819, Shelley in Brecht, Shelley in Adorno, Shelley in Benjamin', in Michael Scrivener, ed., *Reading Shelley's Interventionist Poetry, 1819–1820* (2001), available online at www.rc.umd.edu/praxis/interventionist/ (accessed 21 December 2011).

'Legislators of the Post-Everything World: Shelley's *Defence* of Adorno', *ELH*, 63 (1996): 707–33.

Keach, William, *Arbitrary Power: Romanticism, Language, Politics* (Princeton University Press, 2004).

Shelley's Style (London: Methuen, 1984).

Keats, John, *The Poems of John Keats*, ed. Miriam Allott (London: Longman, 1970).

Kertzer, Jonathan, *Poetic Argument: Studies in Modern Poetry* (Kingston: McGill-Queen's University Press, 1988).

King-Hele, Desmond, *Shelley: His Thought and Work*, 3rd edn (London: Macmillan, 1984).

Kipperman, Mark, *Beyond Enchantment: German Idealism and English Romantic Poetry* (Philadelphia, PA: University of Pennsylvania Press, 1986).

Knudsen, Christian, 'Intentions and Impositions', in Norman Kretzman, Anthony Kenny and Jan Pinborg, eds., *The Cambridge History of Later Medieval Philosophy: From the Rediscovery of Aristotle to the Disintegration of Scholasticism 1100–1600* (Cambridge University Press, 1982), pp. 479–95.

Krieger, Murray, *A Reopening of Closure: Organicism Against Itself* (New York: Columbia University Press, 1989).

Kuhns, Oscar, 'Dante's Influence on Shelley', *MLN*, 13 (1898): 161–5.

Langford, Paul, *A Polite and Commercial People: England, 1727–1783* (Oxford University Press, 1989).

Leavis, F. R., Letter to the Editor, *Times Literary Supplement*, 21 May 1971, p. 593.

Revaluation: Tradition and Development in English Poetry (Harmondsworth: Penguin, 1972). First published 1936.

Lee, Debbie, *Slavery and the Romantic Imagination* (Philadelphia, PA: University of Pennsylvania Press, 2002).

Leighton, Angela, *Shelley and the Sublime: An Interpretation of the Major Poems* (Cambridge University Press, 1984).

Lewis, C. S., *Studies in Words*, 2nd edn (Cambridge University Press, 1967).

Lindstrom, Eric, '"To Wordsworth" and the "White Obi": Slavery, Determination, and Contingency in Shelley's *Peter Bell the Third*', *Studies in Romanticism*, 47 (2008): 549–80.

Locke, John, *An Essay Concerning Human Understanding*, ed. Peter H. Nidditch (Oxford: Clarendon Press, 1975).

Loptson, Peter, 'Hume and Ancient Philosophy', *British Journal for the History of Philosophy*, 20 (2012): 741–72.

Lovelace, Richard, *The Poems of Richard Lovelace*, ed. C. H. Wilkinson (Oxford: Clarendon Press, 1930).

Lucretius Caro, Titus, *De rerum natura*, with an English translation by W. H. D. House, rev. Martin Ferguson Smith (Cambridge, MA: Harvard University Press, 1992).

The Nature of Things: A Didactic Poem, trans. John Mason Good, 2 vols. (London: Longman, Hurst, Rees, & Orme, 1805).

McCaffery, Steven, *Prior to Meaning: The Protosemantic and Poetics* (Evanston, IL: Northwestern University Press, 2001).

McLane, Maureen N., *Romanticism and the Human Sciences: Poetry, Population, and the Discourse of the Species* (Cambridge University Press, 2000).

Macleod, Colin, 'Homer on Poetry and the Poetry of Homer', in *Collected Essays* (Oxford: Clarendon Press, 1983), pp. 1–15.

Malthus, T. R., *An Essay on the Principle of Population*, ed. Geoffrey Gilbert (Oxford University Press, 2008).

Marg, Walter, 'Zur Eigenart der Odyssee', *Antike und Abendland*, 18 (1973): 1–14.

Marx, Karl, *Economic and Philosophical Manuscripts* (written 1844), in *Early Writings*, trans. Rodney Livingstone and Gregor Benton (Harmondsworth: Penguin, 1975).

Maupassant, Guy de, *A Life*, trans. Roger Pearson (Oxford University Press, 1999; repr. 2009).

Mendilow, Jonathan, 'Shelley's Philosophy of Liberty', *Journal of Libertarian Studies*, 6 (1982): 169–80.

Meschonnic, Henri, *La Rime et la vie* (Lagrasse: Verdier, 1989).

Vivre poème (Liancourt: Dumerchez, 2006).

Mills, Howard, *Peacock: His Circle and His Age* (Cambridge University Press, 1969).

Milnes, Tim, 'Centre and Circumference: Shelley's Defence of Philosophy', *European Romantic Review*, 15 (2004): 3–22.

Mönckeberg, Vilma, *Der Klangleib der Dichtung* (Hamburg: Classen & Goverts, 1946).

Montaigne, Michel Eyquem, Seigneur de, *The Complete Essays*, trans. and ed. M. A. Screech, rev. edn (London: Penguin, 2003).

Morton, Timothy, *Shelley and the Revolution in Taste: The Body and the Natural World* (Cambridge University Press, 1994).

Mulhallen, Jacqueline, *The Theatre of Shelley* (Cambridge: Open Book, 2010).

Murry, John Middleton, *The Problem of Style* (Oxford University Press, 1922).

Nelson, Stephanie, 'Shelley and Plato's *Symposium*: The Poet's Revenge', *International Journal of the Classical Tradition*, 14 (2007): 100–29.

Newey, Vincent, 'Shelley's "Dream of Youth": *Alastor*, "Selving" and the Psychic Realm', in 'Percy Bysshe Shelley: Bicentenary Essays', ed. Kelvin Everest, *Essays and Studies*, n.s. 45 (1992): 1–23.

Nietzsche, Friedrich, *Beyond Good and Evil: Prelude to a Philosophy of the Future*, trans. R. J. Hollingdale, rev. edn (London: Penguin, 1990).

Noel-Tod, Jeremy, *The Lyre: British Poetry News*, available online at http://thelyreonline.blogspot.com/2009/12/sir.html, 4 December 2009 (accessed 15 September 2011).

Notopoulos, James A., *The Platonism of Shelley: A Study of Platonism and the Poetic Mind* (New York: Octagon, 1969).

Olson, Paul A., '*A Midsummer Night's Dream* and the Meaning of Court Marriage', *ELH*, 24 (1957): 95–119.

O'Malley, Glenn, *Shelley and Synesthesia* (Evanston, IL: Northwestern University Press, 1964).

O'Neill, Michael, '"Driven as in Surges": Texture and Voice in Romantic Poetry', *The Wordsworth Circle*, 38 (2007): 91–3.

Parnell, Thomas, *Poems on Several Occasions* (London, 1722).

Patterson, Orlando, *Slavery as Social Death: A Comparative Study* (Cambridge, MA: Harvard University Press, 1982).

Peterfreund, Stuart, *Shelley Among Others: The Play of the Intertext and the Idea of Language* (Baltimore, MD: Johns Hopkins University Press, 2002).

'Shelley, Monboddo, Vico, and the Language of Poetry', *Style*, 15 (1981): 382–400.

Pite, Ralph, *The Circle of Our Vision: Dante's Presence in English Romantic Poetry* (Oxford: Clarendon Press, 1994).

Plato, *Complete Works*, ed. John M. Cooper with D. S. Hutchinson (Indianapolis, IN: Hackett, 1997).

Pocock, J. G. A., *Virtue, Commerce, and History* (Cambridge University Press, 1985).

Porter, James I., 'Love of Life: Lucretius to Freud', in Shadi Bartsch and Thomas Bartscherer, eds., *Erotikon: Essays on Eros, Ancient and Modern* (University of Chicago Press, 2005), pp. 113–41.

Potts, Timothy C., 'Conscience', in Norman Kretzman, Anthony Kenny and Jan Pinborg, eds., *The Cambridge History of Later Medieval Philosophy: From the Rediscovery of Aristotle to the Disintegration of Scholasticism, 1100–1600* (Cambridge University Press, 1982), pp. 687–704.

Propst, Louise. *An Analytical Study of Shelley's Versification* (University of Iowa Press, 1933).

Prynne, J. H., Letter to the Editor, *Times Literary Supplement*, 28 May 1971, p. 620.

Pulos, C. E., *The Deep Truth: A Study of Shelley's Scepticism* (Lincoln, NE: University of Nebraska Press, 1954).

'Shelley and Malthus', *PMLA*, 67 (1952): 113–24.

Quinney, Laura, *Literary Power and the Criteria of Truth* (Gainesville, FL: University Press of Florida, 1995).

Rajan, Tillotama, *The Supplement of Reading: Figures of Understanding in Romantic Theory and Practice* (Ithaca, NY: Cornell University Press, 1990).

Ravinthiran, Vidyan, 'Dante and Shelley's Terza Rima', *Essays in Criticism*, 61 (2011): 155–72.

Reiman, Donald H., *Intervals of Inspiration: The Skeptical Tradition and the Psychology of Romanticism* (Greenwood, FL: Penkevill, 1988).

Shelley's 'The Triumph of Life': A Critical Study (Urbana, IL: University of Illinois Press, 1965).

Ricks, Christopher, *Milton's Grand Style* (Oxford University Press, 1963).

Roberts, Hugh, 'Shelley Among the Post-Kantians', *Studies in Romanticism*, 35 (1996): 295–329.

Rossington, Michael, 'Rousseau and Tacitus: Republican Inflections in the Shelleys' *History of a Six Weeks' Tour*', *European Romantic Review*, 19 (2008): 321–33.

'Shelley's Republics', in Heather Glen and Paul Hamilton, eds., *Repossessing the Romantic Past* (Cambridge University Press, 2006), pp. 63–79.

Roubaud, Jacques, 'Prelude: Poetry and Orality', trans. Jean-Jacques Poucel, in Marjorie Perloff and Craig Dworkin, eds., *The Sound of Poetry/The Poetry of Sound* (University of Chicago Press, 2009), pp. 18–25.

Rousseau, Jean-Jacques, *Reveries of the Solitary Walker*, trans. Russell Goulbourne (Oxford University Press, 2011).

Ruston, Sharon, *Shelley and Vitality* (Houndmills: Palgrave Macmillan, 2005).

Saintsbury, George, *A History of English Prosody*, 3 vols. (New York: Russell & Russell, 1961), vol. III.

Santner, Eric L., *On Creaturely Life: Rilke, Benjamin, Sebald* (University of Chicago Press, 2006).
Schmitt, Carl, *Political Romanticism*, trans. Guy Oakes (Cambridge, MA: MIT Press, 1986).
Scott, Clive, *The Poetics of French Verse: Studies in Reading* (Oxford: Clarendon Press, 1998).
Scott, Clive and T. V. F. Brogan, 'Terza Rima Sonnet', in Alex Preminger and T. V. F. Brogan, eds., *The New Princeton Encyclopedia of Poetry and Poetics* (Princeton University Press, 1993), p. 1271.
Scott, William O., 'Shelley's Admiration for Bacon', *PMLA*, 73 (1958): 228–36.
Scrivener, Michael Henry, *Radical Shelley: The Philosophical Anarchism and Utopian Thought of Percy Bysshe Shelley* (Princeton University Press, 1982).
Shelley, Bryan, *Shelley and Scripture: The Interpreting Angel* (Oxford: Clarendon Press, 1994).
Shelley, Mary, *The Journals of Mary Shelley*, ed. Paula R. Feldman and Diana Scott-Kilvert, 2 vols. (Oxford University Press, 1987).
Simpson, David, *Wordsworth, Commodification and Social Concern: The Poetics of Modernity* (Cambridge University Press, 2009).
Small, Helen, *The Long Life* (Oxford University Press, 2007).
Smart, Christopher, *The Works of Horace, Translated into Verse*, 4 vols. (London, 1767).
Smith, Adam, *The Theory of Moral Sentiments*, 6th edn, 2 vols. (London, 1790).
Southey, Robert, *Robert Southey: Later Poetical Works, 1811–1838*, ed. Lynda Pratt and Tim Fulford, 4 vols. (London: Pickering & Chatto, 2012).
Stephen, Leslie, 'Godwin and Shelley' (1879), in *Hours in a Library*, 3 vols. (London: Folio Society, 1991), vol. III, pp. 59–93.
Stewart, Garrett, *Reading Voices: Literature and the Phonotext* (Berkeley, CA: University of California Press, 1990).
Stewart, Susan, 'What Praise Poems Are For', *PMLA*, 120 (2005): 235–45.
Strang, Hilary, 'Common Life, Animal Life, Equality: *The Last Man*', *ELH*, 78 (2011): 409–31.
Tacitus, *The Works of Cornelius Tacitus: With an Essay on His Life and Genius*, trans. Arthur Murphy, 4 vols. (London: Robinson, 1793).
Vicario, Michael A., *Shelley's Intellectual System and its Epicurean Background* (London and New York: Routledge, 2007).
Wallace, Elizabeth Kowaleski, *The British Slave Trade and Public Memory* (New York: Columbia University Press, 2006).
Wang, Orrin N. C., *Fantastic Modernity: Dialectical Readings in Romanticism and Theory* (Baltimore, MD: Johns Hopkins University Press, 1996).
Wasserman, Earl R., *Shelley: A Critical Reading* (Baltimore, MD: Johns Hopkins University Press, 1971).
Waters, William, *Poetic Touch: On Lyric Address* (Ithaca, NY: Cornell University Press, 2003).
Waxman, Wayne, 'Impressions and Ideas: Vivacity as Verisimilitude', *Hume Studies*, 19 (1993): 75–88.

Welsh, Andrew, *Roots of Lyric: Primitive Poetry and Modern Poetics* (Princeton University Press, 1978).

Wheatley, Kim, *Shelley and His Readers: Beyond Paranoid Politics* (Columbia, MO: University of Missouri Press, 1999).

Whitehead, A. N., *Science and the Modern World* (London: Fontana, 1975).

Wilcox, S. C., 'The Prosodic Structure of "Ode to the West Wind"', *Notes and Queries*, 18 (February 1950): 77–8.

Wilkinson, John, 'Following the Poem', in *The Lyric Touch: Essays on the Poetry of Excess* (Cambridge: Salt, 2007), pp. 195–211.

Wilson, Emily R., *Mocked with Death: Tragic Overliving from Sophocles to Milton* (Baltimore, MD: Johns Hopkins University Press, 2004).

Wilson, Ross, 'Clare's Indistinct Array', *Romanticism*, 17 (2011): 148–59.

'Introduction', in Ross Wilson, ed., *The Meaning of 'Life' in Romantic Poetry and Poetics* (London and New York: Routledge, 2009), pp. 1–12.

Wolfson, Susan J., *Formal Charges: The Shaping of Poetry in British Romanticism* (Palo Alto, CA: Stanford University Press, 1997).

'Sounding Romantic: The Sound of Sound', in Susan J. Wolfson, ed., *'Soundings of Things Done: The Poetry and Poetics of Sound in the Romantic Era and Ear'* (2008), available online at http://romantic.arhu.umd.edu/praxis/soundings/wolfson/wolfson.html (accessed 11 March 2013).

ed., *'Soundings of Things Done': The Poetry and Poetics of Sound in the Romantic Ear and Era* (2008), available online at http://romantic.arhu.umd.edu/praxis/soundings/index.html (accessed 17 December 2011).

Wollstonecraft, Mary, *'A Vindication of the Rights of Men' and 'A Vindication of the Rights of Woman'*, ed. Sylvana Tomaselli (Cambridge University Press, 1995).

Woof, Robert, ed., *William Wordsworth: The Critical Heritage*, vol. I: 1793–1820 (London and New York: Routledge, 2001).

Wordsworth, William, *The Excursion*, ed. Sally Bushell, James A. Butler and Michael C. Jaye (Ithaca, NY: Cornell University Press, 2007).

'Lyrical Ballads' and Other Poems, 1797–1800, ed. James Butler and Karen Green (Ithaca, NY: Cornell University Press, 1992).

Selected Prose, ed. John O. Hayden (Harmondsworth: Penguin, 1988).

Wright, John W., *Shelley's Myth of Metaphor* (Athens, GA: University of Georgia Press, 1970).

Yeats, W. B., 'The Philosophy of Shelley's Poetry', in *Essays and Introductions* (London: Macmillan, 1961), pp. 65–95.

Young, Edward, *The Complaint; or, Night Thoughts on Life, Death, and Immortality* (London: Dodsley, 1742).

Index

CAMBRIDGE STUDIES IN ROMANTICISM

General editor
JAMES CHANDLER, *University of Chicago*

1. Romantic Correspondence: Women, Politics and the Fiction of Letters
MARY A. FAVRET
2. British Romantic Writers and the East: Anxieties of Empire
NIGEL LEASK
3. Poetry as an Occupation and an Art in Britain, 1760–1830
PETER MURPHY
4. Edmund Burke's Aesthetic Ideology: Language, Gender and Political Economy in Revolution
TOM FURNISS
5. In the Theatre of Romanticism: Coleridge, Nationalism, Women
JULIE A. CARLSON
6. Keats, Narrative and Audience
ANDREW BENNETT
7. Romance and Revolution: Shelley and the Politics of a Genre
DAVID DUFF
8. Literature, Education, and Romanticism: Reading as Social Practice, 1780–1832
ALAN RICHARDSON
9. Women Writing about Money: Women's Fiction in England, 1790–1820
EDWARD COPELAND
10. Shelley and the Revolution in Taste: The Body and the Natural World
TIMOTHY MORTON
11. William Cobbett: The Politics of Style
LEONORA NATTRASS
12. The Rise of Supernatural Fiction, 1762–1800
E. J. CLERY
13. Women Travel Writers and the Language of Aesthetics, 1716–1818
ELIZABETH A. BOHLS

14. Napoleon and English Romanticism
SIMON BAINBRIDGE

15. Romantic Vagrancy: Wordsworth and the Simulation of Freedom
CELESTE LANGAN

16. Wordsworth and the Geologists
JOHN WYATT

17. Wordsworth's Pope: A Study in Literary Historiography
ROBERT J. GRIFFIN

18. The Politics of Sensibility: Race, Gender and Commerce in the Sentimental Novel
MARKMAN ELLIS

19. Reading Daughters' Fictions, 1709–1834: Novels and Society from Manley to Edgeworth
CAROLINE GONDA

20. Romantic Identities: Varieties of Subjectivity, 1774–1830
ANDREA K. HENDERSON

21. Print Politics: The Press and Radical Opposition: in Early Nineteenth-Century England
KEVIN GILMARTIN

22. Reinventing Allegory
THERESA M. KELLEY

23. British Satire and the Politics of Style, 1789–1832
GARY DYER

24. The Romantic Reformation: Religious Politics in English Literature, 1789–1824
ROBERT M. RYAN

25. De Quincey's Romanticism: Canonical Minority and the Forms of Transmission
MARGARET RUSSETT

26. Coleridge on Dreaming: Romanticism, Dreams and the Medical Imagination
JENNIFER FORD

27. Romantic Imperialism: Universal Empire and the Culture of Modernity
SAREE MAKDISI

28. Ideology and Utopia in the Poetry of William Blake
NICHOLAS M. WILLIAMS

45. Literary Magazines and British Romanticism
MARK PARKER

46. Women, Nationalism and the Romantic Stage: Theatre and Politics in Britain, 1780–1800
BETSY BOLTON

47. British Romanticism and the Science of the Mind
ALAN RICHARDSON

48. The Anti-Jacobin Novel: British Conservatism and the French Revolution
M. O. GRENBY

49. Romantic Austen: Sexual Politics and the Literary Canon
CLARA TUITE

50. Byron and Romanticism
JEROME MCGANN AND JAMES SODERHOLM

51. The Romantic National Tale and the Question of Ireland
INA FERRIS

52. Byron, Poetics and History
JANE STABLER

53. Religion, Toleration, and British Writing, 1790–1830
MARK CANUEL

54. Fatal Women of Romanticism
ADRIANA CRACIUN

55. Knowledge and Indifference in English Romantic Prose
TIM MILNES

56. Mary Wollstonecraft and the Feminist Imagination
BARBARA TAYLOR

57. Romanticism, Maternity and the Body Politic
JULIE KIPP

58. Romanticism and Animal Rights
DAVID PERKINS

59. Georgic Modernity and British Romanticism: Poetry and the Mediation of History
KEVIS GOODMAN

60. Literature, Science and Exploration in the Romantic Era: Bodies of Knowledge
TIMOTHY FULFORD, DEBBIE LEE, AND PETER J. KITSON

61. Romantic Colonization and British Anti-Slavery
DEIRDRE COLEMAN

62. Anger, Revolution, and Romanticism
ANDREW M. STAUFFER

63. Shelley and the Revolutionary Sublime
CIAN DUFFY

64. Fictions and Fakes: Forging Romantic Authenticity, 1760–1845
MARGARET RUSSETT

65. Early Romanticism and Religious Dissent
DANIEL E. WHITE

66. The Invention of Evening: Perception and Time in Romantic Poetry
CHRISTOPHER R. MILLER

67. Wordsworth's Philosophic Song
SIMON JARVIS

68. Romanticism and the Rise of the Mass Public
ANDREW FRANTA

69. Writing against Revolution: Literary Conservatism in Britain, 1790–1832
KEVIN GILMARTIN

70. Women, Sociability and Theatre in Georgian London
GILLIAN RUSSELL

71. The Lake Poets and Professional Identity
BRIAN GOLDBERG

72. Wordsworth Writing
ANDREW BENNETT

73. Science and Sensation in Romantic Poetry
NOEL JACKSON

74. Advertising and Satirical Culture in the Romantic Period
JOHN STRACHAN

75. Romanticism and the Painful Pleasures of Modern Life
ANDREA K. HENDERSON

76. Balladeering, Minstrelsy, and the Making of British Romantic Poetry
MAUREEN N. MCLANE

77. Romanticism and Improvisation, 1750–1850
ANGELA ESTERHAMMER

78. Scotland and the Fictions of Geography: North Britain, 1760–1830
PENNY FIELDING